# MAN'S BEST FRIEND
## ON THE ROAD AGAIN WITH

A Selective Guide to the Northwest's Bed and Breakfasts, Inns,
Hotels, and Resorts That Welcome You and Your Dog

## Dawn and Robert Habgood

**A Dawbert Press Publication**
MACMILLAN • USA

Macmillan General Reference
A Prentice Hall Macmillan Company
1633 Broadway
New York, New York 10019

Copyright © 1996 by Dawbert Press, Inc.

Howell Book House
MACMILLAN is a registered trademark of Macmillan, Inc.

First Edition

ISBN: 0-87605-714-8

Editor: Pamela Gerloff
Interior Artwork: Glynn Brannan

Manufactured in the United States of America
10 9 8 7 6 5 4 3 2 1

# Contents

# Introduction

Like millions of others in this country, we cherish our dogs and their unique place within our family. Our two golden retrievers are an integral part of our lives, and we find it difficult to leave them for extended periods of time. From the earliest days of our marriage, we loved to pack our bags and hit the road in search of new, undiscovered terrain. Each of the regions in our country is so distinct from the next, we thrive on the new pleasures and discoveries around each bend in the road. However, our unwillingness to abandon our pets soon clashed with our traveling spirits.

So thirteen years ago, we started including our dogs on weekend vacations. We began compiling lists of pet-friendly accommodations. Before long, we owned virtually every regional guidebook, but had unearthed only a handful of decent lodgings. Brochures could be deceptive, and the places were not always as nice as we expected. Our dogs did not care, but we did.

Finally, we decided to solve the problem ourselves and went "on the road again" in search of a variety of accommodations that would not only appeal to us, but to other people who wanted to vacation with their dog and who were seeking quality places with character, regional flavor, and charisma.

*On The Road Again With Man's Best Friend* is the result — a series of regional travel guides that are both selective and comprehensive. We include listings of all accommodations that accept travelers and their dogs; however, we highlight only those that merit special attention. For over a decade, we have been traveling to, and writing about, places to stay with dogs, allowing us to provide readers with our personal, first-hand impressions. If we think a place is great, we let you know, and if there are areas that could be improved, we mention them as well. We are able to do this only because we make a point of personally visiting and revisiting each entry in each of our guides.

In looking through this book, prospective guests will discover a wide range of vacation destinations that should appeal to their senses, as well as to their pocketbooks. And remember, traveling with a dog can be a delightful experience, but it is also a responsibility that, if misused, can not only completely ruin your vacation, but can deny the opportunity for others to visit that establishment in the future.

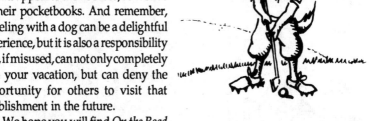

We hope you will find *On the Road Again With Man's Best Friend* to be an informative and helpful guide, and one you will include when planning any vacation with Bowser. We have found our dogs enjoy being "on the road again" just as much as we do.

# How do we Select "the Best" Accommodations?

We choose our dog friendly entries by sifting through all the accommodations that welcome dogs in a given region, looking for places that exude a warmth, charm, and quality that even dog-less vacationers would find appealing. For instance, we include cottage communities that have been around for decades and, although some are rather rustic, attract a strong following of devoted patrons. Intimate B&Bs are added for their personalized attention and ambiance, while resorts are appealing for their diversity of activities. Elegant country inns and small hotels often top our list, but equally important are the family-run farms in the countryside.

Once selected, we pay an unannounced visit to the establishment, always maintaining our anonymity. This allows us, in most cases, to provide future guests with a concise overview and detailed descriptions that are not influenced by any type of special treatment. Because we accept no money from the innkeepers or owners, we can remain objective and you can feel more comfortable without our recommendations.

# How to Use the Book — General Information

Each entry begins with pertinent general information about the establishment, including the address, telephone number, owner or manager's name, acceptable methods of payment, and number, type, and cost of the various guest rooms. We also describe any pet policies, and restrictions regarding children, if any. This section tells you more about each area we cover.

## Types of Accommodations:

**B&Bs:** These are often private homes and guests should treat this experience

as though they are staying with a friend. B&Bs are usually short on amenities and on-site activities, but long on personalized attention. You can expect to find comfortable guest rooms, a common area with perhaps a television and stereo, a Continental breakfast, and a warm and friendly host who genuinely enjoys having houseguests. B&Bs generally do not serve lunch and dinner.

**Inns:** Inns can sometimes be confused with B&Bs. Most have the same type of intimate feeling, but with just a few more rooms. One of the biggest differences is they have either a restaurant or can serve at least breakfast and dinner. Inns are more highly regulated and must meet the various state and national health and access codes. Also, they provide more activities and creature comforts than do traditional B&Bs.

**Cottages:** The cottage complexes we feature vary greatly in size, amenities, and activities — but even the most rustic are very clean and well maintained. Although the cabin or cottage might offer only the bare essentials, there is always plenty to do on the premises or in the nearby area. There is almost always a main lodge with a great restaurant. In some cases, all guests eat here, and in others they have a kitchenette that gives them the option of dining in their cottage or at the main lodge. We usually choose a cottage complex because it offers a picturesque setting with plenty of open space for both owner and dog to explore.

**Hotels and Resorts:** Smaller hotels often label themselves inns because they feel it makes them appear more intimate. We try to warn readers of this early and explain exactly what they can expect. Hotels usually have fifty or more rooms, and are located in large towns and cities. They traditionally deliver a full range of amenities, which could include an indoor or outdoor swimming pool, concierge services, multiple restaurants, a large staff, and a health club. Resorts, on the other hand, are generally located on the outskirts of popular tourist destinations or in the countryside. They offer a wide variety of guest rooms, as well as an expansive list of amenities, activities, and on-site programs.

**Motels/Motor Lodges:** These vary greatly in cost and features, although guests can usually expect standard rooms, a few amenities, and perhaps a restaurant either on the premises or nearby. They do not usually warrant a description, which is why we have provided our comprehensive appendix, "The Best of the Rest," which gives readers the names, addresses, and telephone numbers of these establishments.

## Rooms:

Because guest rooms vary a great deal from one establishment to the next, it is important, when making a reservation, to be very specific about your requirements. Read the descriptions carefully and decide which amenities are important, whether they are a private bathroom, a bedroom with a big closet, a firm mattress, a room on the first floor, or a separate sitting room. Do you want a room that could be out of the pages of *House Beautiful*, or modern conveniences such as televisions or Jacuzzis? Please be specific.

## Rates:

The range of rates listed with each description gives you a good idea of what to expect at a particular establishment. Many of these accommodations offer special discount packages, off-season rates, weekly rates, or interesting theme weekends. Always inquire about what's offered. Almost all of the accommodations listed in our books have "shoulder" seasons too — quiet times immediately before or after the busier times of the year. In addition to saving a little money, people traveling during these months will have a better choice of rooms, be able to eat out without making reservations, and enjoy sightseeing without all the usual crowds. Guests should also be careful to check if the rates are based upon single or double occupancy and if they include local taxes, fees, and so on.

## Meal Plans:

We always indicate the type of meal plan offered by a given establishment.

* Bed and Breakfast (B&B) rates includes a Continental *or* full breakfast.
* European Plan (EP) does not include any meals.
* Modified American Plan (MAP) includes both breakfast and dinner
* American Plan (AP) is all-inclusive, providing breakfast, lunch, and dinner.

## Method of Payment:

While most of the smaller establishments would prefer to be paid in cash or by personal check, the larger inns, hotels, and resorts accept an array of credit cards, abbreviated as follows:

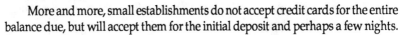

* **AE** - American Express
* **CB** - Carte Blanche
* **DC** - Diners Club
* **DSC** - Discover
* **ENR** - EnRoute
* **JCB** - Japanese Credit Bank
* **MC** - Master Card
* **VISA** - Visa

More and more, small establishments do not accept credit cards for the entire balance due, but will accept them for the initial deposit and perhaps a few nights.

## Children:

We provide this category to inform prospective guests about any additional rules, regulations, or benefits concerning their children. Legally, people traveling with children cannot be discriminated against; however, we have found that there are certainly places where parents with young children would be uncomfortable. When we mention appropriate ages, it is at the request of the innkeeper or manager. More often, though, there are special discounts for young children and those under the age of 12 often stay free of charge when accompanied by a parent.

## Dog Policies:

This category outlines any restrictions concerning guests' canine companions. These can include size requirements, the age of the dog, and management concerns such as leaving dogs alone in the room or walking them off the property. Some establishments offer an array of doggie treats for their canine guests, which could be homemade biscuits or extra dog beds and bowls.

## Opening and Closing Dates:

Seasonal openings and closings are outlined in this section. Many of the accommodations are open all year; however, during the off-season it is fairly common for B&B owners or innkeepers to shut down and go on a short vacation. Always, call ahead to make sure the establishment is open when you are planning to visit.

# Planning Your Trip

In our experience, and we are sure fellow travelers agree, planning ahead of time is the best way to avoid mistakes that make for unpleasant experiences. Here are some of our time-tested guidelines.

## Traveling by Car - Planning & Precautions:

If you've never traveled with your dog before, think twice about setting out on a four-day vacation together. To ease the uninitiated dog into travel mode, start with a day trip, then an overnight or weekend jaunt, then book a longer stay somewhere. If your dog has a tendency to bounce around the car, you should buy a travel crate or a car gate — something to confine him to the rear of the vehicle so that you can drive safely.

Before you set out on your trip, take your dog for a leisurely walk. This will not only give him a chance to work off a little energy, but may also coax him into sleeping during the trip. Do not feed him or give him substantial amounts of water just before leaving. Once in the car, make sure the dog's area is either well-ventilated or amply air-conditioned. Plan frequent pit stops (every two hours or so), where you can exercise your dog on a leash.

Even if the day is not hot, a car can heat up to very high temperatures in very little time. Take the following precautions to prevent heat stroke, brain damage, or even death to your dog:

* Try to park the car in the shade and leave the window open enough to provide ample ventilation.
* Do not leave your dog for long intervals of time.
* Before you leave the car, fill his bowl with cold water to ease any effects of the heat.
* *Never leave a dog in a hot car!*

## Traveling by Plane - Planning & Precautions:

There are certain legal guidelines and restrictions for air travel with a dog. The United States Department of Agriculture (USDA) and the International Air Transport Association (IATA) govern air travel for pets. The airlines themselves have regulations, and they differ, so you should always contact your airline in advance to review their procedures and requirements. Regardless of your carrier, these are important guidelines to consider:

* The dog should be at least eight weeks old and fully weaned.
* The dog cannot be ill, violent, or in physical distress.
* The dog should have all the necessary health certificates and documentation.
* The travel crate must meet the airline's standards and be large enough for the dog to lie down comfortably, turn around, and stand freely in it.

Try to book a non-stop flight, and take temperature into consideration: In the summer, try to fly at night when it's cooler; in winter, fly during the day, when it's warmer.

Plan your trip well in advance and make sure you are following all the rules.

## What Your Dog Needs to Enjoy the Trip:

Just as you have to pack appropriately for your vacation, your dog will need certain items to ensure he has a comfortable and enjoyable time, too. These include:
* A leash and collar with ID tags.
* A few favorite toys, chew bones, and treats.
* A container of fresh drinking water from home.
* A supply of his regular dog food.
* Food and water bowls.
* A dog "bed," whether it is a towel, mat, or pillow, or the dog's travel crate.
* Grooming aids, including extra towels for wet dogs and muddy paws.
* Any medication your veterinarian has prescribed or suggested.
* The dog's vaccination records, especially a rabies certificate or tag.

## When You Arrive:

Many of the hosts and innkeepers we have met have expressed their general concerns about guests who bring their canine companions. So that your visit is an enjoyable one, we wanted to list them so you can keep them in mind.
* Tape the local address and telephone number, indicating where you are staying, onto your dog's tag.
* Dogs should not be left alone in the bedroom unless in a crate or confined to the bathroom with some favorite toys.
* Dogs should be kept leashed while on the grounds. Always clean up after the dog, and try to walk him away from the main grounds.
* Use the dog's bedding to lessen the chance of damage to the furnishings. Never let your dog sit or lie on any of the furnishings.
* Because of health codes, dogs are generally not allowed in any area where food is made or served.

# Disclaimer

Please keep in mind that the hosts, managers, and innkeepers are under no obligation to accept your dog. The management of each establishment listed in our guides has indicated to us, both verbally and in writing, that they have welcomed dogs in the past, had positive experiences, and will accept them in the future provided they are very well-behaved. Prior to publication, each of the establishments was contacted again to ensure they still welcome guests traveling with dogs. We cannot, however, guarantee against last minute changes of heart. Sometimes circumstances exist that require them to decline admitting our canine friends. They may already have a few dogs there, or be hosting a special function that would make it impractical for them to have your dog stay with you. *It is imperative you notify the establishment that you will be traveling with your dog when making your reservations.*

# Oregon

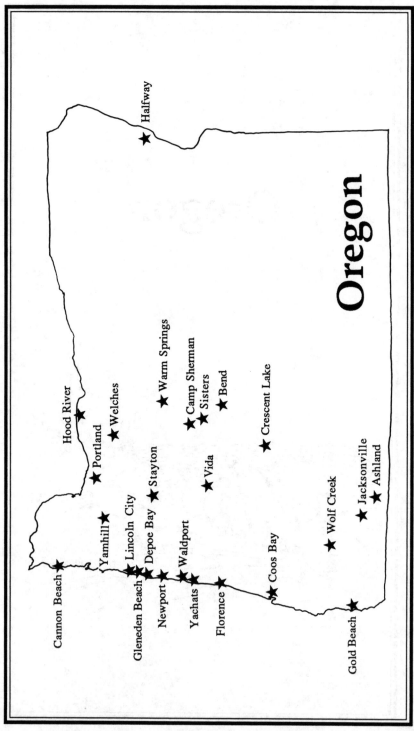

# The Green Springs Box R Ranch

*16799 Highway 66*
*Ashland, Oregon 97520*
*(503) 482-1873*

*Hosts:* Don and Jean Rowlett
*Rooms:* 4 houses
*Rates:* $95-125 (EP), weekly rates are available
*Payment:* Personal checks
*Children:* Welcome
*Dogs:* Welcome in the houses
*Open:* April through December

Any place that offers the coordinates for private planes to land seems as if it would be exceptionally exclusive and remote. Sure enough, the Green Springs Box R Ranch lies in southern Oregon's Cascades; however, it is also only a 30-minute drive from Ashland, home to the Oregon Shakespearean Festival and the Pacific Northwest Museum of Natural History. While some choose to fly in, most drive, as it is an easy jog off Interstate 5 to Route 66 and the ranch.

The Green Springs Box R Ranch has an interesting history, dating back to the turn of the century, when the main ranch house served as a stage coach stop along the Applegate Trail — a trail established in 1846 that ran from the Klamath Basin to Jacksonville. Taking the ranch's history into account, the Rowletts are in the process of putting together their own small museum and an authentic Old Western town. A few historic buildings from around Oregon now rest on this land, including the oldest building in Jackson County, a hand-hewn smokehouse, and a blacksmith's shop. Guests might also want to visit the historic Boot Hill graveyard or investigate the collection of authentic covered wagons, also on the property. History aside, the Green Springs Box R Ranch is also an authentic 1,000-acre working cattle ranch.

The old-fashioned ranch house and modern log cabins overlook lush green meadows and ponds surrounded by pines. The Aspen and Shasta houses are the smallest of the four, accommodating eight people each, while the Landing and Lakeview cabins can house 12 and 16 people, respectively. A single family might reserve one of the smaller cabins, but these are also ideal for groups of friends or extended families. Each cabin configuration is slightly different, but all are fully carpeted and well equipped with all the necessities for a week-long vacation. The largest of these houses contains two bedrooms; however, what the children find especially appealing are the carpeted loft spaces. In these, the hosts supply the foam pads — guests just need to bring their sleeping bags. Many children find the idea of "roughing it" appealing. (Bed linens are supplied for the lucky ones who get beds.) Each cabin's central gathering place is in the living room, where comfortable sofas and chairs surround the natural rock fireplaces. An unlimited supply of wood inspires many guests to have a fire nearly every night. The kitchens are fully equipped and modern, although guests should plan on stocking up on groceries before they arrive. There is also a small store in the area for buying perishables and assorted wares, or guests can head over to the Green Springs Inn and Jenny Creek Café for a casual, hearty meal.

There are no organized activities at the ranch designed especially for children or dogs, although there are ranch tours by wagon or sleigh available. Belgian draft horses — Willy and Waylon — will take guests along portions of the old Applegate Trail. This is a really fun way to get to know the lay of the land. Guests may volunteer to help with some of the chores on the ranch, including feeding the animals or gathering eggs. Most come to relax, though — perhaps fish a bit, or just explore this vast open country with their dog. There are trails right on the property, and the Pacific Crest Trail is also close by. Anyone spending a week here might take the day and drive up the Dead Indian Road. One particularly popular trail begins at the Daley Creek Campground and parallels Beaver Dam Creek. In this typically dry country, many enjoy spending a few hours exploring the creek and the old growth forest throughout this region. But that's not all — there are plenty of other intriguing hikes throughout the area that would also be appropriate for guests and their canine companions.

# The Riverhouse

*3075 North Highway 97*
*Bend, Oregon 97701*
*(800) 547-3928, (541) 389-3111*

*General Manager:* Wayne Purcell
*Rooms:* 220 doubles and suites
*Rates:* Doubles $61-67 (EP), Suites $74-165 (EP)
*Payment:* AE, DC, MC, and VISA
*Children:* Welcome (cribs and high chairs are available)
*Dogs:* Welcome, provided they are not left alone in the room
*Open:* All year

Bend lies in Oregon's high desert, with nothing around it but spectacular scenery. It has grown remarkably over the years; what started out as a small ranching town has developed into a virtual metropolis. In the winter months, Mount Bachelor is the primary draw, but in the summertime visitors flock here for the assortment of outdoor diversions and for the mountain biking in the nearby foothills. While there are plenty of roadside motels in Bend that welcome dogs, one of the standouts is The Riverhouse.

Yes — it is technically a motel; it does lie next to busy Highway 97; and it does have more than 200 rooms. Even more unusual, though, is that the Deschutes River runs right through the middle of the complex, adding an intriguing dimension to this mini-resort. When making a reservation, we suggest that guests request a room overlooking the river, as far away from the main road and restaurant as possible. Our favorite rooms are those in the 150-163 block on the first floor of the two-story riverside building. Almost as appealing are Rooms 122-149. Although these occupy the building next door, they are also a little closer to the restaurant and lounge. A footbridge leads guests across the river to another building. While these rooms are furthest from the main road, they are not quite as private and they look back towards the dining room. We definitely recommend staying away from the rooms situated over the lobby, as they are quite close to the highway and can be very noisy at times.

Keeping all this in mind, once new arrivals drop down into the complex they will discover that the guest rooms are basically oversized, upscale motel rooms. Contemporary oak headboards back pairs of queen beds covered with attractive floral spreads and edged by dust ruffles. Cream-colored walls are devoid of decoration, with the exception of a few framed bird prints. The bathrooms are quite modern, with separate vanities and a full complement of toiletries. A long, low bureau is topped by a television equipped with movie channels (VCRs may be rented). The direct-dial telephones feature voicemail, and clock radios supply pleasing background music. These are the most basic standard rooms. There are also chambers with an in-room Jacuzzi, a fireplace, or a kitchenette. We recommend the riverside guest rooms, though, as they have sliding glass doors that open to private patios. From here, guests and their dogs can walk right out past pine trees and shrubs to the river's edge. When the water is low, many enjoy hopping from one flat rock to the next and exploring further up or down the river bed.

The Riverhouse Restaurant offers an extensive Continental menu. Those who don't get to stay in the riverside rooms can enjoy the same river views from the restaurant. The restaurant's specialties are beef, and include such favorites as filet mignon, prime rib, and tenderloin. We also suggest trying the fresh rainbow trout or the filet of salmon. The portions are enormous, so there is usually plenty left over to share with Bowser. Another feature that is unusual for a traditional motel is that guests may order from the room-service menu and enjoy a quiet meal in the privacy of their room. Afterwards, many enjoy heading to The Fireside Lounge, which, most nights, offers live entertainment, as well as a big screen television.

During the day, there is plenty to keep everyone happy — right on site. As we mentioned, dogs can explore the river, or perhaps follow the road up to the golf course. There is also a jogging path that wends along the golf course and the canal. Children and their parents will undoubtedly gravitate to one of the two swimming pools. If it is warm, most choose the outdoor pool and the adjacent whirlpool that is surrounded by attractive landscaping. For inclement days, there is a covered pool and spa, with an adjacent deck. A separate exercise room and spa are located across the river in one of the other outbuildings.

Just south of Bend, hikers can pick up the Deschutes River trail, which leads them over fairly easy terrain to Benham Falls. Dogs will love dipping their paws in the river, or occasionally stopping for a drink. Also south of Bend, but east of the Deschutes River trail, are a series of caves. These are more interesting for people than for dogs, although canine companions might enjoy the cool interiors on hot days. These caverns are known as the Boyd, the Wind, and the Skeleton Caves and each has a short trail leading to it from the road. One other option is Shevlin Park, just west of Bend, where a leisurely trail follows the Tumalo Creek for nearly five miles.

# House on the Metolius

*P.O. Box 601*
*Camp Sherman, Oregon 97730*
*(541) 595-6620, Fax (541) 595-2402*

**Managers:** *Mark and Toni Foster*
**Rooms:** *5 doubles, 2 houses*
**Rates:** *Doubles $100 (EP), Houses $135 (EP)*
**Payment:** *MC and VISA*
**Children:** *Not appropriate for children as rooms set up for two people*
**Dogs:** *Welcome, with approval*
**Open:** *All year, except for January and February*

If fishing, hiking, and a little roughing it sounds appealing, then we can think of no better spot than the House on the Metolius. The resort is booked a year in advance and vacancies are often difficult to come by, but those who manage to secure one will be forever hooked. (No pun intended).

First-time guests are quick to learn what native Oregonians have known for some time: the eastern slopes of the Cascades are quite arid, making this area ideal for outdoor vacations. The warm summer days and cool nights lend themselves to easy exploration of this region's incredible natural beauty. The House on the Metolius is set amid 200 acres situated at an altitude of 3,000 feet in one of the area's loveliest valleys. A look in any direction gives spectacular views of the majestic Cascade Mountains, stands of ponderosa pines, or mountain meadows dotted with wildflowers. Good hiking and bicycling routes are close, but most people come for the fly fishing, or, in our case, for the total tranquillity. One of the more ideal spots for casting flies and catching trout (rainbow and brown) is on the lower section of the spring-fed Metolius River that wends through the property. Barbless hooks must be used so that the native trout can be caught and then released — hatchery-raised trout are keepers. Those who wish to perfect their angling technique may take lessons in fly fishing at a school right on the premises.

Guests stay in either cottages, duplexes, or triplexes sprinkled about the property — some of these date back to the resort's beginnings in the 1940s. These private accommodations, set among the pines, lie at the edge of the gorge overlooking the river and meadows. All accommodations are rustic, with pine-paneled walls setting the backdrop for the simple rattan chairs and comfortable sofas placed about the living rooms. Handmade quilts cover the king beds, making these the most festive spots in the cottages.

Although the maids don't clean daily, they do provide fresh towels. Wood burning fireplaces are laid with kindling and seasoned logs for when guests first arrive, but they are in charge of fire building duties for the rest of their stay. The kitchenettes are well equipped with all the essentials, including microwave ovens and coffee makers, although most guests prefer grilling on the deck or patio. The House on the Metolius is decidedly isolated; however, within a ten-minute drive are some excellent restaurant options.

This is truly a retreat for those who want to get away from civilization. The only telephone is in the office; a VCR is available, along with a variety of videotapes on fishing. For those who have left their favorite reading materials at home, there is a small library of books. While some cannot pack enough outdoor activities into a day, others enjoy relaxing in the Adirondack chairs placed about the lawns and and just listening to the sound of the wind blowing through the towering stands of pines and the water rushing by in the gorge below. The days are sunny and warm; the nights are cool with an occasional frost. Best of all, though, are the panoramic views of the majestic mountains off in the distance. Dogs, too, love this place, because they have seemingly unlimited space to explore. One suggested day hike takes guests and their canine companions along the Metolius River Trail.

The House on the Metolius has carved out a very special niche in the Cascades. The Fosters are intent on providing a peaceful and quiet retreat, which means they prefer couples to large groups of friends, families, and children. This place is private, with a feeling of exclusivity usually reserved for the well-heeled. We followed a long gravel road before reaching a barely recognizable sign pointing to another dirt lane. We paralleled the property, occasionally glimpsing the undulating lawns, before reaching an electric gate that guards the entrance to The House on the Metolius. For those who are given the code, this gate unlocks a wonderful and secret world along the banks of the Metolius.

# Hallmark Resort

*P.O. Box 547*
*1400 South Hemlock*
*Cannon Beach, Oregon 97110*
*(800) 345-5676, (503) 436-1566, Fax (503) 436-0324*

*General Manger: David Norstedt*
*Rooms: 128 doubles and suites, 4 houses*
*Rates: Doubles $79-165 (EP), Suites $125-219 (EP)*
*Payment: AE, MC, and VISA*
*Children: Welcome (cribs are available)*
*Dogs: Welcome with a small fee*
*Open: All year*

Cannon Beach is named, appropriately enough, after a cannon that washed up on its shores in the 1800s. Modern-day visitors know it for something else entirely: its 235-foot-high Haystack Rock, the third largest freestanding monolith in the world. Equally memorable is The Hallmark Resort, which is dramatically perched on the cliffs overlooking this natural wonder and surrounding sandy beach.

The resort sits unto itself on the hill, in a cluster of attractive shake buildings. It has all the trappings of a larger hotel, with a concierge, an array of amenities, and restaurants just footsteps away. Our top choice for room selection should come as no surprise — the Oceanfront Rooms. These range from a standard bedroom with a queen bed to a studio with a Murphy bed to the one- and two-bedroom suites with a Murphy bed and a separate bedroom. The premise behind the Murphy beds is a good one. During the day they are tucked out of sight, thereby creating a good-sized living room; at night they fold down to form a bedroom — complete with a fireplace and nice ocean views. Most families like the suite arrangement, because the children can sleep in the rear bedroom, while the adults can enjoy the sounds of the waves and the warmth from the fireplace in their living room/bedroom. The decor is fairly typical of many upscale motels, with Scandinavian-style oak furnishings utilized throughout.

Rooms that don't come equipped with kitchenettes do have small refrigerators, ideal for storing all sorts of goodies. Packages of Starbucks gourmet coffee are left next to the coffee makers, so that guests can make their own coffee in the morning before heading into town for a more substantial repast. One interesting item that was provided in the rooms made us chuckle: earplugs. They are left for guests to use during Sou'westers, when the wind is blowing so hard that some find it difficult to sleep. Guests concerned about the storms can keep abreast of the weather in the *Oregonian*, which is delivered to one's door each morning. Other amenities available for guests to use include irons, ironing boards, hair dryers, popcorn poppers, and laundry facilities.

Those who want to save a bit of money can reserve one of the rooms in Hallmark Square, just behind Dooger's restaurant. Guests staying here pay substantially less — and they should, since the rooms overlook a parking lot. While these rooms do not offer exceptional water vistas, they do have access to all other amenities at the hotel. Duplexes located just across the way are far larger and more reasonably priced than anything available on the ocean, making them especially appropriate for families with dogs.

The ocean water may be a bit chilly for the average person, although not for the average dog. But not to worry, the hotel has a really nice indoor pool. Everyone will enjoy spending time in and around it. Sloping ceilings lined with skylights provide plenty of natural light for this space, which is surrounded by a plethora of plants. Bright blue and white tiles provide a fresh, clean feeling to this good-sized area. Guests may swim in the pool; they also have a choice of two whirlpool spas, a wading pool for the little ones, and even an exercise room. Those who want a private spa may wish to reserve an oceanfront room, outfitted with a Jacuzzi tub large enough for two.

Critters of all kinds are handled with care by the management. For instance, recently there has been a problem with raccoons and seagulls feeding in and around the resort; so the management politely requests that guests refrain from offering the wild animals tidbits of food. The management also feels strongly that doggie guests need to leave the beach as clean as they found it. To that end, the management has placed a supply of disposable pooper scoopers at the top of every staircase descending to the beach. In addition, they ask that dogs not be left alone in the rooms or on the patios, as they might disturb the other guests. This should not be a problem, though, as there are plenty of things to do in the area.

Obviously, long beach walks are a wonderful way to spend time with Bowser. Other options include a hike up Neahkannie Mountain or along the Oswald West State Park's beaches and trails, both of which are close to the resort. The village of Cannon Beach is another great place for taking a stroll with Bowser, especially along the road paralleling the beach, as it is lined with small restaurants, art galleries, and kite shops.

# Quiet Cannon Lodgings

*P.O. Box 174*
*372 North Spruce Street*
*Cannon Beach, Oregon  97110*
*(503) 436-1405 or 436-1805*

*Hosts: Don and Joan Holden, Al and Charlotte Hovey*
*Rooms: 2 condominium units*
*Rates: $85-95 (EP)*
*Payment: Personal checks*
*Children: Not appropriate for children*
*Dogs: Welcome with a daily fee of $5; however," they are not to be left in*
*the unit alone"*
*Open: All year*

Each traveler has a different concept of what the ideal vacation should entail. For those who prefer vacations where they can settle into their own apartment, prepare meals at their leisure, and live autonomously, the Quiet Cannon Lodgings are a delightful option.

The Quiet Cannon Lodgings consist of two apartments located in a contemporary, weathered-shingle building at the end of a cul-de-sac on Cannon Beach. They are surrounded by a grove of pine trees, flower beds, and mature plantings. The units are spacious, with large kitchens (loaded with modern conveniences), separate bedrooms with queen beds, and living rooms with fireplaces. Those who enjoy cooking out-of-doors will appreciate the barbecue. The interior decor is contemporary, yet very simple — perhaps this is best, as it does not detract from the views through the walls of picture windows. Best of all, the apartments overlook Ecola (meaning big fish or whale) Creek, which flows into the Pacific just beyond. The larger and more expensive of the two units faces the creek and ocean, while the somewhat smaller one has views of the creek and sand dunes. They both share a long patio, offering yet another way to enjoy this lovely setting.

The apartments' location is what especially endears guests to the Quiet Cannon Lodgings. They can step out the door and immediately sink their toes into the soft sand and explore in any direction. (A small sign attached to the house reminds guests to clean the sand off their dogs before heading back inside). Many guests and their dogs like to take a swim in the fresh waters of the creek or go off in search of ocean life harbored in the tidal pools. One of the more popular excursions is to follow the beach down to the town center and walk back along the quiet side streets. Others are content to relax by the ocean and try their hand at flying a kite — which seems to be a popular pastime in these parts.

While the Hoveys and Holdens greatly respect their guests' privacy, they are also very willing to recommend a favorite restaurant or activity. Al even compiled a 6-page brochure on some of the nearby sights and attractions. Some suggestions include Haystack Rock (the third largest monolith in the world), Les Shirley Park (a Lewis & Clark campsite), and Tillamook Head. The latter choice is part of the Ecola State Park, just two miles north of Cannon Beach. The views that lie along this section of the Oregon Coast Trail are memorable, but Bowser will probably be more interested in sniffing out the little critters that sometimes poke their heads up from behind the craggy rocks. At different points along the trails, hikers may also find sea lions and water fowl in their natural habitat, as well as grazing deer. After an exhilarating outing, guests may want to return home, put on a pot of water for tea, light a fire, and enjoy a peaceful afternoon at the Quiet Cannon Lodgings.

# Coos Bay Manor

*955 South Fifth Street*
*Coos Bay, Oregon 97420*
*(800) 269-1224, (541) 269-1224*

*Innkeeper: Patricia Williams*
*Rooms: 5 doubles*
*Rates: $65-75 (B&B)*
*Payment: MC and VISA*
*Children: Welcome; not appropriate for children under the age of 4*
*Dogs: Welcome, but they must get along with the resident cat. There is*
*an outdoor dog run for dogs who prefer sleeping outside.*
*Open: All year*

We have driven *through* Coos Bay a number of times over the years, but we never thought to stop and spend the night, as we were always heading further north along the coast. It turns out that Coos Bay is an interesting place. It dates back to 1854 and is best known for having the largest deep-water port along the Oregon coast. As a result of its size and its central location, the port is also the largest shipper of timber and timber-related products anywhere in the country. While there is always plenty of activity in port, and huge trucks rumbling along the main roads, there are also lovely neighborhoods in this bustling town. Just before leaving the southern end of Coos Bay, visitors can make a turn west and head up the hill into a quiet, residential neighborhood lined with gracious homes and cottages. Many of the largest and most historic of these buildings were commissioned by wealthy lumber barons at the turn of the century. The Coos Bay Manor is one such home.

There is no sign announcing the Coos Bay Manor, but armed with the address and a good description, it was not hard to find it. Set on a knoll, this gracious manor house is bedecked with wisteria and surrounded by beautiful gardens. This historic Colonial-style house was built in 1912 by two Finnish brothers, the Nerdrums, who worked for one of the local lumber companies. Today, guests will discover it has been nicely restored and is now listed on the National Register of Historic Places. Patricia showed us the black and white picture of the original house. Her initial thought after purchasing the house was to keep it basically the way she had found it. Then she discovered the old photograph and realized all of the work that really should be done to bring it back to its former stature.

She was just the woman to do it too — a friendly and vivacious redhead who seems to have unlimited amounts of energy. We met her in the grand foyer. As we looked around, it was clear to us that her restoration has been a total success. The highlight in here is the central staircase that rises to an open-air banister edging the entire second floor. Patricia, accompanied by her friendly black cat, gave us the grand tour. We started in the living room, where guests were relaxing on the couch in front of the fireplace. Behind it was a long table set with a huge vase of roses picked from the garden. A baby

13

grand piano occupies one end of this formal space, while at the other end an archway leads into the dining room. As with all the other rooms in the house, high ceilings and hand-carved paneling add architectural interest. Many B&Bs have a large communal table set up for meals, which is fine if the mix of guests is a good one. We like the individual tables in here, as they afford breakfast eaters a little more privacy. The expanded Continental meal might include such options as Belgian waffles, pancakes topped with berries, an omelet, and an assortment of breads and muffins. Fresh huckleberries are often available, depending on whether or not the hostess has had time to go out and pick them.

There are few, if any, areas that are off-limits to guests, including the big, old-fashioned kitchen. As we passed through the butler's pantry to get here, we found Patricia in the midst of canning an assortment of vegetables — the aroma was divine. Both this inviting space and the hostess seemed to have two things in common — loads of character and a good deal of charm. After our tour of the first floor, we climbed the staircase to the bedrooms. Our first stop was in the yellow-hued Country Room that occupies the front corner of the house. The brass bed looked especially appealing with its thick featherbed and handmade quilt. When we stopped to admire the delicate embroidered flowers edging the pillow cases and sheets, Patricia modestly told us she had done the handwork. Off in a corner rests a spinning wheel. The Country Room and Garden Room next door are the only two bedrooms to share a bathroom. This bathroom is a large converted closet that is now fashioned with French blue marbled walls that match the room next door.

The Garden Room overlooks the rhododendrons in the back yard and is favored, for some reason, by women traveling alone. We can understand the appeal, as a crisp white handkerchief-patterned duvet covers this featherbed and a white gauze quarter-canopy frames it — the effect is very serene. White wicker furniture forms a small sitting area under the windows. Our next stop was the Cattle Baron's Room, a totally masculine space with a bear skin stretched across one entire wall (it must have been some bear) and a coyote skin along another. There are all sorts of books in here, along with Native American portraits and artifacts. The good-sized bathroom is private and also has attractive marbleized accents. Shutters on windows open to reveal views of the backyard. A favorite room for romantics is the Victorian Room, with its canopied bed and plenty of lace and frills. A sitting area, set near the window, overlooks the front yard. The bathroom in here is virtually the same as it was back in the early 1900s. This large space was opulent for the time, and still has the original wallpaper, oversized bathtub, and fixtures. The rose theme in the wallpaper is carried through to the antique dressing table, which contains a small dish of soaps, shampoos, and lotions that are all accented in various hues of pink. The Colonial Room is perfect for people who need two beds. This room has a pair of four-poster bedsteads covered with simple white spreads. Guests look out these windows onto a pair of huge redwood trees. The small bathroom is situated just outside the door. Its brass basin and marble countertop were salvaged from a friend's house that, unfortunately, burned down. Patricia appreciates details and even showed us where the basin has been worn down from years of use.

French doors from the second-floor landing open to a roof deck, where guests are welcome to sit and take their breakfast, or perhaps, on a clear evening, watch the stars. After a hearty morning repast, most people are ready to head out for the day. Some might choose to take a walk with their dogs through the surrounding neighborhoods. More extensive walks might be had by visiting one of the local state parks. Our first choice is the Sunset Bay State Park. Here, dogs are welcome to visit the sandy beach, or perhaps set out along the three-mile trail leading to the Shore Acres State Park. This was once owned by a gentleman who planted the area with exotic plants from all over the world. There is another path that leads from here down to Simpson Beach. Another popular option is to head north to the Oregon Dune National Recreation area, where mountainous sand dunes provide a wonderful outlet for romping dogs and frolicking children.

---

# Odell Lake Lodge

*P.O. Box 72*
*Crescent Lake, Oregon 97425*
*(541) 433-2540*

*Hosts: John, Janet, and Kelly Milandin*
*Rooms: 8 doubles, 17 cabins*
*Rates: Doubles $38-52 (EP), Cabins $55-200 (EP)*
*Payment: MC and VISA*
*Children: Welcome*
*Dogs: Welcome in the cabins only. Limit of one pet per cabin at $5 per*
     *night. Dogs must be leashed at all times and are not allowed on*
     *the cross-country ski trails.*
*Open: All year*

Odell Lake is one of the largest natural lakes in Oregon. Formed by a glacier thousands of years ago, today it encompasses 3,800 acres and is over 280 feet deep. Mackinaw and native rainbow trout thrive along with Kokanee salmon in these cold waters. Anyone who happens to fall in while fishing will just as quickly hop right out again. We followed a one-lane road along the lake for a short distance before reaching the lodge. Alhough it was late October and there was not another diversion in the area for miles, the Odell Lake Lodge was bustling with adults, children, and a few dogs — all enjoying the warm fall weather. Children were riding their bicycles along the quiet back road, while others could be seen walking the path that skirts along the shoreline. The faint smell of wood smoke was everywhere.

The main lodge is a neat, old-fashioned place, with a dark wood exterior and inviting front porch. This is the centerpiece for the small community, as guests and visitors come here both to enjoy one another's company and to purchase everything from fishing licenses and tackle to drinks and candy. We especially liked the great room, with its light pine walls and big beams. The focal point, though, is the huge stone fireplace that comprises most of the far wall, except for the small windows revealing views of the lake. A lending library of books, games, and puzzles fills two other walls of built-in shelves. Comfortable overstuffed couches and chairs are set everywhere. When we arrived, many of the guests were either reading, working on a puzzle, or sorting through the fishing books while New Age music played softly in the background.

Off in another wing of the lodge, there is a small restaurant. It is equally light and airy, and is privy to some of the best lake views, through a long wall of windows. The meals are all home cooked. The dinner menu has a little something for everyone, with steak and shrimp, pork chops, chicken and mushroom Alfredo, and shrimp scampi topping the list of entrées. A well thought out children's menu is just as reasonably priced. Among the most popular aspects of this hearty affair are the fresh fruit pies that are offered for dessert.

We liked the option of using the restaurant, but the cabins also contain fully-equipped kitchens. We suggest planning ahead and bringing enough supplies for the duration of one's stay — remembering, though, that great food is always available at the lodge. The cabins can be rustic, although there are a few exceptions. The most desirable accommodations line the bluff overlooking the lake (#6-8, 10, 12, 16, and 17); the second tier of cabins backs up to the children's play area, which might appeal to some parents. The cabins can sleep anywhere from 2-16 people. The most common configuration consists of a double bed with bunk beds in either one or two separate rooms, and sleep sofas in the living rooms (when there are living rooms).

Cabins #1-4 are the smallest, and are capable of housing four people — a very close foursome. One small bedroom has a double bed and a bunk bed, while the kitchen/sitting room contains just enough space for a wood stove, table, and a few chairs. Couples traveling with a dog would find any of these smaller cabins to be just fine. If we were to pick one of the cabins as our favorite, it would be #10, as it is newer than the rest and is probably the best designed. Two bedrooms contain queen beds, while the living room is outfitted with a pair of sofa beds. What we like most, though, is the bay window overlooking the lake, and its private lakeside deck. Cabin #12 is huge, and rambles all over the place. This would be a good choice for extended families who would like to stay together. Regardless of one's final choice, all guest cabins have fully-equipped kitchens, private bathrooms, linens, and plenty of firewood for the wood stoves or fireplaces. Barbecues are also available for outdoor cooking.

Not too surprisingly, we found that people and their dogs weren't spending all that much time in their cabins. As we mentioned, they were riding bikes, playing down by the stream, and heading off into the forest for leisurely hikes. The small children's play area down by the lake was very popular, especially the slide and swing sets made out of old logs. Those who may have forgotten something can probably rent it here. Water-oriented rentals range from canoes and row boats to 18-foot motor boats. Mountain bikes are also available. In the winter months, people come here to cross-country ski.

While dogs are not allowed on the groomed, cross-country ski trails, they are welcome on the back-country trails. There are snow shoes and skis available to rent, as well as affable instructors. Guests soon discover that the lodge lends itself to days of relaxation interspersed with explorations of this incredibly beautiful mountainous terrain. There is plenty of space for canines to roam once they get away from the cottages.

Throughout the Deschutes National Forest and Diamond Peaks Wilderness Area, there are countless trails that allow dogs. One popular option, beginning right at the lake, leads hikers to a pair of beautiful, high mountain lakes — Yoran or Diamond View lakes. The Pacific Coast Trail also wends through this region. Those who are interested can pick up a portion of it near Odell Lake and hike up to any of the Rosary Lakes.

# Inn at Arch Rock

*P.O. Box 251*
*70 Northwest Sunset Street*
*Depoe Bay, Oregon   97341*
*(541) 765-2560*

**Innkeepers:** *Greg and Susan Lyons*
**Rooms:** *11 doubles, 1 house*
**Rates:** *$68-95 (B&B), House $125 (B&B)*
**Payment:** *Visa*
**Children:** *Welcome; children under 12  years of age are free of charge*
**Dogs:** *Welcome in rooms 5-8*
**Open:** *All year*

Set on the cliffs looking back toward Depoe Bay, the Inn at Arch Rock is part inn and part unconventional motel. The main inn is a traditional dormered Cape, set on a quiet side street, well off busy Highway 101. After walking into the small reception area and seeing the steep narrow staircase leading to the inn's guest rooms, we suspected that guests traveling with dogs would probably not be prime candidates for these compact spaces. We were instead directed out to either the cottage or the three-room "motel." We thought we would give the motel rooms a chance — after all, we had been pleasantly surprised on plenty of other occasions.

This time was no exception. From the exterior, this is an attractive building bedecked with white shingles and a farmer's porch. The interiors are even more attractive, with hardwood floors and wood-paneled walls that imbue them with some character. A chintz valance above the window or an ivy-patterned wallpaper help enhance the overall decor. What might once have been one large bedroom, is now neatly broken up into a sleeping area, sitting room, and breakfast nook. A queen beds lies under a window toward the rear of the room. A sofa bed and rattan chairs form an intimate sitting area facing the ocean; in another there is a small breakfast table flanked by two ladder back chairs. A series of windows not only allows the sun to permeate these spaces, but also reveals spectacular water views. A tiny kitchenette is surprisingly well stocked, including a large basket filled with microwave popcorn and coffee and tea. Drinks and other perishables may be stored in the small refrigerator. Each morning, guests are offered a simple Continental repast of homemade muffins and cinnamon rolls.

Our favorite room of the three is Room 8, which is decorated around an English country theme. The decor in Rooms 6 and 7 is not as sophisticated, but it is attractive nonetheless. Guests with dogs can also stay in the quaint one-bedroom cottage, which can accommodate four people by utilizing both the queen bed and sofa bed. It is set apart from all the other units, which might make it even more appealing to families with dogs — they don't need to worry as much about an inadvertent peep late at night.

What most people remember about the Inn at Arch Rock are the views and the sounds of the crashing surf. Just in front of the inn is a small lawn — a nice place for relaxing when the surf isn't too wild. The cliffs are also quite famous for their spouting horns. This occurs when the water rushes into small vertical crevices and sprays up to 50 feet in the air. People come to Depoe Bay just to watch this natural phenomenon.When near the cliffs, we recommend that dogs be leashed. It is fun to take Bowser for a walk along these cliffs into town; but visitors need to be careful about the sporadic spouts, as they can unnerve and completely soak both human and beast.

While summertime guests will be able to enjoy the spouting horns, they won't be able to see the winter whale migration just off the coast. Regardless of the time of year, though, most are fascinated with the fishing boats as they navigate in and out of the narrow crevice that is a channel between the open sea and "the world's smallest harbor." Two miles north of Depoe Bay, visitors and their dogs will find Fogarty Creek State Park, which is comprised of more than 150 acres right along the ocean. The park offers some nice picnic sites and walking trails, but many come here specifically to watch the sea lions. The Beverly Beach State Park also welcomes dogs and has easy nature walks through the forest, as well as an expansive beach with intriguing tide pools. Further south, visitors and their dogs are welcome to investigate the 400 acres around South Beach or the 230 acres around Ona Beach.

# Gull Haven Lodge

*94770 Highway 101 North*
*Florence, Oregon   97439*
*(541) 547-3583*

**Owner:** *Mary Fike*
**Rooms:** *3 doubles, 4 suites, 1 cottage*
**Rates:** *Doubles $35-60 (EP), Suites $75-85 (EP), Cottage $49 (EP)*
**Payment:** *DSC, MC, and VISA*
**Children:** *Welcome*
**Dogs:** *Welcome with an $8 daily fee. The extensive pet policy asks that dogs always be leashed and that they be given an outdoor shower before coming inside;  dogs may not be left unattended in rooms and guests must clean up after their pet.*
**Open:** *All year*

As guests navigate the serpentine coastal road, they will come all of a sudden upon the Gull Haven Lodge — a rather funky three-story building perched on a bluff overlooking the crashing Pacific Ocean. There is absolutely nothing around this place except some spectacular natural scenery. The Gull Haven Lodge offers guests not only inexpensive accommodations, but also panoramic ocean views through most of the bedroom windows. What more could anyone seeking a simple, low-key haven along the Oregon coast require?

We arrived on a warm fall day and walked into the cozy skylit office, where a plethora of jade and hanging plants were thriving amid the pseudo-tropical environment. As we waited for the manager to appear, we sampled some of the taffy from a basket set on the counter and leafed through several of the assorted brochures on the surrounding area. An affable assistant suddenly emerged and gave us the grand tour. We soon discovered we really liked the lodge, because it offers a variety of accommodation options for guests and their four-legged friends — ranging from expansive apartments to a single-room cottage. Every room, without exception — whether facing north, south, or west — has outstanding ocean views.

We started our tour in the three-room Gathering Place, which is separate from the main lodge. It is perched on the edge of the rocks, with views from just about every vantage point (except, perhaps, from the tiled shower). The spacious and comfortable living room doubles as a bedroom, with a sofa bed and two window seats that convert into beds. Window-seat sleeping is not normally our first choice; however, we would be willing to reconsider, knowing that in the morning there are terrific expanses of ocean visible through the two walls of plate glass windows. A separate double-bedded room should please those who want a little more privacy. The full kitchen has just about everything to make a cook happy, and when the oven is not heating up the space, the fireplace is.

North Up and South Up, true to their names, are located on the upper floors of the main lodge. These two options are especially appropriate for families or groups of friends. South Up offers a separate bedroom; however, the best views are from the queen bed set just off the dining area or from the window-seat bunks. North Up is a larger four-room apartment with two private bedrooms and still more window-seat bunks. Both of these apartments offer full kitchens, along with large living and dining rooms. Guests who stay here will have the sensation that they are floating between the sky and ocean.

The Shag's Nest is an ideal choice for a couple interested in total privacy – and, of course, water views. This one-room cabin is located down the hill from the other accommodations, on a knoll that abuts the edge of the cliff. Guests may sit out on the small deck festooned with flowering plants, or enjoy the views through three walls of picture windows. A queen bed, set near the fireplace, is a wonderful place to watch the sun set or a tumultuous ocean storm roll in. Guests also have a kitchenette for preparing light snacks and meals. The only potential drawback to this oasis is that the bathroom is located in the main lodge.

For those who do not need all the extra space of an apartment or cabin, we recommend the Lavender or Garden rooms. Both of these cedar-walled rooms are literally fashioned with more walls of windows than they are of wood. These accommodations share a kitchenette and bathroom, but their decor is decidedly less eclectic than the other guest quarters. These have contemporary floral prints on the beds and an array of modern amenities in the kitchenettes. We also liked Northwest Down, which is found on the lower level of the lodge. In addition to being substantially more private, it, too, has a kitchenette.

Guests who would like to walk their dogs have two immediate options. First is a small circle of lawn that separates the lodge from the cliff; we encountered a pair of dogs happily playing on it. It is a good idea to leash Bowser, though, as a burst of speed in the wrong direction can lead to catastrophic results. The second, and more popular, option is to take the dog for a walk down the path that leads over the cliff to a very private cove. Visitors will discover that many of the beaches in this region are found in small coves or along miles of shoreline. Whichever sandy expanse guests and their dogs choose to explore, they will generally find interesting shells, tide pools teeming with aquatic life, or seals and whales swimming just offshore. Those interested in hiking with their dog should look into Cape Perpetua, where there are a variety of dog-walking options. The St. Perpetua Trail leads visitors up to a scenic vista that has commanding views of the coast. Another possibility, called the Spruce Trail, leads to a spruce tree dating back 500 years. (This route should not be confused with the trail called the Whispering Spruce Trail.) The Carl G. Washburne State Park also offers fun hiking opportunities for both humans and dogs, along the China Creek and Hobbit trails.

As a final note, Gull Haven Lodge is not appropriate for guests who are looking for an elegant, oceanside retreat with lovely landscaping, exquisite food, and a variety of built-in diversions. This is, instead, a simple lodge with comfortable accommodations, convenient kitchenettes, and terrific views of the ocean. Those who like low-key seaside retreats, though, will thoroughly enjoy the Gull Haven Lodge.

# Salishan Lodge

*P.O. Box 118*
*Highway 101*
*Gleneden Beach, Oregon 97388*
*(800) 452-2300, (541) 764-3600, Fax (541) 764-3510*

*General Manager: Pierre Alarco*
*Rooms: 205 doubles*
*Rates: Doubles $109-236 (EP)*
*Payment: AE, DSC, MC, and VISA*
*Children: Welcome (cribs, cots, and baby-sitters are available)*
*Dogs: Welcome with a $15 daily charge*
*Open: All year*

The Salishan Lodge is the one of the most luxurious resorts along the Oregon coast — it also happens to welcome dogs. Its dramatic oceanside setting, overlooking Siletz Bay, amid 700 acres of landscaped and natural surroundings, puts this resort on our short list of highly recommended places to stay in the Northwest. Although the resort is expansive, a distinct feeling of privacy pervades. Guest rooms lie in villas set into hillsides, and are mostly linked by covered footbridges and paths that are reminiscent of ancient Japanese palace gardens. A wending drive leads guests past rivers and waterfalls, through fir, spruce, hemlock, and cedar groves, until they reach their villa. (There are eight guest chambers per villa.) Contemporary lines, coupled with weathered-wood siding, cause the villas to blend with the surrounding landscape. This feeling of seclusion continues inside, as each room is not only well designed, but also soundproofed. Many guests will be thoroughly impressed with the magnificent views revealed through the walls of sliding-glass doors. Not all windows overlook the bay; some pan out over dense forests or the verdant golf course. Many of these rooms contain hemlock-beamed cathedral ceilings and walls painted in subtle earth tones that produce an atmosphere of understated elegance and character. Lithographs by artists of the Northwest are limited to two per room. Although we would have enjoyed seeing more, they deftly capture the unique rugged beauty of this idyllic place.

The newer Siletz Bay rooms are the most distinctive guest chambers, offering exceptional bay views, separate sitting areas, and stone fireplaces. The Salishan Chieftain rooms contain slightly less formal furnishings, but similar views. Those who are more interested in spending their money on their recreational pursuits, rather than on their room, may request the simplest and least expensive Salishan rooms. These spaces do not contain separate sitting areas, but in all other respects are well appointed and furnished. The decor is very attractive but not especially noteworthy, except in the Siletz Bay rooms, where everything is upgraded to create a more luxurious setting. In all cases, though, every effort has been made to maximize the views; so whether guests are lying in bed or sitting on the couch in front of the fire, they can enjoy the lovely vistas. The extra large bathrooms received special attention, with their Corian sinks, whirlpool tubs, baskets of toiletries, and separate showers.

The resort's amenities are bountiful. Golfers will appreciate the challenging, 18-hole, par 72 golf links (built in the Scottish tradition on land reclaimed from the ocean). The three indoor and one outdoor tennis court will appeal to some, while others may prefer working out using the exercise equipment in the Fitness Center. This complex also houses an indoor swimming pool, hydrotherapy pool, saunas, and circuit weight training. Children will enjoy the game room and expansive playground.

Dogs, on the other hand, will thoroughly relish exploring the three-mile long beach. Digging for clams and mussels, searching for seashells, and watching migrating whales are favorite activities for human counterparts. The resort even furnishes comprehensive maps of the area's nature trails and running loops for guests to investigate with their canine cohorts.

It is easy to work up an appetite, and even easier to satisfy it in one of the resort's five restaurants. One of the most popular meals is the famous Sunday brunch, which is presented in the Cedar Tree restaurant. Guests may select from a seemingly endless list of items, which can including eggs Benedict; Belgian waffles; apple smoked salmon hash; sourdough, buckwheat or buttermilk pancakes; and authentic English bangers (sausages). The Dining Room, situated on three levels, is the most formal of the restaurants, and serves an extensive array of seasonal native seafoods and game. We munched on the crispy sourdough bread while perusing the extensive menu. Our choices included the double lamb chops topped with roasted garlic and peppers; veal loin with a ragoût of woodland mushrooms; the Tillamook cheddar cheese fondue with sourdough bread; and the Oregon seafood soup with oysters, baby shrimp, smoked salmon, and Dungeness crab. Subtle burgundy and mauve tones, coupled with the picturesque views of Siletz Bay and the surrounding forest, set the mood for a memorable dining experience. For simpler fare, there is the informal Sun Room, which is an especially sunny spot in the morning.

It is difficult to sum up this terrific resort in just a few paragraphs, except to say that prospective guests truly need more than a day or two to fully appreciate the beauty and overall peacefulness of the Salishan Lodge.

# Jot's Resort

*P.O. Box J*
*Highway 101 at the Rogue River*
*Gold Beach, Oregon 97444*
*(800) FOR-JOTS, (541) 247-6676, Fax (541) 247-6716*

*Owners Virginia McKinney*
*Rooms: 19 singles, 79 doubles, 3 suites, 20 cottages*
*Rates: Singles $80 (EP), Doubles $90 (EP),*
*        Suites and cottages $120 -300 (EP)*
*Payment: AE, DC, DSC, MC, and VISA*
*Children: Welcome (cribs, cots, and baby-sitters are available)*
*Dogs: Welcome in the ground floor units with a daily fee of $10*
*Open: All year*

Jot's Resort has been around for over 20 years, and with good reason. It not only occupies a portion of the Rogue River's northern banks but is also a great base for fine fishing further upstream. Jot's is easy to find — just before crossing the expansive bridge into Gold Beach, look for the sign and a rather steep driveway leading down to a small complex of one- and two-story buildings. The reception area and tackle shop are situated in the middle of this compound, opposite an outdoor swimming pool and an indoor spa and pool. As we arrived, we found an enthusiastic group of guests preparing to head up the Rogue River by way of jet boat.

The accommodations at Jot's Resort are basically glorified motor lodge rooms. Located in several buildings at the mouth of the river, all guest rooms overlook the water as well as the town of Gold Beach. The decor in each room is comprised of Danish-style furnishings and neutral color schemes. Each guest chamber is outfitted with a cable television, a direct-dial telephone, and a large bathroom. In each bedroom, an additional vanity sits just outside the bathroom. Sliding glass doors open to porches or decks.

A separate, two-story building offers more modern accommodations with an enhanced list of amenities. These are especially suitable for families, as they contain living rooms with cathedral ceilings and fireplaces, kitchens for preparing meals (perhaps the catch of fish from the day), and skylit lofts that afford additional sleeping space. The newer rooms also have private decks and equally fine water views. Some of the best features, however, are found outside, where the distant sounds of the crashing waves combine with the sight of shore birds, sounds of sea lions, and the pulsing lighthouse beacon.

For us, the accommodations are almost secondary to the numerous diversions available in and around Jot's. In addition to fishing, there is beach combing, digging for clams, Windsurfing, whale watching, or crabbing. Anglers come prepared to catch the fish of the season, which includes salmon from May to November, cutthroat trout during the summer, and giant sturgeon and steelhead year round. The resort's extensive sport shop is brimming with everything one might require. The folks running the marina have plenty of rental boats, but they can also arrange for guided river expeditions and deep sea fishing charters. Land-based fishing opportunities for cod, perch, snapper, ocean chinook, and Coho salmon are just a short cast away. Another favorite pastime is riding the jet boats, which offer scenic 64-mile — and wild 104-mile — round trip expeditions along the Rogue River.

Dogs who grow weary of pacing the banks looking for waterfowl and aquatic life will be entertained with some of the local day hikes. The neighboring Siskiyou National Forest is just south of Gold Beach. Within this park is the Chetco Gorge Trail, which leads hikers and their canines along the Chetco River to Eagle Creek. There are even places along the way for swimming, which will certainly appeal to furry friends. The Samuel H. Boardman State Park, also south of Gold Beach, has 1,400 acres of hiking trails that allow leashed dogs. When guests return at the end of the day, they should probably park their dogs for a nap and then take a swim in either the outdoor heated pool or the indoor pool and spa. Other attractions include miniature golf or hitting the links at the nearby nine-hole golf course.

Whatever the day's diversions, guests need look no further for their evening meal than the Rod 'n' Reel, a favorite eatery among visitors and locals alike. In addition to offering a bar and a lounge with nightly entertainment, the restaurant provides an intimate setting and an extensive menu. Salmon, jumbo prawns, and the house special, the Admirals' Delight, top the seafood menu, while prime rib and filet mignon highlight other portions. After dinner, we enjoy heading back to the room, opening the sliding glass doors, and letting in the sounds and the smells of the sea while we drift off to sleep.

---

# Clear Creek Farm

*P.O. Box 737*
*Halfway, Oregon 97834*
*(541) 742-2238, Fax (541) 742-5175*

*Hosts: Barbara, Matt, and Denise Phillips, Mike and Rose Curless*
*Rooms: 4 doubles, 2 cottages*
*Rates: Doubles/Cottages $60 (B&B), $10 per child, $16-19 per teenager*
*Payment: VISA*
*Children: Welcome*
*Dogs: Welcome*
*Open: All year*

Anyone unfamiliar with northeastern Oregon may be surprised to find a climate very different from that of its western counterpart. While western Oregon gets an abundance of rain and cool ocean winds, the eastern region is much hotter and drier, because the Cascades obstruct the path of the ocean storms. Clear Creek Farm is in the far reaches of northeastern Oregon, just a short distance from Idaho. The closet town is a hamlet known as Halfway — an appropriate name for a town that used to be the halfway point for the stagecoach that ran between Pine Town and Carson. Today's visitors will more likely view it a bit differently, as the farm and town lie halfway between Upper Hell's Canyon and the Eagle Cap Wilderness, two spectacular natural recreation areas.

Clear Creek Farm is a real working ranch, and has been for well over 100 years. Buffalo roam across its 160 acres, which are also planted with orchards and gardens fed by ponds and a year-round stream. In the spring, the acreage is dotted with colorful wildflowers. This is a rustic place, which tries to reacquaint people with a simpler lifestyle and the beauty of nature. As with most ranches, Clear Creek Farm consists of an old-fashioned farmhouse and various other rustic outbuildings. While guests traveling with a dog may stay in any of the accommodations, we prefer the two outbuildings because of their additional privacy.

One of these is really a modified, open-space barn. This not only sounds unique, it is unique. The artist who built the barn designed it to be rustic and intimate, and in keeping with its surroundings. One of the two bedrooms contains both a king and a queen bed, while another offers a pair of bunks. Guests who stay here also have views of the ponds and mountains from their covered porch. Barbara said guests *think* they will rock on the porch to enjoy these views, but the *reality* is there are so many other pleasant diversions that few return to their room until after nightfall. Another popular guest chamber lies just behind the barn, in a second converted building containing a queen bedstead and two bunks. A modern bathhouse is immaculate, supplying guests with plenty of hot, running water.

These outbuildings are closed in the winter months, so those who venture out this way between October and April will stay in the cozy farmhouse. It contains four guest bedrooms, which are named after their predominant color — blue, pink, etc. Guests with children might be interested in the extra bedroom, which contains both a pair of  bunk beds and a crib and is often used as a nursery. The early American antiques are simple and attractive, as are the other collectibles and furnishings. The bathroom is shared and is always clean and tidy.

Everyone looks forward to the full country breakfast, which Barbara laughingly describes as "one hell of a breakfast." In the summer, it is cooked in the unusual, open-air summer kitchen just off the back of the farmhouse. It includes homemade breads, such as sourdough and cinnamon, eggs, bacon, and buffalo sausage. Dutch babies, delicious puffed pancakes baked in a casserole, are the house specialty. Fresh fruits, berries, and vegetables from the farm and its orchards are always featured. (The farm is especially famous for its delicious peaches.) In the afternoons, freshly squeezed lemonade and other refreshing libations are made available to guests returning from their day's adventures. The morning meal is so good, we asked about lunches and dinners. Barbara told us they now offer a *Guests of the Ranch* package that includes a lunch and dinner, served at guests' convenience, for an extra charge of $20. (The *Guests of the Ranch* package also entitles participants to take advantage of all aspects of ranch life, if they are so inclined. This might encompass everything from a simple chore like feeding the chickens to something a little more complicated, such as vaccinating the buffalo.) Barbara also mentioned that there are several good restaurants in town, and one exceptional eatery that is well worth splurging on at least once during a visit.

With acres to explore and so much to do, guests who opt for a week-long vacation at the farm rarely run out of things to do. There is a creek for fishing and a pond for swimming. Of course, long walks and hikes are always a highly recommended activity. Bowser will discover that the resident dogs like to accompany hikers on these adventures, as well. We still chuckle over the story about one guest who was accompanied by her pet crocodile. Bowser just might be lucky enough to befriend one of these more unusual pets during his stay. Children love helping milk the goat, pick berries, or visiting with the other farm animals.

Those interested in venturing further afield will discover that the famous Hell's Canyon is just a short distance away. There are also white-water rafting and jet boat trips, an abundance of steelhead, sturgeon, and trout to be caught, interesting auto tours, backpacking, and extensive horseback riding trails available throughout the region. The climate ranges from desert-like conditions on the canyon floor to cool alpine air with crystal blue lakes at the higher elevations. At the end of a busy day, it is always nice to return to the Clear Creek Farm's low-key, homey atmosphere, either to watch the setting sun or to relax in the rejuvenating hot tub.

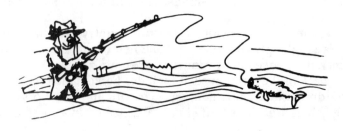

# Pine Valley Lodge
# Halfway Supper Club

*P.O. Box 712*
*1563 North Main Street*
*Halfway, Oregon  97834*
*(541) 742-2027*

*Innkeepers: Dale Beatty and Babette Russell*
*Rooms: 6 doubles*
*Rates: $55-65 (B&B)*
*Payment: Personal checks*
*Children: Welcome (a crib is available)*
*Dogs: Welcome with notice and approval*
*Open: All year*

If the *Hells Canyon Journal* could give the Halfway Supper Club a "four forks up" rating, then we felt it was worth investigating too. Actually, our curiosity was initially sparked by the Clear Creek Farm's recommendation, when Barbara Phillips told us it serves some of the finest food around. Little did we know it also has six extraordinarily unusual guest rooms.

From the exterior, the Pine Valley Lodge looks like many of those western lodges lining the highways — plenty of natural wood, wraparound porches, and steep roofs. We thought the array of antlers displayed over the front door made the place look especially authentic. New arrivals can just step inside, put their Stetson on the hat rack, and turn around to an unusual place filled with an eclectic, yet sophisticated, mix of furniture, collectibles, and art. Hardwood floors and naturally finished wood walls support the beamed ceilings in the great room. This chamber is filled with a wonderful assortment of antiques, ranging from classic armchairs to rustic sofas, all covered with bright fabrics reflecting Native American and western-style prints. It is difficult to know where to look — there is almost too much to take in visually. A mounted fish hangs on one wall next to a rip saw blade, while on another are a pair of fishing rods. A milk painted hutch is nestled against another wall, alongside a lightly stained oak table topped by a lamp. The lamp's base is also a little unusual, as it is formed by figurines of a man and woman entwined in dance. Games abound, including backgammon, Mah-Jong, and cards, as well as stacks of books covering a myriad of subjects.

Keeping all this in mind, it is the use of color that galvanizes this place. The ceilings in the great room are a cranberry red, as is one wall in the intimate dining room. The other pine-paneled wall in here is painted a deep teal reminiscent of the tropics. Draped dining room tables and chairs don't always match, but neither do the candle holders, which range from crystal to silver. It doesn't matter — it all somehow works beautifully. Guests should note that even they must make reservations for dinner, as there is limited seating, and limited hours — the dining room is open from 6 to 8 p.m. The appetizers might include a French onion soup made with sweet onions, white wine, and brandy, or Babette's tomato and basil brochette. There are also plenty of meat dishes on the menu. The hefty New York strip steak comes in either 14- or 16-ounce portions, or guests may try the more diminutive filet mignon. Both arrive grilled and served with twice-baked potatoes and fresh vegetables. Lamb chops are marinated in lemon and rosemary and then grilled, as well. There is also a fish of the day, and if guests catch their own, Babette will be happy to prepare it for them. Diners should take care not to be fooled by the whiskey cake; it is actually loaded with chocolate. Others might prefer the more delicate crème caramel — Cuban style.

After a meal of this magnitude, the short walk to the bedroom is a welcome relief. Guests should ignore for a moment that they share a single bathroom, because the unique bed chambers more than compensate for this. One of our favorites is the Bayou Room. The highlight is a massive four-poster bed with carved-wood, snowy egrets seemingly poised for flight from the tops of the finials. Royal blue, emerald green, and dusty rose all combine — on a lampshade, on a rustic armoire, and in the fabrics covering the pillows. The Western Room features one wall painted a pale green, while the eaves are an eye-catching hue of yellow. A day bed, covered with a Hudson Bay blanket and intricately patterned pillows, rests under one of these steep eaves. Native American patterned blankets cover both the oak framed bed and an old armchair. Each room is a fascinating study of color and artistic presentation, especially in one bedroom, whose walls and ceilings are painted a turquoise blue and stenciled with flowering hibiscus. Light and dark woods combine to create the unusual antique bureaus. Down comforters grace every bed, except in the summer, when white chenille spreads are substituted.

In the morning, Babette cooks an extensive breakfast that includes her fresh breads and preserves. This will give guests enough energy to take their canine cohorts out to explore the surrounding territory. Halfway is located at the gateway to the famous Hell's Canyon. From here, it is easy to access the nearly three quarters of a million acres of trails, scenery, and isolation.

Deciding which part to investigate first is up to guests and their dogs, but wherever they end up, there will undoubtedly be some bighorn sheep, elk, bear, and even bobcats and cougars. Rattlesnakes and other reptiles also inhabit the area — so we advise treading carefully. Visitors can head on up to Cornucopia and take hikes through the two million-acre Wallowa-Whitman National Forest. This is relatively undisturbed and wild countryside that appeals to most anyone who has a sense of adventure... and we have to say, the Pine Valley Lodge provides the perfect base from which to explore it.

# Columbia Gorge Hotel

*4000 Westcliff Drive*
*Hood River, Oregon 97031*
*(800) 345-1921, (541) 386-5566, Fax (541) 386-3359*

*Owner:* Boyd Graves
*Rooms:* 42 doubles, 4 suites
*Rates:* Doubles $150-270 (B&B), Suites $295-365 (B&B)
*Payment:* AE, DSC, MC, and VISA
*Children:* Welcome
*Dogs:* Welcome; must be leashed in the public areas
*Open:* All year

Simon Benson, a Portland lumber baron, built the Columbia Gorge Hotel in 1921. He thought it would be the perfect destination for those traveling along the Columbia Gorge Scenic Highway. He wasn't the first person to be enamored by these cliffs or the gorge, though. Robert Rand had discovered this picturesque region some 17 years prior to Benson's arrival, and had constructed a summer resort. Moreover, Rand decided to give the hotel a name in keeping with its Native American meeting ground status — the Wah Swin Gwin Hotel. When Benson purchased the property from Rand, he tore down the existing structure, but left the grounds, trails, and landscaping intact. We like to think of the Columbia Gorge Hotel as an amalgamation of both these men's visions. The majestic hotel is all Benson, while the estate-like setting is vintage Rand.

This combination of internal and external features attracted a renowned patronage for many years, with such notables as Presidents Roosevelt and Coolidge staying here, as well as actresses Myrna Loy, Jane Powell, and Clara Bow. Rudolph Valentino also became such a frequent guest that the management eventually named a room after him. In keeping with Benson's vision, this Spanish-style structure did become a landmark property. Unfortunately, even with all its notoriety, the Columbia Gorge Hotel eventually fell on hard times. After being sold some years later, it was converted into a nursing home. Finally, in the 1980s, Boyd Graves purchased the hotel and began a re-restoration process that continues to this day.

Through Graves' extensive efforts, the hotel once again achieved landmark status and is listed in the National Register of Historic Places. The open lobby is impressive, with high ceilings, lavish draperies framing the windows, and vintage 1920s' furnishings. Gilt-edged mirrors rest above long tables set with fresh flower arrangements. Sofas and chairs are grouped for private conversations in the Valentino Lounge, where the marble fireplace is kept well-stoked during the cold winter months. The most popular tables are those near the floor-to-ceiling windows that overlook the gorge. Once settled in here, most guests are quite content to wait awhile for their table in the adjacent dining room.

The Columbia River Court dining room is an equally elegant

space — especially at night, when brass chandeliers and candles illuminate these inviting chambers. One of our favorite sections is the elongated enclosed porch, which is graced with walls of windows. The most desirable tables are those set under these windows, or just across from them. The largest of the dining areas is also lovely, but patrons would have to strain their necks to achieve the same views. Fortunately, everyone, regardless of their table, receives the same fine service and delectable food. This seasonally-changing menu offered appetizers that included a shrimp and cilantro tart; a crèpinette of pheasant made with wild mushrooms and served with a walnut and sage crème fraîche; or the house smoked salmon risotto. Entrées ranged from the scallops in a huckleberry and lavender vinaigrette and loin of venison encrusted with pistachios to the Pacific spot prawns sautéed in lobster oil with cilantro, tomatoes, and lemon zest. The dessert specialty is the apple tart — Columbia Gorge style. Local apples are blended with a rich caramel and then baked in a sweet puff pastry. It is then flambéed at the table with orange licquer— a fitting end to a most memorable meal.

After dinner it is easy to linger awhile, but eventually it is time to head upstairs for bed. We could have walked or taken the modern elevator, but we preferred using the old-fashioned elevator that must be operated by a hotel staff person. A walk down these historic halls reveals little change from the days of Benson, and after opening the bedroom doors, we were pleased to discover that this feeling also permeated the guest chambers. Each bedroom is fashioned with formal combinations of deep greens, blues, and maroons reflected in the floral fabrics that cover the traditional furniture. Hand-carved canopy beds and fireplaces highlight the specialty rooms, but generally, guests find simpler brass or two-poster bedsteads, a simple chest of drawers, an armoire, and little else in the way of decoration. Modern amenities are also quite minimal — color televisions and telephones. The spacious tiled bathrooms are a bit old-fashioned but they are also spotless, and the baskets of toiletries are thoughtful extras. We especially appreciated the rose and handmade chocolates laid on the pillow each night. Moreover, we found that the strong historic appeal, coupled with the unparalleled views, provide an ambiance that is hard to match. Each of the rooms overlooking the gorge is blessed with a slightly different perspective of the river. Some of our favorite chambers are in the west wing near the waterfall. Guests can open the window at night and feel the breezes, while listening to water cascade over the falls to the river below. Families may reserve the suites (two bedrooms connected by a bathroom) that overlook the mature gardens situated on the opposite side of the hotel.

In the morning, guests can gather the newspaper resting outside their door and head downstairs to enjoy the hotel's "World Famous Farm Breakfast" — one that is so unique its name has been trademarked. The breakfast originated at the Snoqualmie Falls Lodge over 25 years ago, but has expanded since then. As the hosts like to remind their patrons, "It's not a choice, you'll get it all." You may wish to begin with fresh fruit, and possibly an apple fritter with sugar and spice. This may be followed by oatmeal served with brown sugar and sweet cream, or possibly three farm fresh eggs. Fresh grilled trout may be substituted for the bacon, smoked pork chop, or the apple and maple-flavored sausage. We suggest taking a short break before sampling the hashed brown potatoes, baking powder biscuits with apple blossom honey, and the stack of buttermilk pancakes. Coffee or champagne are often the preferred complement to this expansive offering. Best of all, a patient canine cohort will thoroughly enjoy any leftovers.

After everyone has enjoyed breakfast, guests may wish to gather up Bowser and explore the ten acres of lush gardens that surround the hotel. It is a park-like setting, with wonderfully landscaped grounds, footbridges, and trails. A creek meanders through the property, eventually reaching the edge of the cliffs and dropping over 200 feet to the river below. The spectacular Wah-Gwin-Gwin Falls are, in themselves, reason enough to visit the hotel. For active guests, there are a variety of things to do in the nearby area.

Windsurfing has become "the" activity of choice among the residents; but only for experts, as the winds are strong and tricky, making the board sailing rigorous and exciting. Hiking is another wonderful option for human and beast and there are plenty of trails just off Interstate 84. Down the road, west of the Hood River, is a particularly easy climb along Tanner Creek to the Wahclella Falls. Another popular option is found just south of the Bonneville Dam. This trail leads hikers a short distance to the Wauna Point overlooking the dam, and then on to the scenic Dublin Lake.

# Hood River Hotel

*102 Oak Street*
*Hood River, Oregon  97031*
*(800) 386-1859, (541) 386-1900, Fax (541) 386-6090*

*Owners: Pasquale, Jacquie, and Kesia Barone*
*Rooms: 32 doubles, 9 suites*
*Rates: Doubles $49-95 (EP), Suites $79-145 (EP)*
*Payment: AE, DC, DSC, MC, and VISA*
*Children: Welcome (cribs, cots, high chairs, and baby-sitters are available)*
*Dogs: Welcome with a $15 daily fee*
*Open: All year*

The Columbia River, referred to as "the Gorge," serves as a natural boundary between Oregon and Washington. This region is a haven for Windsurfing enthusiasts who flock here from across the country to challenge the high winds and squirrelly currents. Windsurfing is what initially drew Pasquale down from Canada on vacation some years ago. Once he arrived, he could think of little else but Windsurfing the Gorge. But his instincts as a developer prompted him to look past the river to the low-key town of Hood River. There he discovered the dilapidated, turn-of-the-century Mount Hood Hotel. He decided to purchase and completely restore it. In 1989, the revitalized four-story brick hotel once again opened its doors to the public.

As new arrivals walk into the reception area of the Hood River Hotel, with its original hardwood floors, detailed moldings, and Victorian antiques, they will feel a strong sense of the building's history. This light and airy chamber is blessed with an abundance of sunlight, which streams in from all over: through the French doors, through a wall of floor-to-ceiling paned windows, and through a pair of 20-foot high windows flanking the fireplace. It would seem difficult to create a sense of intimacy in such a cavernous space as this; yet an intimate effect is cleverly achieved by providing guests with cozy sitting areas broken up by a plethora of potted floor and hanging plants. The brass lamps and chandeliers cast a soft glow throughout this inviting chamber; at night, this lovely effect accentuates the teal and coral color schemes.

We checked in at the small reception area set toward the rear of this space. Since it was off season, we had our pick of guest rooms. As most visitors will quickly discover, the guest rooms vary considerably, in both size and furnishings. Turn-of-the-century reproductions are standard, whether they consist of canopy, brass, and four-poster beds, or cherry bureaus, mirrors, or dressing tables. Oriental patterned rugs accent the fir floors. Calico or chintz curtains frame the windows, which coordinate with the comforters and dust ruffles on the beds. We thought the dried flowers, whether shaped into a wreath over a bed or arranged in a vase, provided soothing accents of color, as did the rose or green painted trim. When the wind isn't blowing off the river (which is fairly rare), ceiling fans circulate the air. Heat is provided by wonderful, old fashioned radiators. The most requested rooms are those that overlook the river, but the rooms with views of the interior courtyard are also appealing. Some guests, especially families, may require more space than is found in the standard rooms; they may wish to consider the spacious suites, with their sitting areas and full kitchens. Not too surprisingly, many of the hotel's bathrooms have been created from spaces that were formerly closets.

In the evening, guests need not venture far for their meal, as fine Northern Italian cooking is as close as the hotel's lobby. We were pleased to find that Pasquale's Ristorante is as popular with the locals as it is with guests of the hotel. The casual, European atmosphere in the café revolves around the enormous mahogany bar, which is backed by glass and brass. We had difficulty choosing between the calamari sautéed in garlic, olive oil and white wine; the Pacific oysters on the half shell; or the cream cheese and pesto torta. The pasta dishes are fairly typical, ranging from the fettuccine Alfredo and spaghetti vongole to tortellini with basil, and angel hair pasta with pesto and garlic shrimp. Veal Marsala, pork and beef tenderloin, and filets of salmon or halibut, with either garlic dill or lemon dill butter tops off the main menu. In the morning, after savoring a frothy cup of cappucino, guests may sample such dishes as the eggs Florentine, a frittata, Belgian waffle, or the crèpes stuffed with Hood River spiced apples.

There are enough hills to climb in Hood River to work off any culinary indulgences. The historic Hood River train is just down the hill. A bit further, guests will spy the Windsurfers testing their prowess on the Gorge. A short drive from the hotel, there is also golf, horseback riding, and, in the wintertime, downhill skiing.

Along the road leading from Portland to Hood River are various hiking options — for both people and dogs. The closest option is the Wygant Peak trail, where climbers are treated to terrific views of the surrounding area and the Gorge far below. A far more difficult climb is the trail leading up Mount Defiance, beginning at the Starvation Creek State Park. The falls along the Eagle Creek trail continue to lure enthusiasts of all hiking abilities (and their eager canines), as much for their spectacular chain of waterfalls as for their abundance of natural beauty. Among the more popular hiking trails are the Deschutes River Canyon, Dog River, Old Dalles Road, and Buck Creek. Each offers a different perspective of this spectacular region.

# Jacksonville Inn

*175 East California Street*
*Jacksonville, Oregon 97530*
*(800) 321-9344, (541) 899-1900*

*Hosts: Jerry and Linda Evans*
*Rooms: 8 doubles, 1 cottage*
*Rates: Doubles $80-135 (B&B), Cottage $185 (B&B)*
*Payment: AE, CB, DC, DSC, MC and VISA*
*Children: Welcome*
*Dogs: Small dogs welcome with approval; owners must bring dog bed,*
*      dog must be housebroken*
*Open: All year*

Jacksonville is a beautifully preserved historic town, nestled into the mountains of southern Oregon. It was founded in 1852, when the promise of gold in the surrounding hills seemed to guarantee prosperity for its residents. Fortunes were made, grand estates were constructed, wealthy merchants built stores, and government buildings were erected. Prosperity appeared to have no end. However, the veins of gold eventually dried up and many residents moved on, leaving behind their rich heritage. Today, Jacksonville has nearly 100 buildings that are a part of the National Register of Historic Places. The main street, and those immediately surrounding it, are still historically intact, giving visitors a good feeling for life as it might have been back in the 1800s. The Jacksonville Inn is no exception. It was built in 1863 by two merchants who operated it as a general store. The original two-story brick structurenow houses guest rooms, a restaurant, and an excellent wine store.

We first visited the inn about six years ago. While it was attractive then, it is even more so now. One reason the Jacksonville Inn is so ideal for people traveling with dogs is that guests access the bedroom wing through a separate outside entrance. Each guest room is named after either a local or famous personality. For instance, the Peter Britt room is named after the renowned photographer who took award-winning pictures of Crater Lake. Vance Colvia was the first Bozo the Clown, and the voice behind many of the Disney cartoon caricatures. Madame Jeanne de Reboan was the operator of the town's "boarding" house.

The unique personalities and sense of history behind these names carry through into the bedrooms. Early American oak antique beds, tables, and chairs are usually featured, although our room contained a scrolled iron bed and another room down the way was outfitted with a canopy bedstead. This feeling of authentic Americana fits in well with the exposed brick walls and beamed ceilings. The decor is sophisticated, with coordinated, floral Waverly prints that are used on everything from wall treatments and comforters to the fabrics covering the armchairs and sofas. The Gin Linn room is one of our favorites, especially in the morning when the sun streams through the lace curtains into the yellow floral bedroom. Across the hall is a more masculine room, with an enormous square oak headboard and a couch covered in a sophisticated black and white print. Our bedroom was like a garden room with a green and white trellis wallpaper. The tiled bathrooms are totally modernized, and have baskets of toiletries — the Peter Britt room even offers a Jacuzzi. Extras not usually associated with historic inns include individual climate controls, direct dial telephones, and televisions tucked away in oak armoires. We also appreciated the glass ice buckets for chilling our wine, the small refrigerators for storing snacks, and the tray of fruits, cookies, and candies.

Anyone looking for a little more privacy may reserve the historic cottage set just a few blocks from the inn. Guests staying here are treated to luxurious accommodations. The lovely pencil-post canopy bed is positioned so that guests can lie in bed and still enjoy the crackling fireplace. Some may enjoy setting a peaceful mood by lighting a fire and listening to music on the stereo, while others might prefer to rent a movie and settle in for a leisurely evening in their room. The cottage's kitchenette is well stocked with supplies, and the bathroom is appointed with both a Jacuzzi and a steam shower.

Cottage guests need walk only a short distance for the delicious morning meal, served by the inn exclusively to its guests. We started with fresh fruit and coffee, with our main course options including Belgian waffles, French toast, and omelets. We finally decided upon a delicious egg, spinach, and mushroom gâteau in a puff pastry with a sherried cream sauce. A popular champagne brunch is featured on Sunday. The Jacksonville Inn's restaurant is always highly rated, and most patrons enjoy the cozy ambiance found in the basement. The gold-flecked mortar in the sandstone and brick walls creates an intimate atmosphere, which is enhanced by a roaring fireplace and candlelight flickering from the elegantly set tables. The multi-course meal may be accompanied by any of the 700 wines from the expansive cellar. The menu is primarily Continental and quite extensive, featuring a good selection of vegetarian and heart-healthy foods, along with more tantalizing offerings such as filet mignon with a bernaise sauce (the house specialty), prime rib, and veal marsala.

Jacksonville is a great town for leisurely walks, and dogs will feel right at home. (We even saw a couple of canines hanging out inside one of the old-fashioned bars.) The famed Britt Music and Art Festival is held here each year in July. Day hikes are another popular option, especially for those willing to drive south a short distance to Applegate Lake, which is situated in the Rogue River National Forest. Hikers and their dogs can follow the Grouse Creek Trail or take a different route along the trail that edges Applegate Lake. One final option is the Little Squaw Trail, which wends around both Little and Big Squaw Lakes. Whether people and their dogs decide to investigate the sights and attractions around town or explore the assorted hiking opportunities available nearby, they will thoroughly enjoy the warm and convivial atmosphere found at the Jacksonville Inn.

# The Hideaway Motel

*810 Southwest 10th*
*Lincoln City, Oregon   97367*
*(541) 994-8874*

*Hostess: Sharon Odenthal*
*Rooms: 6 doubles*
*Rates: $65-95 (B&B)*
*Payment: MC and VISA*
*Children: Welcome (cribs available)*
*Dogs: Welcome for a daily fee of $5*
*Open: All year*

We were a little skeptical that a nice, quiet lodging could be situated in a busy seaside town like Lincoln City. But sure enough, nestled just a short distance from the fast food restaurants, the nondescript seaside motels, and the general hubbub is the Hideaway Motel. The private residences in this neighborhood are an attractive blend of three-story houses, cottages, and even a few nice trailers. In the midst of this is the Hideaway Motel, which frankly is a complete misnomer — this is a charming, light blue shake cottage with white shutters that bears no resemblance to a motel. It is set on a cliff, with the blue Pacific and sandy beach providing a lovely vista. During our visit, a crane was attempting to rebuild an eroding path that leads guests to and from the beach. The cottage, on the other hand, is in no danger of going anywhere.

This is a low-key place; most guests enjoy it for its casual, beachside setting. Of the six suites available, the largest and most requested is the Master Suite. This is the one unit that doesn't have stairs. Guests just open the door, make a jog to the right, and enter a cozy two-bedroom suite. We were drawn to the living room's bay window and its expansive views. Best of all, families or a group of friends will discover that six guests can easily be accommodated in this suite, between the two bedrooms and the sofa bed. The full-kitchen is well equipped, and includes a dishwasher. We could imagine almost looking forward to a Sou'wester blowing in, as an excuse to light a fire and relax amid the cozy surroundings. Just upstairs from the Master Suite is the intimate Crow's Nest. Aptly named, it is tucked under the eaves of the house's mansard roof. The window up here is also built into the end eave and provides dizzying views out to the ocean. The Sunset, Honeymoon, and Royal suites have equally lovely water views, while the Canyon Suite, true to its name, overlooks the wooded canyon, which is often lush with colorful wildflowers. Guests requiring a little extra space may wish to reserve either the Canyon or Sunset suite, as both offer living rooms and private decks.

Regardless of room choice, guests are certain to enjoy the casual ambiance at the Hideaway. The pine-paneled walls nicely complement the mix of maple and oak furnishings. With the exception of the Honeymoon Suite and Crow's Nest, each suite does have a fireplace supplied with unlimited amounts of wood. Kitchens are outfitted with most everything one would require to make an impromptu meal. Equipped with microwaves, coffee makers, and popcorn poppers, they're great places for preparing light snacks and *hors d'oeuvres*. Guests who return to the Hideaway year after year do so for its proximity to the water and beach, coupled with the lulling effects of the crashing waves and fresh salt air.

One of the best routes for walks with dogs is along the road that circles back down the hill to the beach. There is also a small grassy area near the beach's entrance, where visiting dogs can romp with the local canines. Once out on the sand, it is easy to be gone for hours, as it is possible to walk for awhile before turning around and heading home. Lincoln City is also centrally located for pleasant day trips. The Cascade Head Trail, just off Highway 101, is comprised of waterside forests that provide all sorts of options for hikers and their dogs. Another alternative, for those who are interested in boating or fishing expeditions, is the Devil's Lake State Park in Lincoln. There is also a trail up Mount Hebo that many hikers enjoy investigating; it begins in the Mount Hebo Campground. Our canines very much enjoyed this pleasant hike, as it offers plenty of meadows, forests, and streams.

# Starfish Point

*140 Northwest 48th Street*
*Newport, Oregon   97365*
*(541) 265-3751, Fax (541) 265-3040*

*Owners: Neil and Kathleen Atkinson*
*Rooms: 6 suites*
*Rates: $150-170 (EP)*
*Payment: AE, DSC, MC, and VISA*
*Children: Welcome  (a crib and high chair are available)*
*Dogs: Welcome with a $5 daily fee*
*Open: All year*

Starfish Point is a wonderful name, but it contains even more fabulous accommodations, nestled into a wooded hillside overlooking the ocean. These attractive, contemporary condominium suites were originally built as luxury time-share units — but unfortunately, the project went bankrupt. Thankfully, the Atkinsons bought the place, imbued it with additional charm, and opened it to the overnight guests. We couldn't be more pleased at discovering this tempting retreat along the Oregon coast.

The small complex is set on the edge of Newport, but is well concealed from Route 101 by mature trees and bushes. As we entered the complex, it was hard to imagine what lay inside the dove gray wood-sided buildings. Perhaps this was best, because once we saw the interiors it was as if we had stumbled upon a hidden treasure. The architect who designed these spaces created intimate spaces. Each room is set on a different level and privy to spectacular hillside and ocean views, through walls of glass. We had the impression of being situated alone on a hillside with only the green forest surrounding us with the blue Pacific below.

These interior spaces flow nicely together, with few wasted corners. Guests step in through a small tiled foyer and down into the central living room, complete with color television and a stereo. Each unit is fully carpeted and fashioned with good-quality rattan furniture and bright cotton floral fabrics. This common area opens onto two more glass-walled rooms — the formal dining room and the octagonal captain's study. Guests who sit in either of these spaces will find their eyes continually drawn out to the natural world just beyond the expanses of glass. Depending on the suite, guests walk either up or down from the captain's study to the equally lovely master bedroom with its private bathroom. In one suite, tiny cobalt blue tiles surround the two-person Jacuzzi. We think the candles in here are a nice addition for those wanting to set a particularly romantic mood.

We feel the most desirable units are those situated on the end of the building, with unobstructed views of the ocean. The master bedroom in these particular buildings offers a window with wonderful views of the water and beach. Because these were built as time-share units, very little expense was spared when it came to quality. Therefore, guests can expect to find modern kitchens equipped with an array of state-of-the-art appliances, such as Jenn-Aire ranges. Starfish Point is as ideal for families as it is for a pair of couples (although the two couples would have to flip a coin for the upstairs master suite). Each suite also has a private deck allowing guests to venture outside and soak up some Oregon sun.

Dogs are definitely welcome additions at Starfish Point. Although they don't have acres of grounds to romp on, they need only persuade their owners to take them down a path leading through dense pines to Agate Cove. Once at the shore, human and canine can walk for hours together, either up toward Yaquina Head or down toward Newport. There are also three state parks south of Newport — South Beach, Lost Creek, and Ona Beach. All allow dogs to explore their paths, beaches, and tide pools. Another option is the Beverly Beach State Park, where there are even more spectacular hillside and oceanside walks to be enjoyed with a beloved canine companion.

---

# The Benson

*309 Southwest Broadway*
*Portland, Oregon 97205*
*(800) 426-0670, (503) 228-2000, Fax (503) 226-4603*

*General Manager:* Charles Indermuehle
*Rooms:* 233 doubles, 57 suites
*Rates:* Doubles $155-190 (EP), Suites $200-600 (EP)
*Payment:* AE, CB, DC, JCB, MC, and VISA
*Children:* Welcome (cribs, cots, and baby-sitters are available)
*Dogs:* Welcome
*Open:* All year

Built at the turn of the century, The Benson Hotel remains a French baroque architectural classic, set among the more contemporary high-rise buildings dotting Portland's skyline. Simon Benson commissioned this building, and others, after making his fortune in Oregon timber. He went to great lengths to secure the finest materials and craftsmen to build his hotel, even going so far as to import Circassian walnut from Russia. Some years ago, when we first wrote about The Benson, the physical structure was in need of repair and restoration. We are pleased to report that after a thorough restoration process, it is once again a showplace. Besides refurbishing the public areas and revamping the two restaurants, the management has pumped over $16 million into the renovation of the guest rooms.

The elegant lobby was, and continues to be, the hotel's showpiece. Its walls are paneled in dark red walnut, while huge, cut-glass chandeliers hang from the ornately-carved, coffered ceilings. Massive columns break up what would otherwise be a cavernous space, providing a number of intimate sitting areas. One of our favorites spots is over by the marble fireplace, especially during afternoon high tea. Oriental rugs cover the Italian marble floors, while an impressive collection of antiques and fine furnishings are placed about this handsome chamber. Immense flower arrangements provide fragrant aromas and colorful accents.

While each guest chamber has been thoughtfully updated, it still adheres to the historic integrity of the hotel. We noticed (especially when walking along the upstairs hallways) that even the original guest room doors, complete with inlaid wood, had a rich patina to them. The finialed headboards contain inlaid woods in the same hues as the doors, while the classic furnishings (such as writing tables, sofas, and chairs with ottomans) fill out the rest of the guest chambers. Taupe and cream color schemes, combined with subtle black accents lend a certain opulence to these rooms. In addition to gilt-edged mirrors and lovely botanical prints, many of the walls are graced with hand-colored architectural prints.

The Benson Rooms are perhaps the most popular chambers, as they offer intimate sitting areas in the bedrooms. The once rather small, antiquated bathrooms have been enlarged and modernized, and now boast of shower/tub combinations, hairdryers, baskets of toiletries, and terry robes. Guests who reserve the most deluxe suites will discover Jacuzzis in the bathrooms and wet bars in the spacious living rooms. Regardless of room choice, guests will find big baskets of gourmet goodies placed on the honor bar and televisions concealed in the armoires. The Grand Suite is the most opulent accommodation at the hotel, with a four-poster, king-size bed resting in one huge alcove, and a black lacquered dining room table set on the edge of the living room. (President Clinton stayed here in 1993.) Its corner location makes it an especially light and airy chamber. While few guests will be interested in paying the hefty sum for this luxurious suite, they will be happy to learn that many of the other corner guest rooms offer similar views.

The London Grill, with its light wood paneling and arched ceilings, is a favorite among visitors and locals alike. This contemporary motif is reflected in the nouvelle menu as well. Dinner patrons might start with the Japanese lobster tails served in a rich garlic butter, the smoked salmon and caviar, or the lobster bisque. Our entrée selections included an intriguing Northwest hunter's plate consisting of stuffed quail, a venison chop and wild mushrooms, although guests could also dine on the rack of lamb laced with garlic mustard and herbs, the Dover sole with an herb lemon butter sauce, or the yellow fin tuna, sautéed with garlic and ginger and served with a lemon Szechwan sauce.

We especially recommend The Benson Hotel to travelers whose dogs are used to the city. We would recommend the RiverPlace Hotel (which is situated alongside two parks) to those with canines who require a lot of exercise. The area around the Benson Hotel consists mostly of sidewalks and stores, offering very little nearby green grass or open space on which to burn off a little energy. The Esplanade is a short distance away and will give Bowser more than enough room to run and play. It is also fairly easy to jump in the car and head to a few of the more dog-oriented destinations just outside the city. One option includes the Powell Butte Trail, that offers a three-mile hiking trail and terrific views of the more distant mountains, as well as some fine local scenery. Another popular destination is situated some 30 minutes outside Portland, just off Interstate 84. There, a rather easy trail leads up to and around the picturesque Latourell Falls.

# Mallory Hotel

*729 SW 15th Avenue*
*Portland, Oregon 97205*
*(800) 228-8657, (503) 223-6311, Fax (503) 223-5222*

*Manager: Linda Anderson*
*Rooms: 124 doubles, 18 suites*
*Rates: Doubles $50-90 (EP), Suites $80 (EP)*
*Payment: AE, DC, DSC, MC, and VISA*
*Children: Welcome (cribs and cots are available)*
*Dogs: Welcome with a $10 fee, provided they are not left alone in the*
     *room*
*Open: All year*

Situated just a short walk from the city's more popular shopping areas, the Mallory Hotel is a tall, tawny building offering guests comfortable accommodations at a very affordable price. Originally built in 1912, the hotel underwent a substantial face lift in the late 1980s. Despite the extensive nature of the work done here, we feel there are still a few details that could use a little more attention — but because the price is right, we're willing to overlook a couple of well-worn aspects. Although the Mallory Hotel may not be one of the city's premier luxury hotels, it remains a favorite destination for many visitors, as it still retains much of its old world charm and unpretentious atmosphere.

We climbed the long, wide staircase to reach the expansive lobby. The wall of mirrors here makes the space appear all the more cavernous. Comfortable couches, flanked by green wing chairs, form the various sitting areas, while glass chandeliers, suspended from gilded, boxed-beamed ceilings, make the room seem to twinkle. We actually sat here awhile looking up at the ceilings — they were that intriguing. The lobby and its adjacent restaurant are the two most resplendent spaces in the hotel. The dining room is a favorite for Sunday brunch, and is as formal as the lobby; but in the dining room, balloon shades frame the floor-to-ceiling windows. We happened to be visiting on a Sunday, when the hotel was packed with locals and guests alike enjoying the Mallory's famous brunch.

The staff is quirky, but lovable — sort of like the characters in the television show *Seinfeld*. The front desk assistants, for instance, are all very friendly and genuine — not like the ultra-polished types we sometimes encounter whose frequent refrain is "My pleasure" (but who clearly aren't taking much, if any, pleasure in what they are doing for their guests). When we checked in with the front desk, the staff couldn't supply us with a brochure, but they had plenty of stories to tell us about the hotel. One of these was about the resident ghost — Mr. Mallory. He is not an ordinary ghost, but one who reputedly pounds on the wall with what sounds like a hammer. Some patrons think this is really neat (in theory), but after the first "tap, tap, tap" most scamper down to the front desk asking to be moved to another room. We didn't get to see Mr. Mallory's room, but did check out many of the others.

Physically, the Mallory's guest rooms look much the same as they probably did in the 1930s. Some of the double rooms are still in need of a little attention, while others are very attractively, albeit eclectically, furnished, with some of the chairs and sofas appearing as though they were carryover's from the hotel's earlier years. Most of the bedrooms have either a king bed or a pair of twin beds covered with simple, white cotton spreads. The rather Spartan decor is complemented by standard amenities such as color televisions and refrigerators. The private bathrooms have colorful tiles reminiscent of the Art Deco period (they probably are originals from that period), and, in many cases, guests must step up to reach them. Without exception, though, everything is extremely neat and clean. Some of our favorite bedrooms are the corner rooms on the upper floors. These are substantially larger than the other chambers, and some boast expansive views of the city and Mount Hood.

As we've noted, while the Mallory Hotel might be a bit dated, it still offers good value and a lot more pizzazz than some of the larger chain hotels in the region. Guests who stay here are not only close to the opera and theater district, but are also just a short car ride from the city parks and the waterfront area. In addition to investigating the waterfront and nearby parks, we also suggest driving south to the Tryon Creek State Park. Here, hikers and their leashed dogs can follow some of the short nature trails or the longer hiking trails, through beautiful forests and alongside picturesque creeks. Maps are supplied, so bring a picnic lunch and spend the day exploring the more than 600 acres available to visitors.

# RiverPlace Hotel

*1510 Southwest Harbor Way*
*Portland, Oregon   97201*
*(800) 227-1333, (503) 228-3233, Fax (503) 295-6161*

*General Manager: David Frazier*
*Rooms: 39 doubles, 35 suites, 10 condominiums*
*Rates: Doubles $155-205 (B&B), Suites $185-600 (B&B),*
*        Condominiums $395-395 (B&B)*
*Payment: AE, MC, and VISA*
*Children: Welcome (cribs, cots, high chairs, and baby-sitters are available)*
*Dogs: Welcome; guests must sign a damage waiver form*
*Open: All year*

The RiverPlace Hotel has always been one of our favorite city hotels in the Northwest. When we first reviewed it, the prestigious Alexis group was managing its overall operations. Today, it is a part of the Westcoast Hotels group and we are pleased to report that it is just as appealing as ever, perhaps even more so. The RiverPlace lies on the northern banks of the Willamette River in a section of Portland known as the Esplanade. On one side of the hotel are six-story condominiums, shops, restaurants, and boutiques; on the other, vast expanses of grass leading down to a marina. Long ago the area was seedy; however, with the arrival of the hotel in 1985, this section of the city has become a very desirable destination for travelers and local residents alike.

Architecturally, the hotel gracefully combines the old with the new. Its turrets and rotunda roof, crafted with bleached wood and brick, make it reminiscent of the massive, turn-of the-century great cottages. Oversized windows draw in ample amounts of natural sunlight and provide good views of the river, marina, and adjacent park. The interior is a little more contemporary, though, with an abundance of light oak and marble, forming clean lines. Bright colors seem to permeate the interior spaces — on the chintz-covered sofas and chairs grouped into intimate sitting areas, in the fresh flower arrangements set on antique tables, and in the abundance of ornamental potted palms and ficus trees. All these combine to create the residential feeling that guests find so appealing.

The bedrooms are as elegant as the common areas. These were recently updated and offer a variety of color combinations. In some, burgundy and navy blue are integrated into the surroundings; in others, pale yellows and French blues imbue a sophisticated style. Fine reproduction antiques include wing chairs with ottomans, overstuffed sofas, teak coffee tables, and expansive writing desks. Brass sconces and framed botanical prints grace the walls. Our favorite rooms are those with woodburning fireplaces, wet bars, and whirlpool bathtubs, although all guest bathrooms feature Corian sinks, baskets of European toiletries, and thick terry cloth robes. Anyone planning an extended stay may wish to reserve one of the hotel-managed condominiums. These provide substantially more space and a varied assortment of amenities — especially ideal for families staying here with their dogs. In the evenings, complimentary sherry is served before dinner, and guests returning to their rooms afterwards will find that their beds have been turned down and gourmet chocolates rest on their down pillows. In the morning, a gourmet Continental breakfast and a newspaper are delivered to the room.

The hotel's former no-tipping policy disappeared with the Alexis management group; however, there are still a few complimentary services, such as shoe shines, valet, and concierge. One of the most impressive features is the fact that the hotel has three restaurants overlooking the water, each of which offers a different atmosphere and river view. The Esplanade restaurant is the most formal, specializing in local cuisine, with an emphasis on fresh seafood. The veteran chef, John Zenger, has recently begun to make some exciting menu changes. When we visited, three dishes seemed especially noteworthy: the wild mushrooms, mountain cheeses, Fino sherry, and garlic, baked in an herbed filo; Dungeness crab and bay shrimp cakes; and Manila clams steamed in a chipotle broth. Entrées included the grilled marlin with Kona crab hash and lime mustard sauce; the red pepper linguini with mesquite-seasoned chicken; and the salmon with a pistachio pesto crust and a fresh tomato coulis. But it is not only the dinner menu that is bringing rave reviews; it is also the popular brunches. Not surprisingly, Eggs Benedict is on the menu, although an even more interesting version, with a Thai twist, is what most patrons are talking about. In this concoction, poached eggs are set on Dungeness crab and bay shrimp crab cakes, then covered with a light, red curry hollandaise. At The Esplanade, there is also an emphasis on healthy, light dishes such as the ten-grain flapjacks served with a lemony berry compôte, and the egg-white omelets filled with items such as wild mushrooms, scallions, chopped fresh herbs, or a tomatillo salsa. The Bar offers a more casual and intimate dining setting, with its woodburning fireplace and jazz pianist setting the overall mood. In the summer months, most people gravitate to the outdoor Patio for their meals.

The RiverPlace Athletic Club, situated just a half block from the hotel, is outfitted with tennis, squash, and racquetball courts, as well as three swimming pools, aerobic classes, a massage therapist, and a weight room. The hotel's steam room is private, and may be reserved for an hour at a time. Those who prefer outdoor exercise (for example, Bowser), will appreciate the ease of access to the landscaped walkways around the Esplanade. Some might shop or eat their way along this waterfront park; however, the wide expanses of grass are far more extensive than the shopping and are certainly more intriguing for Bowser. Just a short drive away is the Hoyt Arboretum which offers pleasant walks through the stretches of forest and metropolitan areas. At the arboretum, visitors and their dogs will find the Wildwood Trail along with some other trails that walkers and their dogs can follow for either short or long distances. Wending alongside lush lawns, a thriving marina, and winding river is sure to keep both canines and their human counterparts well occupied.

---

# Lake Creek Lodge

*Star Route*
*Sisters, Oregon   97759*
*(800) 797-6331, (503) 595-6331*

**Hostess:** *Roblay McMullin*
**Rooms:** *16 houses and cottages*
**Rates:** *$60-150 (MAP), $70-170 (EP), Additional*
*person $35-50 (MAP)*
**Payment:** *Personal checks*
**Children:** *Welcome (cots are available)*
**Dogs:** *Dogs are not allowed in the summer season, but are welcome in*
*the off season for an $8 daily fee. Dogs must always be leashed*
*when on the property and walked in dog-walk areas.*
**Open:** *All year*

The Lake Creek Lodge, set in the heart of the Deschutes National Forest, is surrounded by spectacular mountain peaks and alpine valleys. The nucleus of the resort consists of a small complex of cottages and houses that are encircled by 60 acres of pine forests, emerald lawns, well-tended flower gardens, and the Lake Creek Pond. We arrived on a quiet fall afternoon. Although few people were out and about, there was still a sense of vitality about the place. Bright flowers bloomed along the walkways; a dozen or so guests were relaxing in the Adirondack chairs; and parents were fishing with their children at the pond.

The resort, we later learned, dates back to 1935, and the original owner lives in a small cottage on the property. She is 88 years old, and still tends to her extensive flower gardens. We also suspect she has had a lot of influence in creating the array of flower gardens scattered about the rest of the property. Some of the small, brown clapboard cottages also date back to the resort's beginnings; however, there are newer and larger knotty-pine houses that offer modern amenities as well. The older cottages generally accommodate up to four people in their one- and two-bedrooms. While these are fashioned with a bathroom, they do not have a living room or kitchen. A refrigerator is set out on the small porch, allowing guests who stay here to store their drinks and perishable snacks. These rather sparsely furnished cottages are often reserved as "grandparent" units. The children and grandchildren, on the other hand, generally stay in the newer houses. This gives the extended family a central gathering place, but allows the grandparents to slip off and enjoy a little quiet time.

The houses are decidedly more expansive and are outfitted with a large central living room and a variety of bedroom configurations. The light pine walls and large windows brighten these spaces, while the fireplaces add a bit of warmth and character. The attractive furnishings are comfortable, and a few knickknacks add a homey touch to the expansive chambers. Colorful handmade quilts cover the pine bedsteads and cotton curtains frame the paned windows. Although the overall ambiance is a little on the Spartan side, everything is very neat and clean.

The low-key setting, along with the abundance of diversions and the affable nature of the staff, are some of the reasons many visitors have been coming here for generations. All guests, and especially children, love the warm, fuzzy feeling of the Lake Creek Lodge. Children are not only permitted to be first in line at dinner, but are also invited to enjoy their meal with their peers in a separate dining room. This is a very relaxed set-up for both the children and their parents. The weekly "wiener roast" is always fun for the kids, while the adult contingency can enjoy the varied entrée selections in the main dining room. These range from salmon and prime rib to lamb and fried chicken. Guests will quickly discover, however, that the meals are merely a small component of a vacation at the Lake Creek Lodge.

Toddlers like having their own small, shallow pool, while older "water-safe" children may use the full-size swimming pool. The pond is stocked each year with trout, and is reserved for children under the age of twelve. Adults are not disregarded, though, as the clear, spring fed Metolius River runs right through the property. Fly-fishing is the only type of fishing permitted on this river, and it has certainly tested the skills of many an angler. In addition to the swimming and fishing, guests can play basketball, paddle or standard tennis, shuffleboard, horseshoes, and volleyball. While Bowser cannot romp about the grounds, we found the jogging trails that edge the forest to be ideal for burning off a little steam.

Day hikes are also quite popular. One of our favorite routes begins at the Canyon Creek Campground and follows the Metolius River Trail through canyons and past many natural springs. Hikers and their dogs are certain to encounter plenty of wildlife along the way, especially if they are quiet. Another option is the Black Butte Trail, which leads to a spot with panoramic views of the valleys and of the Mount Washington, Mount Jefferson, and Three Fingered Jack. In the winter, many bring their cross-country skis and take their canines on excursions along some of the aforementioned trails. Although dogs are not allowed at the Lake Creek Lodge during the height of the summer season, we found that the shoulder and off-season are not only less crowded, but are also some of the best times to explore and enjoy the picturesque region surrounding the Lake Creek Lodge.

# Bird and Hat Bed & Breakfast

*717 North Third*
*Stayton, Oregon  97383*
*(503) 769-7817*

*Hostess: Jacqulin Kirby*
*Rooms: 3 doubles*
*Rates: $40-53 (B&B)*
*Payment: Personal checks*
*Children: Welcome for a $5 additional nightly fee*
*Dogs: Welcome*
*Open: All year*

The Willamette Valley is fast becoming a wine aficionado's Mecca. Its rich soil and moist climate causes the grapes to develop slowly, which allows wine makers to create some fairly complex vintages. These wines are beginning to win accolades at some of the country's most prestigious festivals. Before all this notoriety, though, this was traditional farm country with the land dedicated to dairy production and crops more basic than grapes. While this region has not quite reached the status of Napa Valley, in many ways this makes it all the more appealing for visitors who are in search of an up-and-coming wine producing region. We like it because it lies at the edge of some spectacular national forests, near scenic covered bridges, and amid plenty of natural lakes.

Within this small community is a quaint B&B called the Bird and Hat. Longtime residents probably would refer to it as the old Brewer House, as it was built in 1907 by Dr. Charles Brewer. Over the years, this humble abode has served many purposes — part private residence and part commercial enterprise. Dr. Brewer practiced medicine here for many years; at one time it was a beauty shop, at another time, a gift shop; and a little more recently, it was a small restaurant. Today, the residential quality has been restored under Jacqulin's tutelage.

We found this charming house to be especially appealing from the street, with its gambrel roof flowing down to an inviting farmer's porch. The house is situated on a corner, but is surrounded by small, flowering fruit trees, rose gardens, and mature shrubs. One side of the house is also shaded by an enormous old tulip magnolia. We followed a stone path around the side of the house where we discovered Jacqulin's extensive organic vegetable garden. Since we were visiting in the fall everything was still quite lush; we cannot even begin to imagine how beautiful it would be in the spring and summer.

Guests are treated like members of the family, and as we arrived another couple was wistfully departing. It is easy to feel comfortable here. The first floor is an inviting open space, with hardwood floors, walls of windows, and plenty of places in which to curl up with a good book. The highlight is the living room, with its white brick fireplace. A couch is set in front of the fireplace, and guests often sit here and enjoy the fire, listen to music, or watch a movie on the television or VCR. A wide archway leads from this inviting chamber into the dining room — another sunny space. A lace-covered table is the site for the morning repast. Jacqulin is more than happy to prepare just about any dish for her guests, and she often tries to incorporate fresh fruit or vegetables from her gardens. Eggs Benedict can be served just as easily as an overstuffed omelet or a stack of pancakes covered with fresh fruit. Whatever the meal, it is always substantial.

Upstairs there are three bedrooms. The largest of these is situated in the front of the house, with a small private porch. Light pours in through the windows, although it seems even brighter because of the pale peach and green color schemes that are used throughout this space. This is a good room for families because of the additional sleeping areas. A virtual mountain of pillows covers one day bed tucked into a corner; behind another wall is another tiny room, which looks as if it were converted from a former walk-in closet. When Jacqulin's grandchildren were babies, this was their crib room. It still works well for those staying here with children. Darker colors prevail next door, especially on the bed, which is backed by a dark oak, hand-carved headboard. Navy blue is the predominant color tone, but it is balanced with just enough creamy colors to give it some life. A little balcony opens to views of the tulip tree. The separate sink in here is convenient, as the shared bathroom is situated across the hallway. We especially like the bedroom towards the rear of the house. The four-poster mahogany beds are covered with navy floral comforters, and an antique armoire is placed against one wall. Especially appealing is the adjacent wall of double hung windows that make the room feel like an old-fashioned sleeping porch. As we looked out through the windows, we spied a little rock-lined pond that appeared natural amid all the greenery. It is built with old cattle feeding troughs — we thought it was a clever way to recycle something.

It is rarely a problem finding something to do around Stayton; the difficulty is deciding what to do first. One of the simplest and most pleasant activities is just walking around this unassuming rural town. As we mentioned, a few trendy establishments, such as the gourmet restaurants, are beginning to creep into town and this is starting to change the flavor of this farming community.

Naturalists, however, will be impressed that this region is renowned for having the largest concentration of waterfalls anywhere in the country. Some of the highlights include the Silver Creek Falls and Salmon Falls. The 8,000-acre Silver Falls State Park is the largest in Oregon and welcomes human visitors and their dogs. Another popular destination is the Willamette National Forest, where there are ample hiking opportunities. Phantom Bridge is one of our favorite hiking destinations in the area. The trail leads people and their dogs past Dog Rock (how appropriate) and on to the Phantom Bridge, which is a naturally created rock bridge. People can either marvel at it or walk right out on it. Coffin Mountain is another great day hike, easily accessible from the town of Marion Forks. One last option is situated outside of Quartzville and is called Chimney Peak. Hikers can reach the top of the peak by following the McQuade Creek Trail.

# The Wayfarer Resort

*46725 Goodpasture Road*
*Vida, Oregon 97488*
*(503) 896-3613*

**Hosts:** *Karen and Mike Rogers*
**Rooms:** *13 cottages*
**Rates:** *$65-175 (EP),Weekly rates are available*
**Payment:** *MC and VISA*
**Children:** *Welcome (cribs and baby-sitters are available)*
**Dogs:** *Welcome with a one-time fee of $5, provided they are leashed*
**Open:** *All year*

The Wayfarer Resort is located just 25 miles east of Eugene, yet guests feel very removed from the urban world. It lies in a dense forest on the banks of the McKenzie River and the glacier-fed Marten Creek — a region that traditionally lures those who love fly fishing. After crossing the 50-year-old covered bridge that spans the McKenzie River, visitors meander along a country road, where sunlight filters through the cedars, birches, and spruces, casting a soft glow upon the forest floor.

We arrived at the Wayfarer Resort late one afternoon to find a few guests quietly casting their flies into the creek. This is a low-key, storybook kind of place, where most of the red cottages are clustered along the river's edge, overlooking the forest on the opposite banks. These guest quarters are simply constructed, with open-beamed ceilings and natural knotty pine walls. The furnishings are comfortable; big sofas and deep chairs are perfect for curling up and watching the crackling fire or reading a favorite book. Picture windows in many of the cottages frame views of the river and forest, as do the sliding glass doors that lead out to good-sized decks. Each cottage also has an outdoor barbecue and a fully-equipped kitchen. Handmade quilts adorn the beds, which vary from twin to king-size.

The cottages range from an intimate studio to the spacious Octagon cottage with two bedrooms and two bathrooms. The semi-circular central stone fireplace is the centerpiece for the Octagon Cottage's large common room, which also is outfitted with a piano, television, and wet bar. The kitchen is fashioned with a variety of modern amenities including a Jennair stove. While the interior is quite comfortable and impressive, guests will undoubtedly spend much of their time on the expansive wraparound deck overlooking the rushing river. If we could make only one suggestion, it would be to try to reserve one of the cottages directly on the creek — it is well worth the additional stipend.

In addition to the excellent fly fishing, guests can play badminton, volleyball, horseshoes, or tennis. The swing set and a stocked pond are geared for young children, while adults can take advantage of the golf opportunities at the Tokatee links. Rafting trips and hiking trails are also conveniently located nearby. Just west of Vida and north of Blue River is one popular hiking option — the Tidbits Mountain Trail, set in the heart of the Willamette National Forest. This is a pleasant hike through a forest that eventually leads to an area offering a lovely view of the valley below, and of some of the surrounding mountains. Castle Rock, also situated just west of Vida, is another great hiking opportunity for those looking for a more leisurely outing with their canine. As with all good hikes, there is always a reward at the end — usually a fabulous view. This one is no exception.

Most guests do not come to The Wayfarer Resort to be pampered and catered to; they prefer the self-sufficiency it offers, enjoying its natural surroundings and relaxing amid the uncomplicated and unpretentious ambiance.

# Edgewater Cottages

*3978 S.W. Pacific Coast Highway*
*Waldport, Oregon 97394*
*(541) 563-2240*

*Innkeepers: Cathy Sorenson and Chuck Turpin*
*Rooms: 9 cottages*
*Rates: $45-220 (EP)*
*Payment: Personal checks*
*Children: Welcome (a crib is available)*
*Dogs: Welcome, providing they are housebroken, stay off the furniture,*
*    and are not left unattended. Daily fee of $5-6.*
*Open: All year*

The Edgewater Cottages have been operated by the same family for the past 30 years. Set along the dunes overlooking a sandy beach, most of these cottages are privy to beautiful views of the water.

There are no cliffs around here, just ocean, sand, and surf — making this an ideal vacation spot for guests with older children or dogs, since there is little need to worry about anyone getting into much trouble.

As we drove down the coastal road, we almost passed right by the complex. A weathered sign, partially obscured by a line of pine trees that fronts the complex, pointed to the entrance. These are not cookie cutter cottages set in a row; instead, we discovered a hodgepodge of gray-shingled cottages — some nestled into a knoll and others along the beach. Mixed in with these rentals are private residences, providing a combination of locals and guests. When we visited, we noticed that some of the older cottages were being re-shingled, but in general, they offer the kind of charm that many have come to associate with a low-key beach vacation.

Our first stop was the Crow's Nest, an intimate space that sleeps two. It does not have direct water views, but that didn't matter — we could smell and hear the ocean. Although the walls are knotty pine and the floors hardwood, red highlights give it a more contemporary look. We stepped across the hemp rug to warm ourselves in front of the red enameled wood stove. As we looked back into the room, we spied the tiny kitchen fashioned with red countertops. Off to the side was a queen bed with a red quilt, and over to one corner a white flag was festooned with a red crab on it. A sliding glass door leads out to a very private sun deck.

The Chart House is one of the most reasonably priced rooms at just $45. It is a studio apartment set into a knoll, with views of the sandy beach through the sliding glass doors and plate glass windows. We like the effect of the thick rope that frames the entrance to this space, as well as the dark, knotty pine walls that collectively give these quarters a nautical feeling. The Chart Room consists of a queen-bedded room and a small living room with a freestanding fireplace. Guests may also reserve the Chart Room's Crew Quarters, which adds a second bedroom to this configuration. The double bed and a pair of twin day beds look quite spiffy under their red, white, and blue sailboat cotton spreads.

Just upstairs there are two even sunnier spaces, the Wheel House and the Commodore's Cabin. Though these, too, have knotty pine interiors, the expanse of glass found in the sliding doors and windows makes these chambers bright. The tiny Wheel House is a cozy studio; but it is well equipped with a complement of amenities. Whether guests are lying in their bed or sitting at the breakfast table, they may enjoy good views of the ocean. The raised-hearth brick fireplace keeps things toasty. The modified kitchenette has a small refrigerator, two burners, a microwave oven, and a coffee maker. The Wheel House can connect to the Commodore's Cabin, just next door. This latter space has two bedrooms and a living room with a rock fireplace — but what makes it truly noteworthy is the sliding glass door that opens onto a sheltered sun deck.

There are individual cottages available as well. These include West Wind, Rustic, Pine Rest, and the granddaddy of them all: Beachcomber. The latter can accommodate eleven guests, while the smallest, Pine Rest, sleeps just two. Beachcomber can also be split up into a wide array of sleeping and living combinations. With the exception of Chart House, all the units have some cooking capabilities. No matter which configuration best suits guests' needs, they will find each kitchen stocked with at least the bare minimum of what we consider to be the essentials for a beach vacation: nutcrackers for crab, cork screws, wine glasses, and coffee makers.

Guests will need to purchase their groceries before arriving at the Edgewater Cottages, as there are not any large supermarkets within easy driving distance of the complex. Each of the cottages is outfitted with televisions, and VCRs and video tapes can be rented at a store just down the road. The telephone is located up in the office and guests are welcome to use it for making local calls. Every unit is also equipped with some sort of fireplace, and there is an unlimited supply of firewood. Since these units are basically housekeeping units, the innkeepers ask that guests leave them in the same condition as they found them. Fresh linens can be exchanged during the stay, along with toiletries, towels, etc.

The beach is so beautiful here that we could walk for miles with our dogs and never get bored — tired maybe, but not bored. It is just as pleasant to sit in one's room in the mornings and evenings and just watch the ocean crash onto the shore. To the east of Waldport, guests will find the Drift Creek Wilderness, which many hikers and their dogs love exploring. It is unusual to find any old growth forests in this region that have been left untouched by the lumber industry; however, this is one of them. The Horse Creek Trail is another popular option for hikers. Those who prefer to stay close to the ocean can also spend the day investigating the state parks that line the coastline. The Governor Patterson Memorial State Park, in Waldport, offers just over 10 acres to explore with Bowser. The Ona Beach or Lost Creek State Parks are often preferred options, with hundreds of acres to investigate. The inn's hosts are also happy to suggest intriguing outings that guests and their canine companions may enjoy.

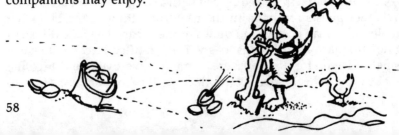

# Kah-Nee-Ta Resort

*P.O. Box K*
*Warm Springs, Oregon   97761*
*(800) 554-4SUN, (503) 553-1112*

**General Manager:** *Steve Whitaker*
**Rooms:** *139 doubles and suites, 25 cottages, teepees*
**Rates:** *Doubles/Suites $100-300 (EP), Cottages $90-200 (EP),*
        *Teepees $50-55 (EP)*
**Payment:** *AE, CB, DC, DSC, MC, and VISA*
**Children:** *Welcome; children under five years of age are free of charge*
**Dogs:** *Welcome in the cottages, with a fee of $14*
**Open:** *All year*

More than 100 years ago, the Warm Springs, Wasco, and Paiute Indians were "given" 600,000 acres of land in eastern Oregon. For decades, they lived off this barren land, with moderate success. Then, in 1958, the United States government built the Dalles Dam, which, unfortunately, destroyed Celilo Falls, a traditional Native American fishing area. The government compensated the tribes for their losses, and with the money, the tribes then commissioned a study on how to ensure the economic future of their people. It was decided to take these funds and buy back reservation land near some natural hot springs. In 1964, they purchased the land in a valley that had originally been owned by an Indian woman named Kah-Nee-Ta. They built a small resort, which included a swimming pool, mineral baths, cottages, and assorted teepees. It became known as Kah-Nee-Ta's village. In 1972, the expansive main lodge was constructed on the hill above the village, and more recently, a 9-hole golf course, restaurant, and the Indian Head gaming facility have been added.

The Kah-Nee-Tah Resort looms almost like a mirage against the spectacular golden rocky hills. The main lodge was designed to resemble an arrowhead; however, from below, it appears more like an ancient cliff dwelling. There are two separate parts to the resort, the main lodge on the bluff and the village a mile and a half down the road. The lodge rooms are decidedly more luxurious than the accommodations at the village; however, they do not allow dogs — so we will focus on the cottages in the village.

The cottages are surrounded by rocky ledges, hills, and a scattering of trees. They are aligned in the shape of a cross, with each leg featuring a combination of one- and two-bedroom cottages.

These are rather rustic affairs, with open-beamed ceilings and simple furnishings, but they are also a great value for families and their dogs. (The dog fee is a little much, but not when compared with most kennels.) The small sitting rooms in each cottage are set alongside the kitchens. There are only a couple of restaurants at the resort — a mom and pop restaurant in the village and the more formal Juniper Room up at the lodge. While the food is just fine in both places, guests staying in the cottages usually prefer preparing their own meals. The Neesha Cottage is probably the most deluxe of the group, with a pair of bedrooms, a full kitchen, a living room with a fireplace, and a Jacuzzi. All the cottages have cable television and private bathrooms with shower/tub combinations.

Another reason the village is so popular is that there is a naturally-heated mineral spring pool here, along with whirlpools and a wading pool. A host of kiddy-oriented options are prevalent, as well as volleyball, horseshoes, miniature golf, and a playground. More adult-oriented activities can be enjoyed throughout the resort, which includes golf and a newly opened 24,000 square-foot casino. Guests of the village are more than welcome to head up the hill and relax in the lounge, an open beamed-ceiling space that resembles an enormous teepee with windows. A massive, gray granite fireplace is surrounded by cushioned benches. While at the lodge, many check out some of the other diversions available at the resort, including playing tennis, having a massage, or renting a mountain bike to further explore the surrounding terrain.

The strong Native American heritage of the Confederated Tribes of Warm Springs comes through at the Kah-Nee-Ta. Guests may wish to sample the resort's famous Bird-in-Clay dinner; they can enjoy an authentic salmon bake with the ritual singing and dancing, or they can simply study the many Native American crafts that are on display throughout the main lodge. As an aside, an even more impressive array of artifacts can be found in the Museum at Warm Springs, which houses an exhibition that has been collected and carefully preserved by the tribes. (The tribes have built traditional houses to help maintain an authentic setting.) We recommend spending some time watching the live drumming and singing that are often occurring, and, if possible, visiting the Wasco wedding ceremony.

All sorts of activities abound at the resort, and all are available for a very reasonable fee. There is horseback riding, river rafting, tennis, bicycling, fishing, or golf. Hiking, of course, is free of charge. Dogs will immensely enjoy this latter option, as there is plenty of wide open country surrounding the resort. This is dry country, and we highly recommend bringing plenty of water for both human and beast during outings. Some enjoy following the path of the

Warm Springs River, while others like to hike over the hills and follow the horse trails that wend through the countryside. Whichever recreational pastime appeals to guests and their dog, we're sure all will come away from the Kah-Nee-Ta Resort with a whole new appreciation of the Native American heritage.

---

# Old Welches Inn

*26401 East Welches Rd.*
*Welches, Oregon 97067*
*(503) 622-3754*

*Innkeepers: Judi and Ted Mondun*
*Rooms: 3 doubles, 1 cottage*
*Rates: Doubles $75-95 (B&B), Cottage $150 (EP)*
*Payment: MC and VISA*
*Children: Most appropriate for children over age 12*
*Dogs: Welcome "if they are fully house trained and very friendly."*
*    They must get along with Judi's dog Sadie.*
*Open: All year*

The Old Welches Inn was built in 1890 by Samuel Welch, and was one of Mount Hood's earliest resorts. The hotel didn't survive, but the house did — and stayed within the Welch family for the next 80 years before the Monduns bought it. Judi told us that even though the house was in a total state of disrepair, the Welches were hesitant to sell it, fearing that whoever bought it would tear it down and build a monstrosity — realizing the inherent value of this riverside property. Fortunately, Judi and her husband also feel strongly about preserving the past. So after they purchased the old place, they shored up the foundation and renovated every inch of the house. Today, guests will find a charming old farmhouse, painted white and highlighted with bright blue trim and shutters. The house still overlooks the river, as well as the golf course, and beyond to the mountains that rise steeply from the valley floor.

We arrived one morning to find Sadie, an Akita Shepherd mix, and Judi out tending to the gardens. As we passed through the white picket fence, we meandered about the yard, which is fashioned with shade trees and free-flowing flower gardens. Sadie bounded up to greet us and then escorted us to the farmhouse. While the guest rooms in the main house are fine for those traveling with a dog, the cottage is perhaps the best choice. Built in 1901, this cottage — like many of the other cottages around the valley — were rented to people for the summer. By the 1930s all the cottages except for this one were owned by individuals. Today, this cottage has the same white and blue color treatments that are found on the main house. Once inside, we emerged into a living room filled with well-worn furniture set around a river rock fireplace. This cozy chamber is well stocked with games and books, as well as a television. Oddly enough, though, the best river views are reserved for the cook, through the small windows over the sink. The kitchen is outfitted with a few condiments, which include such items as popcorn, snacks, herbs, and coffee and tea. Some guests enjoy preparing their own breakfasts, while others might be able to persuade Judi to make them breakfast on a slow day. Of the two bedrooms, the largest has a queen bed while the other is furnished with a pair of twin bedsteads. The master bedroom has an old-fashioned radio that provides a little entertainment; the other guest chamber has the best views of the river, through a pair of small windows. We love the sloping hardwood floors in the cottage — so off-kilter that the doors have been shaved, so they can open and close across the floors. The fairly rustic ambiance is nicely complemented by a faint scent of wood smoke.

Guests staying in the cottage may come and spend as much time as they would like in the main house. The first floor of this antique home flows beautifully, and seems especially light and airy because of the  walls of windows and the cream-colored Berber carpeting. The living room seems like the natural place to congregate, especially on the overstuffed sofas in front of the fireplace. The sun porch is just as popular, with its three walls of windows, comfortable furnishings, and lovely views. During the day, some come in to just soak up the sun; while at night, guests gather here to watch a movie on the big screen television. The hosts have more than 60 videos that guests may choose from.

The three bedrooms are found upstairs. Judi tells us that men generally prefer Columbine, which overlooks the river. In the fall, she puts the hunter green and burgundy flannel sheets on the cannon ball-style bed. Duck decoys and hunt prints add to the masculine feeling in here. The Sweet Briar room, on the other hand, is somewhat more feminine, with its brass and white iron bed covered in a pale pink, green, and white comforter. This guest room also overlooks the river. The only drawback, for some, is the double bed. The largest chamber is called Trillium, and it overlooks the the golf course. In here, English chintzes predominate, whether on the bed or the overstuffed chairs. Judi sets chocolate out on little china plates in each of the guest rooms. Cotton towels are laid out for guests to use in the two shared bathrooms, which happen to be fully stocked with soaps and shampoos. In the morning, guests staying in the main house enjoy breakfast in the dining room, where plants thrive and there are views of the rock-walled porch and river.

While the house is beautifully restored, it is the property that guests and their canine are most likely to enjoy. When the Monduns bought the house, the grounds were covered with thorn bushes and dense foliage. As they cleared it, they discovered all sorts of old bottles and other bits of rubbish down by the water. They cleaned up all the debris, planted gardens, built rock walls, and even came across an old set of stone steps that hadn't been used in years. They built a river rock patio and a wonderful gazebo, along with an outdoor fireplace. We thoroughly enjoyed sitting out here at the end of the day, while listening to the soothing sound of the river and the smaller stream feeding into it.

It is always pleasant to walk the dogs along the country road the runs past the golf course and continues into the hills. Mount Hood is only a fifteen minute drive from the inn, and the Salmon-Huckleberry Wilderness is even closer, with almost as many trails to access. Just outside of Zigzag, hikers and their dogs will find the Salmon River Trail; the Salmon Butte Trail; or a climb to the Devil's Peak Lookout — which reveals exceptional views of Mount Hood. Dogs are welcome throughout this wilderness area and in the neighboring Mount Hood Wilderness Area.

# Wolf Creek Tavern

*P.O. Box 97*
*Wolf Creek, Oregon  97497*
*(503) 866-2474*

*Innkeepers: Mike and Joy Carter*
*Rooms: 8 doubles*
*Rates: $55-75 (EP)*
*Payment: MC and VISA*
*Children: Welcome*
*Dogs: Small dogs are welcome with a $10 non-refundable deposit*
*Open: All year, except for two weeks in January*

The Wolf Creek Tavern is a fun place to spend the night en route to another destination. Some have come here after spending a couple of days hiking through the Siskiyou National Forest, while others use it as a stopover on their way to Ashland's Shakespearean festival. Whatever reasons draw visitors to this old stagecoach tavern, they will be impressed with its authentic ambiance. There are also plenty of visitors who come by to have their picture taken in front of the tavern. While there is some question as to when the Wolf Creek Tavern was built, most historians place it somewhere in the late 1870s and early 1880s. During its heyday it was one of the many stops on the overland route between Portland and Sacramento that gave both horses and passengers a chance to rest and eat.

Its more recent history includes a few famous travelers, including Mary Pickford and Clark Gable, as well as author Sinclair Lewis. However, one room is dedicated to perhaps the most famous notable ever to be a guest here — Jack London. He finished writing *The End of the Story* while staying at the tavern with his wife, Charmain. Guests are not as likely to run into as many famous personalities today; however, they will find the place intriguing. We hopped off Interstate 5 and dropped quickly into Wolf Creek, which consists of a handful of stores and the historic Wolf Creek Tavern. This Greek Revival building, complete with two rows of porches, rests alongside a stand of shade trees. It is in terrific condition, but that was not always the case. When the Oregon State Parks Service took it over in 1977, it was dilapidated, and it took over two years to restore it. Great pains were taken to ensure that the restoration was authentic. The trim was hand milled to match the rest of the tavern, and authentic period colors were carefully mixed and applied so that the tavern came as close as possible to reflecting its former heritage. Today, it is listed on the National Register of Historic Places.

As guests walk through the hallways, they will surely feel this sense of history. Just inside the front door is one of our favorite rooms, the "men's sitting room," which now serves as the intimate bar. There is usually a fire crackling in the fireplace, and those who look carefully will find that the original boot marks are still in evidence from when the men propped their feet up near the fire. On the other side of the hall is the more refined ladies' parlor, with its fireplace (no boot marks here), marble topped tables, and a scattering of antiques.

Most people who come upon the Wolf Creek Tavern are curious about its history. If they've talked to enough people, they will discover that the tavern also serves good, reasonably priced food. The dining room lies to the back of the building, and feels nearly as authentic as the rest of the place. We recommend choosing a table in the second dining room, as it contains one of the tavern's original fireplaces. Patrons can order something as simple as a cobb or shrimp salad for dinner, or opt for something more substantial. While pasta and vegetarian dishes can be found on the menu, there are also heartier options, including old-fashioned pork roast served with mashed potatoes and gravy, English bangers, Cornish pasties, and chicken fried steak. Mind you, these are not for the cholesterol conscious, but for those craving one night of old fashioned indulgences.

Bedtime usually comes early around here, as there isn't much night life in Wolf Creek. There is one bedroom in the original tavern that is furnished with American antiques, including an oak bed, a marble topped table, a mirrored armoire, and lamp globes decorated with hand-painted flowers. Most guests will stay in the newer wing, which was built in 1927. These rooms were designed in a style in keeping with the rest of the tavern. There are two floors of rooms; we liked the ones facing the rear, overlooking the lawn and gardens, as they are more peaceful. These simply decorated spaces contain double brass beds, oak bureaus, and have windows framed by sheer white curtains. Some guests prefer the first-floor rooms, as they allow easier access to the outside for impromptu walks with Bowser. Even though the Wolf Creek Taverns attracts plenty of history buffs, along with the curious, the Carters go out of their way to ensure that the privacy of their overnight guests is always maintained.

There are plenty of grassy areas behind the inn — as well as some quieter streets away from the busy main road — that are great for walking a dog. There is also Wolf Creek, which is on the edge of the Siskiyou National Forest. To get here, follow a tiny back road from Wolf Creek into Galice. Once here, visitors and their dogs will find plenty of hiking opportunities. Those who want to continue with the historic nature of their trip can choose hikes that lead them to old mining operations dating back to the gold rush era. The Dutchy Creek Valley has a trail that meanders through dense forests, then by some old mine tailings and excavating apparatus. Another popular route through this area is the Briggs Creek Trail, which also passes by some of the old mines.

# The See Vue

*95590 Highway 101*
*Yachats, Oregon   97498*
*(503) 547-3227*

**Manager:** *Robert Barzler*
**Rooms:** *9 doubles, 1 suite, 1 cottage*
**Rates:** *Doubles $43-57 (EP), Suite $58-65 (EP), Cottage $43-50 (EP)*
**Payment:** *MC and VISA*
**Children:** *Welcome*
**Dogs:** *Welcome with a $5 per pet nightly charge. Maximum of two*
*dogs per room.*
**Open:** *All year*

We were some six miles south of Yachats when we spotted The See Vue. From the road, it looks very much like any other motel found along the Oregon coast — but there was something subtly different about this place, something that caused us to pull off the highway and take a closer look. We were glad we did. This may have been an ordinary motel when it was first constructed, but ten years ago it was transformed into the eclectic, kitschy spot that it is today. New owners bought it a year or so ago, but the longtime manager has stayed on to maintain the feeling that has made The See Vue so popular with returning guests. The building's exterior is fashioned with naturally-weathered shakes, a plethora of planters filled with blooming flowers, and other mature shrubs, giving The See Vue plenty of visual appeal.

Though the rooms may be lined up in typical motel style, the unusual names on the doors hint at out-of-the-ordinary interior decor. Stepping inside The Sea Rose Suite, The Salish, The Princess and the Pea, The Santa Fe, and Granny's Rooms, preconceived impressions of a traditional motel disappear. These places have character — whether they're filled with granny's antiques, Southwest memorabilia, or original works of art. We like the natural board walls in some, the beamed ceilings in others, and, in some cases, the beachstone fireplaces. The Far Out West Room is found at the end of the building; when we stepped inside, we were somewhat taken aback by the animal skin stretched on the wall over the bed — but it does fit in well with the old west theme, which includes western wool blankets, authentic pictures, and country antiques. Around the corner is a 1950s-style kitchen with plenty of windows revealing ocean views. We also loved Granny's Room, with its hand-carved mahogany double bed backed by a collection of decorative china hanging on the wall — all of which are illuminated by old-fashioned fringed lamps. The white-washed board walls in the kitchen also feature a few pieces of china, along with a collection of woven baskets. Of course, all the culinary necessities are also provided. The Salish, too, captured our attention with its original Northwest Native American mural painted on its walls. The Princess and the Pea would appeal to those with a penchant for the whimsical, as wicker collectibles and assorted knickknacks abound, including an array of old-fashioned musical instruments. The Princess theme might have been derived from the brass rubbings of a knight and his lady. This is the sort of chamber where most find it easy to relax — a crackling fire, a good book, and a picturesque sunset over the Pacific.

Families traveling with their dog will be most comfortable in the Sea Rose Suite, which consists of a double-bedded room, along with a separate alcove that can accommodate a single bed. The loft space and family room with a sofa bed make this suite even more versatile. A full kitchen allows guests to prepare simple snacks and meals that may be enjoyed in the adjoining dining room. With the exception of the Sea Rose Suite, most of the rooms are generally quite cozy. Guests requiring a little more privacy may wish to reserve the cottage. While it is situated closer to the highway, it is nonetheless set off by itself. Stained glass windows enliven one wall of this small abode, while another offers nice vistas of the ocean.

The See Vue lies on a bluff near the edge of the ocean, but there is a large grassy area that dogs are welcome to explore; it is slightly protected by low bushes and a split rail fence. (Visitors must be vigilant about poop patrol). As not all the units offer kitchens, some guests will be happy to learn about the Sea Perch, located just next door, which serves an excellent homemade breakfast. Locals and visitors alike come here for their buckwheat pancakes, Belgian waffles covered in berries, fresh baking powder biscuits and gravy — and endless refills of coffee. We also ordered deli sandwiches to go before we headed out for the day.

Visitors and their dogs need not travel far to find great hiking opportunities or intriguing beach walks. The Carl G. Washburne State Park is probably the closest option. Some trails meander through the coastal mountains, while the Hobbit Trail leads back down to the beach. Anyone who wants to stay near the water can also drive to the Sutton Creek Sand Dunes, where people and their dogs can meander along the sand dunes and observe the array of wildlife. Finally, there is Devil's Elbow State Park. The park has a trail leading up to Heceta Head, where there are terrific views to be enjoyed by both human and beast.

# Shamrock Lodgettes

*P.O. Box 346*
*Yachats, Oregon 97498*
*(800) 845-5028, (503) 547-3312, Fax (503) 547-3843*

**Hosts:** *Mary and Bob Oxley*
**Rooms:** *12 doubles, 7 cabins, 1 apartment*
**Rates:** *Doubles $67-90 (EP), Cottages $86-106 (EP),*
*Apartment $65 (EP), Children $5-7*
**Payment:** *AE, DC, CB, DC, MC, and VISA*
**Children:** *Welcome (cribs and baby-sitters are available)*
**Dogs:** *Welcome in the cabins and the apartment with a $2 daily fee*
**Open:** *All year*

Yachats is a quiet community set directly on a low-lying section of the Oregon coast. There is plenty to do here: long walks with dogs on sandy beaches, fishing, or searching for bloodstones, petrified wood, and agates along the shoreline. The Shamrock Lodgettes are some of the more interesting accommodation options in the area, especially because of the four acres of park-like land that buffers guests from any noise emanating from Highway 101.

A meandering drive wends past stands of pines, clusters of azaleas and rhododendrons, and a sprawling, emerald green lawn until it reaches the cozy log cabins. Although there are a few different types of accommodations at the Shamrock Lodgettes, those who bring a dog will be asked to stay in the cabins. (We feel these are preferable to the motel units.) Self-sufficiency is the key here, as each cabin is considered a housekeeping unit and is outfitted with an efficiency kitchen ("efficiency" denoting no ovens), towel and linen exchange upon request, daily garbage pickup, and firewood drop off. While not as pampered as one would be at a traditional inn, guests are well-taken care of. The Oxleys deliver a daily paper to guest room doors, offer color cable television (with in-room movies) and direct-dial telephones, and are always available to assist with any special requests.

The four oldest cabins, constructed in the early 1950s, are named after various rivers in Oregon. Alsea, Siuslaw, and Umpqua have two double beds in the master bedroom and a sofabed in the living room — enabling them to easily accommodate five guests. Siletz, on the other hand, is one of the largest of the cabins, with two good-sized bedrooms, a sofabed in the living room, and a panoramic ocean view. Yaquina is another two-bedroom cabin that can sleep up to seven people. Osage and Apartment #7 are suitable one-bedroom accommodations. But enough about the basics, because what truly impressed us about this cottage resort was the character we found inside.

Natural wood pervades these spaces, with authentic log walls and pine boards lining the ceilings and floors. The color schemes vary from natural hues of gold to a deep red. While all the living rooms are fashioned with either a stone fireplace or a freestanding wood stove, we especially enjoyed the homey quality of the stone fireplaces. The furnishings are almost secondary, but guests should expect to find camp furnishings such as Adirondack chairs, pine tables, leather chairs, and comfortable sofas — perfect for afternoon naps. Not all the cabins have direct views of the water, but it is worth requesting one that does.

We like this area because there is plenty to do with a dog. The most popular option is to walk about the grounds and down along the shore. Should Bowser tire of this routine, guests might bring him over to Tillicum Beach, Yachats State Park, or Neptune State Park. The latter is a 300-acre park with an abundance of wildlife and natural wonders. One of the more notable natural wonders is the famous Cook's Chasm, a spectacular gorge that has been carved out by the ocean over the centuries. Hiking trails also dot this area. Cape Perpetua is probably the best spot for day hikes with a dog. (For a detailed description, see Gull Haven Lodge in Florence.) There is an abundance of information in the reception area, covering vacationer's options ranging from scenic sights and attractions to nearby restaurants and shopping areas. When deciding to explore this region, visitors should keep in mind that it gets more than 100 inches of rain a year. We suggest bringing a raincoat, and perhaps an extra towel or two for drying off Bowser after a day spent outside. At the end of the day, most human guests look forward to visiting the small spa on the property, featuring a hot tub, a sauna, and the services of a licensed massage therapist.

One final note: the Oxleys have owned the Shamrock Lodgettes for 25 years and their guests usually book a year in advance for the following summer. Thus, for those who are interested in visiting, we highly recommend making reservations well in advance.

# Flying M Ranch

*23029 N.W. Flying M Road*
*Yamhill, Oregon 97148*
*(503) 662-3222*

**Hosts:** *Bryce and Barbara Mitchell*
**Rooms:** *4 singles, 24 doubles, 7 cabins*
**Rates:** *Singles $65 (EP), Doubles $65-75 (EP), Cabins $80-200 (EP)*
**Payment:** *AE, DC, DSC, MC, and VISA*
**Children:** *Welcome (cots are available), Children are free of charge*
**Dogs:** *Welcome, but must be leashed when exploring the grounds*
**Open:** *All year, except Christmas*

Anyone who loves the west's vast expanses of open land, but who doesn't want to travel too far to get it, will be intrigued with the Flying M Ranch. Surrounded by more than 600 hundred acres of land (this is where the vast part comes in), the Flying M Ranch is situated at the end of a bumpy and winding five-mile-long road that was once the old stagecoach route. With every bump we gained a greater appreciation for what stagecoach travelers must have experienced along this road more than 120 years ago. The ranch is set in the Oregon Coast Range near the base of Trask Mountain. Those with small planes can fly in and land on the ranch's 2,200-feet grass runaway, disembarking directly in front of the main lodge.

This place has plenty of things to recommend it, especially for those who like horseback riding. Anyone ten years of age or older can choose between the short, day-long or overnight trail rides. Those choosing the latter will likely end up spending a night at the log cabin on Trask Mountain. Along the trail, riders will enjoy some spectacular scenery, as well as fine fishing in the many streams. Guests return to the ranch's wonderful home-cooked meals and comfortable accommodations — along with some country and western dancing for those who are still able to muster enough energy after a long day in the saddle.

Most of the ranch's activity revolves around the massive timber lodge, which guests enter by way of the large double doors, that are outfitted with axes as door handles. This cavernous space is dominated by bleached log walls adorned with bear and moose heads set alongside animal skins, rip saws, apple presses, antlers, saddles, and other assorted collectibles. The equally enormous restaurant, effectively divided in half by a massive stone fireplace, offers an array of western-style entrées (buffalo, venison, and elk) and is especially known for its barbecue. Towards the rear, guests will find the Sawtooth Lounge, which serves up live music, along with terrific views of the river from its bar — a six-ton log.

The accommodations vary, and lie just across the river from the lodge. Guests may choose from rooms in either the Bunkhouse Motel or the cabins, or really "rough it" and reserve one of the 100 or so campsites for a nominal fee. The Bunkhouse Motel is a large single-story building with a wraparound porch, offering 24 simply decorated and furnished guest quarters. While these rooms don't have televisions or air conditioning, each does contain a pair of queen beds, wall-to-wall carpeting, and modern bathrooms with stall showers. The rooms facing the river are our first choice, primarily because of their river views and large shade trees lining the banks. The cabins, on the other hand, range from the single-bedroom Wrangler's and Rustler's Roost cabins to the more expansive two-bedroom Royal Hideout and Dement cabins. Most have a living room with a sofa bed, a wood stove or fireplace, and a kitchen. Anyone requiring additional amenities should consider the Honeymoon Cabin, where they can bask in the luxury of a Jacuzzi tub, a color television, and a true country decor.

When not on horseback, guests will find numerous activities available, ranging from swimming in the huge pond to more organized events such as tennis, basketball, horseshoes, volleyball, and softball. Besides meeting most human needs, the ranch's 600 acres, abundance of wildlife, picturesque setting, and refreshing river will ensure that Bowser has as energizing a vacation as his human counterparts.

# Washington

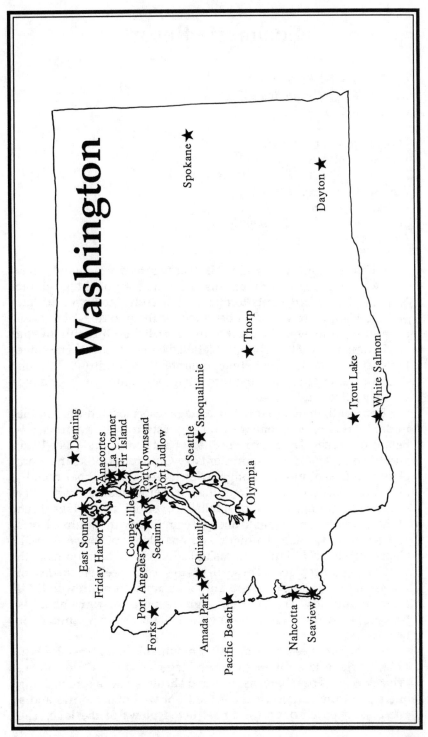

# Washington

Deming ★

Anacortes ★
La Conner ★
Fir Island ★

East Sound ★
Friday Harbor ★

Coupeville ★
Port Townsend ★
Port Ludlow ★

Sequim ★

Port Angeles ★

Seattle ★
Snoqualimie ★

Olympia ★

Forks ★

Amada Park ★
Quinault ★

Pacific Beach ★

Nahcotta ★
Seaview ★

Thorp ★

Spokane ★

Dayton ★

Trout Lake ★
White Salmon ★

# Lochaerie Resort

*638 North Shore Road*
*Amanda Park, Washington 98526*
*(360) 288-2215*

*Hosts:* Bob and Gina Harper
*Rooms:* 6 cottages
*Rates:* $50-65 (EP), Extra persons $8 per night
*Payment:* Personal checks
*Children:* Welcome
*Dogs:* Welcome for a $10 nightly fee
*Open:* All year

On the Olympic Peninsula, it isn't easy to find accommodations that welcome dogs. Perhaps this is because all of the Olympic National Park is off limits to our furry friends. Moreover, if they were to visit, there wouldn't be much for them to do. There is an exception, however, in the region near Lake Quinault in the wilderness areas of the Olympic National Forest. Visitors who come here can explore this incredible, mountainous country with their dogs and, along the way, find rare foliage and immense trees amid the magnificent rain forest.

Best of all, there is a low-key cottage resort located right in the midst of this region that welcomes guests traveling with well-behaved canines. The Lochaerie Resort has been around since 1926, and lies on the northern shores of Lake Quinault. Unlike the more elaborate Lake Quinault Lodge, with its restaurant, boat rentals, and variety of accommodations, the Lochaerie consists of a smaller grouping of cottages set upon a hillside overlooking the lake. Each of these weathered, shingled abodes, complete with multiple eaves and covered porches, is unique and has plenty of visual appeal. Guests can expect to find old-fashioned kitchens, bathrooms with showers, and fireplaces. These places also come well stocked with linens, flatware and china, and unlimited amounts of firewood. All are neat and tidy. The only thing guests need to worry about is bringing their food and choosing the cottage that best suits their needs.

All the cottages are named after mountains in the area. Built in 1932, Christie is a one-bedroom cottage set upon Onion Rock. Privacy is at its best here, as trees and shrubs create a screen along one side of the cottage, leaving the front wall of windows and a good-sized porch open to unobstructed views of the lake. The cottage has a brick fireplace and can accommodate three, but is ideal for two. Angeles, built in 1936, is another one-bedroom cottage that is fashioned with a river rock fireplace. It has large windows that face both the lake and the dense forest. Also built in 1936, and containing a river rock fireplace, is Storm King. It is larger than the first two and even has a loft that kids are sure to enjoy. It is privy to lake, mountain, and sunset views. Two of the most rustic cottages, built in 1926, are Ellinor and Olympus. Each has one bedroom, although Olympus is also outfitted with a sleeping porch that allows it to comfortably accommodate a total of four guests. Finally, there is Colonel Bob, which is the most modern of the cottages. The rooms in here don't have as much character as the other cottages, but guests who stay here are close to the beach.

These cottages are the perfect base for exploring the region. Some are happy to bring books and games and spend their time by the fire. Others will want to combine this with a little fishing, hiking, or informative nature walks. The fishing on Lake Quinault is excellent and guests can test their angling skills right from the resort. There are also 200 miles of hiking trails accessible to visitors and their dogs throughout the Olympic National Forest. Explorers may want to look for remnants of logging throughout the region, or head deeper into the forest to find mushrooms or ancient cedar trees. Two nature trails begin at the South Shore Road. Dogs are also permitted to hike from trails beginning at the Lake Quinault Lodge, the Quinault Ranger Station, and the Falls Creek Campground. One of the more difficult hikes in the area is the one that ascends Colonel Bob Mountain, but the views from here are tremendous.

We think that low price, coupled with the inherent character of these cabins, make this an ideal choice for those who want to be independent, cook their own meals, and take advantage of all this area has to offer. The only additional things we would recommend are for guests to bring their own rain gear and few extra towels for drying off Bowser.

# Albatross Bed and Breakfast

*5708 Kingsway West*
*Anacortes, Washington 98221*
*(800) 484-9507 ext. 5840, (360) 293-0677*

**Hosts:** Barbie Guay and Ken Arasim
**Rooms:** 4 doubles
**Rates:** $75-85 (B&B)
**Payment:** MC and VISA
**Children:** Welcome, but most appropriate for children over the age of 4
**Dogs:** Welcome, but please bring dog's bedding
**Open:** All year

The morning ferry from Anacortes to Vancouver Island and the San Juan Islands leaves early — a bit too early for those coming from any distance. We have long thought it would be nice to have a place to stay in Anacortes, so that rolling out of bed to catch the ferry could actually be a pleasant, if not leisurely, experience. We finally found just the spot at the Albatross Bed and Breakfast.

The Albatross B&B is located at the edge of a residential neighborhood, overlooking a marina, various out buildings, and the more distant water. The Cape Cod-style house and the couple who own it are equally fascinating; however, we will begin with the house. In 1927, the E.K. Wood Mill Company built this cedar house for its mill manager. From about that time until 1943, the company operated one of the largest lumber mills in the state. Unfortunately, all that remains of that facility is a 600-foot-long planing mill. The rest of the buildings were torn down to make room for private homes, which, today, line the hills sloping down toward the water.

The Albatross rests on a street corner in a residential neighborhood. We initially had trouble finding the B&B, as there wasn't a sign with its name on it. Then we spied a bright blue building with white trim that was partially obscured by mature plantings. Ken, who is exceptionally friendly, greeted us and gave us a tour of his home. We half expected to be surrounded by the fragrant smell of cedar, but instead discovered that the exposed cedar was only in the guest wing and that its aroma was faint. Although the scent of cedar had diminished with the years, the deep red hues of the wood had only grown more beautiful. Two unusual features, beaded ceilings and extra thick doors — double the normal width — were especially noteworthy. Our first stop was in the Scarlett O'Hara room. Ken explained that friends of theirs bought an antique bedroom set out of an old Southern mansion. The friends later moved, didn't have room for it, and offered it to Ken and Barbie. This appealing addition to the B&B dates back to the 1850s; its focal point is the half-tester bed with its original velvet canopy, headboard, and footboard. Also present are a matching Lincoln rocker and a marble-topped commode. The commode holds a Victorian lamp with a cranberry-fluted shade of a thousand eyes. Ken and Barbie even have an old-fashioned "necessary chair," although guests won't need it, since a private, modern bathroom is only steps away. The other most popular bedroom lies at the opposite end of the hall. Known as the Monet room, it, too, contains some antiques, but it is named for the florals and lovely color schemes for which Monet is renowned. The Captain's Room is another intriguing space, which contains plenty of nautical paraphernalia sure to delight seafarers and landlubbers alike.

Guests are encouraged to use the living room as their sitting room. Most people are initially drawn to the two walls of plate glass windows offering distant water views. Later in the evening, when the sun has set, guests' attention shifts inward to the fireplace and the comfortable sofa. As we walked from one room to the next, we began to have a better understanding of Barbie and Ken — they are collectors. They collect all sorts of things, notably, fine art, bears, and clocks. More importantly, they know the history behind most pieces in their collections and can give guests a little story on just about everything in the house. But the two most extensive collections are Ken's antique cars and Barbie's — surprise, surprise — Barbie dolls. She displays these in the living and dining rooms, including some wearing Bob Mackie-designed gowns. One Erté doll gown called *Stardust* has over 7,000 decorative beads sewn into the fabric. The curious may wish to inquire about some of the B&B's original paintings. We learned that one actually shimmers — because of the gold dust mixed into the paint. With all these collectibles, guests will feel right at home — and they'll have a myriad of intriguing things to browse through during their stay.

In the morning, guest (even those trying to catch an early ferry) are treated to a hearty meal at the lace-covered dining room table. Barbie can make just about anything, and is happy to adjust her meal to fit guests' special needs. She usually begins breakfast with a fruit plate, which is then followed by homemade pancakes, Belgian waffles, or perhaps a baked-egg dish. Bacon and sausage are also available. Afterwards, guests may catch their ferry, just relax, or perhaps walk down to the water with Bowser. There are grassy areas along the shore that are great fun for running a dog.

Barbie and Ken own a boat called the Charisma, which they charter to guests and others who want to spend a morning or early evening on the water. Ken told us about one great spot where people can walk with their dogs — Washington Park. This is a great seaside park that has plenty of places for picnicking or exploring with a canine. (There are more than 200 acres of grass, forest, and trails that lie on Fidalgo Head.) Other good hikes include the trail around Cranberry and Heart Lakes and the Mount Eerie Trail. Longer day trips can take visitors to Deception Pass, where there are even more hiking options available. Guests should keep in mind, though, that all of these areas are easily accessible from Seattle, so they tend to be crowded during the summer months. After a busy day, guests will probably want to return to the Albatross B&B for a little tea and more homemade baked goodies.

---

# The Victorian B&B

*P.O. Box 761*
*602 North Main*
*Coupeville, Washington   98239*
*(360) 678-5305*

*Innkeepers: Al  and Marion Sasso*
*Rooms: 2 doubles, 1 cottage*
*Rates: Doubles $80 (B&B), Cottage $100 (B&B)*
*Payment: DSC, MC, and VISA*
*Children: Welcome in the cottage only*
*Dogs: Welcome in the cottage only*
*Open: All year*

Whidbey Island lay hidden from most navigators until 1792, when Joseph Whidbey discovered it quite by chance. One day, while sailing through the area, he observed an uncharted river that seemed to flow in the wrong direction. Whidbey secured a small boat and set out to explore the strange passageway, discovering, in the process, an intriguing island. The waterway leading to the island was ultimately called Deception Pass and the island named after Joseph Whidbey. Coupeville was the first settlement on the island. It was established in the 1850s — which makes it the second oldest town in Washington state.

The Victorian Bed and Breakfast is equally historic. This Italianate Victorian home was built over 100 years ago by Jacob Jenne. It is one of a group of homes, all of similar architectural style, that comprise a portion of the town's historic district. Guests may not have water views, but they do feel a strong sense of history when staying at the inn. The Victorian Inn occupies a corner location, and is surrounded by mature shade trees. Its rich shade of blue, with rose highlights inset into the decorative trim, causes The Victorian to stand out from its neighbors. Bay windows seem to add definition to every ell, but the interior remains hidden from view by lace curtains. Guests step across the little half-porch and through the front door into a Victorian parlor, where Marion displays all sorts of handmade items available for purchase. Upstairs are two guest rooms decorated around a causal country theme — one in blues, the other in pinks; both are quite feminine in decor.

The cottage is separate from the main house, but connected to it by a small courtyard framed with white lattice. It actually lies behind the house, on a side street, making it feel all the more private. This cottage, too, is historic, and, from the exterior, it looks like something out of a storybook. The cottage is difficult to see from the road, especially in the spring, when the pink and white wisteria cascade over the porch roof and down to the lavish display of pink lilacs. The aroma produced by this combination of flowers is thoroughly intoxicating. During the rest of the year, the pink hues are maintained with climbing roses entwined on the white trellis. The four-room cottage's interior spaces are quite cozy, but ideal for anyone traveling with a dog. A separate bedroom contains a queen bed, a bureau, and the convenience of a television and VCR. There is a small sitting room with a trundle bed that sleeps two and also doubles as a sofa. As with the rooms in the main house, there is a low-key country feeling to the interior, with draped tables, small flowered prints, and muted color schemes. The convenience of a kitchen is helpful, especially when preparing an impromptu snack or a hearty breakfast for Bowser. Humans are treated to their morning meal either at the inn or out on the courtyard. The menu varies, but guests may expect the usual selection of coffee, teas, and juices, along with, perhaps, the broiled grapefruit, homemade muffins, and the house specialty, a Dutch Baby pancake filled with strawberries or baked apples. Bacon may also be requested.

One of the many appealing things about staying here is that guests and their dogs can easily walk around Coupeville's waterfront. We like to avoid the main road when heading downtown, instead turning right out of the cottage and following a back road to the main street, which runs parallel to the harbor. The closest recreational outlet is the 200-acre Fort Ebey State Park, which is within a few minutes' drive of Coupeville. It was built in 1942 to offer some defense to Seattle, should the city be attacked via the Strait of Juan de Fuca. Today, visitors and their leashed dogs can visit the armaments or walk on the trails that wend through the park. One of the obvious, and more popular, choices is a trail that wends along the edge of the water. Another doggie option lies at Fort Casey, just south of town. Here, there are over 400 acres of fields, picnic sites, and trails to investigate.

# The Purple House

*415 East Clay Street*
*Dayton, Washington  99328*
*(800) 486-2574, (509) 382-3159*

*Innkeeper: D. Christine Williscroft*
*Rooms: 4 doubles, 2 suites, 1 cottage*
*Rates: Doubles $85 (B&B), Suites $125 (B&B), Cottage $125 (B&B)*
*Payment: MC and VISA*
*Children: Welcome*
*Dogs: Welcome*
*Open: All year*

Dayton is not necessarily the first town people think of for a weekend getaway, but it is a surprisingly good choice for those who enjoy hiking, fishing, or cross-country skiing with their dog, as the Umatilla National Forest is just minutes away. Although visitors might equate Dayton with the mountains, it is primarily a farming community. Its roots date back to the 1860s when gold lured prospectors to this region. Those who decided to stay built the Victorian homes we see here today. In the 1880s, the railroad, too, came to town, connecting Dayton with the rest of the west for nearly 100 years. Unfortunately, the train is gone, but the depot remains as a reminder of the town's history. Many of the Victorian homes, as well as the various civic buildings, have been beautifully preserved and form the town's two historic districts.

The Purple House shares in the town's rich history as well. It was built in 1882 by a Dr. Pietrzycki, who was both a physician and a philanthropist. This Queen-Anne Victorian is impressive, though it is a smaller version of the more expansive examples found in other parts of the country. Resting on a quiet side street, it is partially obscured by shade trees and other mature plantings. When Christine bought the house about ten years ago, it was in need of renovation. She spent many years working on her home and furnishing it with her many antiques and collectibles.

Christine left Germany more than 30 years ago, yet she has preserved her rich heritage and shares it with her guests. Here in Washington's countryside, guests are treated to an authentic European B&B. When new arrivals walk in the door, they are generally greeted by Christine's two Shih Tzus, Molley and Melley, who will no doubt want to show guests and their canines around the place. The front parlor is one of the more interesting areas in the house, with one wall of eight-foot-high windows overshadowed by the 18-foot ceilings. As one might imagine, this was not an easy room to fill, but Christine has done a wonderful job with her collection of Oriental antiques, assorted carvings, and a lovely silk screen. In most rooms a grand piano would be the highlight, but in this spacious chamber it barely fills one corner.

Couples traveling together usually reserve the two upstairs bedrooms that share a marble bathroom. Christine thinks this is especially suitable, as there is also an expansive library up here, and deep comfortable chairs ideal for sitting in and reading. One bedroom contains an antique sleigh bed that was covered with black paint when Christine first bought it. She spent hours taking the paint off to reveal the rich grain of the wood underneath. She likes to put feather comforters and pillows on the beds; however, for guests who are allergic; the other room's bed has a lovely Nettlecreek blanket on it.

Those who want a private entrance may choose between the first-floor bedroom or the carriage-house bedroom. The former is fashioned in rose tones, highlighted by a floral comforter on the queen bed. This already-bright space is lightened further by French doors that open directly onto the deck around the swimming pool. The bathroom in here is private, and is outfitted with a sunken bathtub. One final accommodation lies out in the carriage house. This offers the most flexibility of all the guest rooms, as it is separate from the main house. While it may lack some of the sunlight of the other bedrooms, the queen bed does face a glowing fireplace. Guests may prepare snacks in the kitchenette, although most people leave the food preparation up to Christine. She creates delicious European breakfasts, and, with a little notice, can produce delightful dinners.

In the morning, guests awake to the smell of freshly-baked breads. Christine says, almost apologetically, that she isn't really fond of American bread. We thought that just fine, as she creates the most fabulous and memorable breads using recipes brought from her homeland. Some are hearty breads; others are more reminiscent of rich pastries. The meal generally starts with a plate of bread and fresh fruit, followed by quiche or an overstuffed omelet. Christine is very flexible, and will prepare meals to order as well. Among her favorite food items are raspberries grown locally, specifically for her. Guests who may have missed her baked goods at breakfast may sample her pastries during afternoon tea.

After breakfast, some guests might want to take their canines for a leisurely walk along the quiet streets. The Chamber of Commerce supplies a map of the historic districts, making the outing all the more interesting. The Blue Mountains are within a short driving distance of The Purple House. In the wintertime, many come here to downhill and cross-country ski. (Bowser would probably prefer the latter.) Great day hikes and plenty of overnight hiking opportunities are also available in these mountains. The Panjab Trailhead is about an hour's drive from the inn. While the trail can keep hikers busy for days, it is also a good option for shorter outings. Another popular option can be found along the Eckler Mountain Road, where there is the Teepee Trailhead. Hikers may head up or down, depending upon their mood. Those who follow the trail into the valley will end up at the East Butte Creek. Another popular hike off Eckler Mountain Road is the Meadow Creek Trail.

Christine is a flexible, gregarious hostess. We especially like her pet policy, which shows her true affinity for dogs. It reads as follows: *You and your well-behaved owners are welcome. The Purple House's resident Shih Tzus, Molley and Melley, love making friends of all sizes. Owners should inquire about providing for your comfort when making their reservations.*

# The Logs Resort

*9002 Mount Baker Highway*
*Deming, Washington 98244*
*(360) 599-2711*

**Hostess:** *Hazel Ohlsen*
**Rooms:** *5 cottages*
**Rates:** *$73 (EP), $10 for each additional person, $6 per child*
**Payment:** *Personal checks*
**Children:** *Welcome*
**Dogs:** *Welcome, with approval, for a $3 daily fee*
**Open:** *All year*

Anyone who is looking for a rustic retreat, offering an assortment of outdoor activities and an abundance of natural beauty, should think about spending a week at The Logs Resort. A meandering country road lined by dense forests and a scenic river eventually leads to a dirt drive and the sign for the resort. Guests follow this driveway under a canopy of trees laden with hanging moss to a good-sized main house, resting upon the banks of Canyon Creek and the Nooksack River. Initially it may not look like much, but this house and cabins are The Logs Resort. With the change of seasons come copious amounts of rain, and occasionally the river crests; on some occasions the rain has flooded not only the riverside swimming pool but every other low-lying area as well. The rise in water level also carves deep grooves in the rocky river bed. Fortunately, the long-term damage is minimal, and those familiar with this low-key, unpretentious resort return each year to find the same handful of rustic cabins set amidst the forest, river, and more than 70 acres of grounds.

Each of the log cabins offers a different perspective of the surrounding forest and picturesque valley, but all provide the same basic amenities and general room configurations. The natural wood walls and timber-beamed ceilings nicely complement the simple decor and furnishings. All of these abodes contain two bedrooms, each with a pair of bunk beds and a private bathroom. The cozy living room, whose focal point is a stone fireplace, is also simply decorated and appointed. The foldout sofa bed gives guests the potential of transforming the living room into a third bedroom. Besides supplying linens and towels, Hazel stocks the kitchen with utensils, china, and pots and pans. There is always a substantial supply of wood stacked just outside the front door. While most guests enjoy the rustic ambiance of their accommodations, the primary draw to this spot is the pull of Mother Nature.

The surrounding valley, its array of recreational activities, and the scenic river area (complete with its associated wildlife) create the perfect environment for visitors and their canine companions to enjoy. We especially like the solar heated swimming pool perched on the banks of the river, although guests can also play horseshoes, badminton, and volleyball. Various swings are suspended from tall evergreens. Anglers will appreciate the excellent trout and salmon fishing, while Bowser might prefer striking out with his human friends on the hiking trails that cut through the Mount Baker National Forest. Others may be interested in taking a short drive to the town of Glacier, where a series of hiking trails can be found — all of which allow dogs. The trails in this area offer spectacular natural beauty for all types of hikers. Some combine hiking with blueberry picking, especially along the Excelsior Pass Trail that leads to the Damfino Lakes. The equally pleasant Skyline Divide hike offers incredible vistas, along with spring wildflowers. This exceptionally easy trail leads hikers up to three lakes — Hildebrand, Elbow, and Doreen. Some visitors may prefer to confine their adventures to the resort, where they might choose to pick blueberries or follow the riverbed in search of fossils.

Those who visit during the winter months will find cross-country and downhill skiing at the Mount Baker Ski area (only 20 miles from the resort). The Logs Resort is a great destination just about any time of year, particularly for those who are looking for a low-key cabin experience they can share with their dog.

# North Beach Inn

*P.O. Box 80*
*Eastsound, Washington  98245*
*(360) 376-2660*

*Owners: The Gibson Family*
*Rooms: 11 cabins*
*Rates: Daily $85-125 (EP), Weekly $550-1,025 (EP)*
*Payment: Personal checks*
*Children: Welcome*
*Dogs: Welcome*
*Open: March - November*

Orcas Island is a paradise for people who love exploring the outdoors with their dog. The highlights, of course, are Moran State Park and Mount Constitution. The island is more than just a state park, though; at nearly 60 miles, it is also the largest of all the San Juan Islands. Visitors are dropped off by ferry at the southern side of this horseshoe-shaped island; from there they need to drive north to Eastsound. Along the way, first-time visitors will get a good feeling for the island, with its pine forests, rolling green hills, and dramatic craggy shoreline.

Eastsound is the largest town on this lightly populated island, and it still exudes an old-world feeling. Just outside of town is a low-key retreat that is equally old-fashioned — and it should be; it has been here since the 1930s. Time seems to stand still at the North Beach Inn, and its owners, the Gibson family, don't see any need to speed up the clock. Their weathered cottages line a beautiful strip of stony beach and are surrounded by nearly 100 acres of upland — making this a most private retreat. When guests need a place to hide from the modern world and all its technology, this is the place to do it — there are no telephones, televisions, beepers, or fax machines. Guests just need to bring enough supplies to stock the cabin (there is a one-week minimum in July and August) and then just settle into the slow-paced rhythm of the place. Those who come to the North Beach Inn should come prepared to be charmed by the simplicity of this place.

The cottages are all similar to one another; but guests should keep in mind that they are just a few notches above camping. While this might appeal to dogs and children, adults need to know how to plan for such a vacation. Guests can expect a full kitchen and a barbecue for cooking, separate sleeping areas, and a fireplace. The furnishings are an eclectic mix of what appears to be hand-me-downs from well meaning friends. Linens are supplied, or guests may bring their own. But with the surrounding beach, ocean, and forests in the area, guests spend most of their time outside.

People like to have bonfires on the shore at night, run their dogs along the beach, and take long walks through the forest. Most will discover, much to their delight, that it is easy to reconnect with the natural world after just a few days. Guests may want to bring a kayak, or rent one locally, and explore these calm waters and fjord-like bays. When it rains, which is rare, it's time to head inside, build a fire, and read or play games. There are some good restaurants on the island, but they are a bit of a drive from the resort. Once guests arrive, most tend to settle in for the duration.

If they do leave, it is generally to make the short drive over to the 4,600-acre Moran State Park. Here, visitors will more than 31 miles of hiking trails traversing the park, all of which welcome dogs.

The varied scenery is truly spectacular. Some like to hike to the top of Mount Constitution, which, at over 2,400 feet, rises dramatically from sea level. A shorter hike leads to Twin Lakes, or people and their canines may prefer to spend the day at Mountain Lake. Visitors can always get around the island by car, but it is often more fun — and more interesting — to tour by bicycle. They may either rent or bring their own mountain bikes, which can easily navigate the dirt roads and sandy trails that lead to the some of the more isolated portions of Orcas Island.

---

# South Fork Moorage

*Box 633*
*2187 Mann Road*
*Fir Island, Washington 98238*
*(360) 445-4803*

*Houseboat Captain: Jessy Demick*
*Rooms: 2 houseboats*
*Rates: $80-115 (EP)*
*Payment: Personal checks*
*Children: Welcome — but call first; they should be swimmers*
*Dogs: Welcome with approval*
*Open: All year*

The South Fork Moorage is another one of our unique finds — two unusually fine houseboats nestled on the serene Skagit River. Jessy tells a wonderful story about how it all started. During the Depression, one of the houseboats, the Karma, floated on Lake Union. It was one of forty dwellings used as inexpensive housing for those who could afford little else at the time. Jessy and Karma crossed paths some 25 years ago, when he discovered the partially submerged houseboat slowly making its way into the murky waters of Lake Union. He recovered it, began an extensive restoration process, and over the next quarter century, moved it from harbor to harbor looking for an ideal home. He finally found a permanent place to keep it on Fir Island, and just six years ago purchased the property that adjoins the moorage. Jessy recently added another houseboat — the equally appealing Teahouse.

Now there are houseboats, and then there are *houseboats* — these are *houseboats*. They aren't visible from the country lane where visitors enter, as there is a mounded earthen dike, and plenty of trees and bushes creating a natural barrier between the lane and water. We parked in a small dirt parking area, then followed a raised wooden walkway that leads to the river. First in line is the Teahouse, aptly named because it does resemble an authentic Japanese teahouse. Its exterior walls of pale gray wood flow up to the gentle peaks of the shingled roof, inset with subtle skylights. We thoroughly enjoyed the porches off either end, fashioned with benches and assorted pots overflowing with flowers. These decks nicely expand the amount of sitting areas the vessel can offer, while providing a pleasant sanctuary from which guests can enjoy their surroundings. The Teahouse is also graced with many paned windows, the largest of these facing the river. The living room, with its wide window seats and breakfast table, is outfitted with one wall of glass doors that open directly to the porch. Privacy is created, when needed, by drawing the pretty cotton floral curtains. Beyond the sitting room is a tiny galley, a head, and a cozy bedroom that is just right for two.

The Karma is the granddaddy of them all, though. Its redwood shingles and deep green trim accentuate a boat outfitted with an array of nooks, crannies, and levels. One side is fashioned with Palladian windows, while on another, there are tiny paned windows interspersed with exquisite stained-glass windows. The varying hues of color that fall across the lustrous woods in the interior are soothing to the eye and mind. To come aboard the Karma, guests must navigate through a miniature door. As we stepped down into the living room, we entered what would eventually be one of our favorite congregating spots. This inviting chamber is fashioned with one wall of plate-glass windows, a fireplace, and plenty of thickly-cushioned seats. On one side of the room, there is a lovely Palladian-shaped, stained-glass window. The galley kitchen opens up into the living room, so the cook never feels isolated. At the other end of the Karma lies the first-floor bedroom, but it was the sleeping loft, with its wall of stained glass, that proved most intriguing. Skylights provide guests with more than enough natural light during the day. The deep green background of the floral cotton fabrics used on the Karma look all the more handsome against the varnished teak. The head in both these boats is, of course, of the marine variety — so guests should be careful of their usage. Although Jessy does not supply breakfast, he does stock the kitchen with two welcome amenities: champagne upon arrival and coffee for the next morning. Barbecues are available for outdoor cooking. Those who may be concerned about their privacy, need not be, as a small sign is posted at the beginning of the boardwalk indicating "Guests on Board."

Though Jessy obviously has a love for the water, he now lives in a little farmhouse that overlooks the river. We visited late in the season, but his extensive gardens were still in various stages of bloom. During our wanderings, we encountered a few cats cruising the property — which is probably the biggest reason why visitors should heed the sign about keeping Bowser on a leash. There are plenty of places that are lots of fun for taking long walks with a dog. The lane running near the houseboats is generally quiet and parallels the dike on one side and farms on the other. In the summer months, Jessy will take guests and their dogs up river to Mt. Vernon or Burlington and let them canoe or kayak back down the river. Some of the more popular off-river options include a visit to the Padilla Bay Estuary, where there are various nature trails to follow that welcome leashed dogs. Another possibility includes heading over to Whidbey Island, where the Deception Pass State Park is located. It, too, welcomes hikers and their canines. While the park can get a little crowded at times, it is easy to find a little solitude on the miles of trails that wend through the dense forests, along the cliffs, and down near the water.

---

# Kalaloch Lodge

*H.C. 80, Box 1100*
*Forks, Washington 98331*
*(206) 962-2271*

*Manager: ARA Leisure Services*
*Rooms: 18 doubles, 40 cabins*
*Rates: Doubles $48-70 (EP), Cabins $70-135 (EP)*
*Payment: AE, MC, and VISA*
*Children: Welcome (cribs and cots are available)*
*Dogs: Welcome in the cabins ($10 fee)*
*Open: All year*

The Kalaloch Lodge occupies one of the most scenic locations in the Olympic National Park. From its cliff-top position, visitors enjoy spectacular panoramic ocean views. At this juncture along the coastline, the sandy beaches stretch almost endlessly, linked during low tide, isolated from one another when the tide rolls in. It is for these reasons — beautiful beaches and incredible views — that the lodge is usually booked well in advance on both weekends and holidays, year round.

Many guests consider the accommodations secondary to the beautiful surroundings. The lodge consists of a weathered, gray-shingled and blue-trimmed main building (built in 1952) with eight guest rooms, a motel, and either the bluff or traditional log cabins. Guests traveling with dogs are allowed only in the cabins, so we will focus on these accommodations. The cabins have brass beds, kitchenettes, and Franklin-style fireplaces. (The staff supplies ample amounts of wood.) Rustic and simple, they offer few amenities but plenty of character. One cabin has the luxury of a whirlpool tub; however, this is the exception — the other bathrooms are equipped with the basics: a toilet, sink, and stall shower. The kitchenettes are not, we repeat, not equipped. So those planning on preparing their own meals should bring everything they need from home. The cabins serve as clean and comfortable quarters; it is really the view and the surrounding environs that bring guests back year after year.

Although there are basic kitchen facilities, many want to feel as if they are truly vacationing, so they opt to take their meals in the hexagonal restaurant. The Galley restaurant is decorated in a nautical motif and boasts ocean views. Here, dining patrons may sample the lodge's numerous seafood entrées, which are freshly caught and well prepared. Guests may choose from such standards as salmon, prawns, oysters, cod, and scallops, as well as a few beef and chicken dishes. A coffee shop sits apart from the main dining room, offering the same food without the ocean view and at a less leisurely pace. (It is ideal for those with children.) Meals can be expensive, and guests should consider themselves a captive audience — there are no other restaurant options (or anything else, for that matter) in the nearby area.

There is much to do in and around the lodge. In many respects, this region is like a huge wildlife refuge, with water fowl and animals living comfortably alongside humans. The local beach is sandy, flat, and inviting — for everything except swimming. Guests may rent clam shovels at the lodge's grocery store and dig for razor clams (in season). Some enjoy collecting seashells, hiking, or just watching the migrating gray whales each season. Of course, the area is also famous for its flora and fauna, found amid the lush rain forests. The Hoh and Queets rain forests are within a short driving distance of the lodge. Guests should keep in mind, though, that the entire Olympic National Forest and Park are off-limits to dogs. So people staying at the Kalaloch Lodge need to feel content keeping their dog within the confines of this seaside domain. All outings on the hiking trails that wend through the interior forests must be done without Bowser.

Kalaloch means "lots of clams," "easy living," or "land of plenty," depending on one's interpretation. Just as the word holds different meanings for each individual, so will the breadth of one's vacation here. Many come to relax and contemplate, some to explore every nook and cranny, and still others to enjoy the fishing and clamming. Guests who visit during the winter months might find a little more rainfall, but we have to say, the off-season is perfect for those who are looking for total peace and quiet.

# San Juan Inn

*P.O. Box 776*
*50 Spring Street*
*Friday Harbor, Washington 98250-0776*
*(800) 742-8210, (206) 378-2070, Fax (360) 378-6437*

**Innkeepers:** *Skip and Annette Metzger*
**Rooms:** *8 doubles, 2 suites*
**Rates:** *Doubles $78-95 (B&B), Suites $135-175 (B&B)*
**Payment:** *AE, DSC, MC, and VISA*
**Children:** *Over 6 years of age are welcome (cots are available)*
**Dogs:** *Small dogs under 40 pounds are welcome with a daily fee of $10*
**Open:** *All year*

Of the 172 San Juan Islands located in Washington's Banana Belt, San Juan Island is the second largest, and certainly one of the easiest to reach from either Washington State or British Columbia. The ferry boat comes into Friday Harbor, which makes this town the natural hub for the island. Artists' galleries, restaurants, and historic homes commingle with the more tourist-oriented spots along the steep streets that climb from the tiny ferry terminal. Best of all — especially for those who equate Washington state with rain — very little rain falls upon the San Juans in a year. Visitors can often depend on good weather in the spring and fall — a time when the locals finally begin to outnumber the tourists.

Since 1873, the San Juan Inn has been an integral part of the island's history. Over the last century, the building had an array of uses, ranging from private residence to hotel to "wireless" station and restaurant. Throughout it all, the function common to all was accommodating overnight guests. For many years, guests had picturesque harbor views; we are sad to report, however, that other buildings now block these once scenic vistas. Today, the most enjoyable sight is of the inn's intimate gardens.

We have made several visits to the San Juan Inn over the last decade. While much remains the same, there have been some welcome changes. With the exception of the wood-paneled lobby (which is still looking a bit worn and a touch too historic), we found the entire inn appealing. An old fashioned, front desk bell summons the resident innkeeper, who then escorts guests to the second floor's small, Victorian-inspired, bedrooms. Each is named after one of the ferries, sporting such names as Kaleetan and San Juan.

Most chambers are exceptionally cozy, with just enough space for a white iron double bed, although some slightly larger spaces easily accommodate brass queen beds. One of our favorite rooms is Kaleetan, with green striped wallpaper and shuttered windows that open to overlook the gardens. In the afternoon the sun streams into this inviting space. In the other chambers, wicker chairs, porcelain washstands, and marble-topped tables seem to fill every inch of wall space. In keeping with the Victorian theme, pale hues usually predominate, especially in the pastel paints and the floral wallpapers. Dried wreaths and fresh flowers add colorful accents. We have always liked the calico cat doorstops; this time we actually came across the inn's cat, curled up in one of the wicker chairs. Private bathrooms have been added since our first visit, although there are still six rooms that share the spacious bathrooms for "ladies" and "gentlemen".

Toward the rear of the inn, on the second floor, is the parlor. Pinks and lavenders provide a nice contrast against the white wicker furniture. At night, the wood stove is stoked and guests can bask in its warmth, while watching the twinkling harbor lights. In the morning, a Continental breakfast of freshly brewed premium coffee, tea, and juices is complemented by baskets of fruit and muffins. This repast may be enjoyed in the parlor, but we prefer taking ours out to the English rock garden. This is a peaceful spot with daffodils blooming in the spring and roses throwing off splashes of color and a sweet aroma throughout the summer. A grassy knoll is shaded by an ancient holly tree, providing a perfect napping or picnicking spot later in the day. We arrived in the fall, and while the daffodils were no longer in bloom, the orange Japanese lanterns, growing next to the moss-covered brick patio, were in full splendor.

Just off this patio is the inn's most private space — the Garden Suite. This expansive chamber is a favorite among honeymooners and families alike. The oversized king bed is covered in a green quilted spread, while the sitting area holds a sofa bed. Just off this expansive space is the full kitchen. The modern bathroom, aside from containing a Jacuzzi, is also fashioned with a shower built for two. The rest of the guests, who don't have access to a private Jacuzzi, will appreciate the outdoor hot tub located in the garden area. A bucket of zorries awaits those who don't want to wander about in their bare feet.

The San Juan Islands may not offer a plethora of hiking trails, but visitors and their canine cohorts will find plenty of open space and farmland tucked into the gently rolling hills. It isn't necessary to jump on a boat for whale watching; guests can just head over to Lime Kiln State Park, where there are several good vantage points for whale, dolphin, and seal watching. Years ago, the park was used for mining the lime that went into the production of Portland cement. Today, though, the park's visitors are more enamored with the migrating whales than with its former history. A fine adjunct to this trip is a visit to the Whale Museum in Friday Harbor, which offers everything one could imagine in the way of whale information and exhibits. Many may also enjoy taking Bowser out to the British Camp, where visitors gain a better feeling for how the British military lived in the mid-1800s. A path leads to the summit of Mount Young, and from this vantage point visitors will gain a greater appreciation for the beauty of this picturesque island.

# Westwinds

*4904 H. Hannah Road*
*Friday Harbor, Washington   98250*
*(360) 378-5283*

**Owner:** *Christine Durbin*
**Rooms:** *1 house*
**Rates:** *$165-245 (B&B)*
**Payment:** *MC and VISA*
**Children:** *Welcome*
**Dogs:** *Welcome*
**Open:** *All year*

The address for Westwinds indicates it is in Friday Harbor, but it really is not. It is actually situated well off the beaten path on the western side of San Juan Island. We literally traveled over hill and dale to find this B&B, passing rolling hills dotted with farms and livestock. Our inland adventure, gradually led us to the ocean, where we rounded one corner to discover breathtaking views of the Juan de Fuca Strait and beyond, to the snow-covered Olympic Mountains. Even though we could see snow on the distant mountains, the blackberries along the side of the road were bountiful, causing us to stop for a moment to sample a few handfuls while enjoying the wonderful views. We headed off half wondering if we were not terribly lost, when around another corner we found Hannah Road. This led us up a steep hill to a dirt road and a small sign pointing the way to Westwinds.

Flanked on one side by pines, and on the other by ponds and pastures, we followed the dirt lane a short distance to the corral, where we came across Chris's miniature ponies. We stopped to say hello to these very endearing creatures, before continuing up the last steep incline to the house. We found Chris outside gardening with her Golden Retriever, Brandy. Actually, Brandy was lying in the sun and Chris was gardening.

After getting to know Chris, we can understand why people rave about her and Westwinds. She is relaxed and friendly, and also recognizes that guests often enjoy their privacy. She therefore makes the entire house available to them (she lives next door). This makes it as ideal a destination for couples seeking a romantic retreat, as it does for families who need a little more space. Dogs will also love it here as well, as there are five acres to explore and an entire house to get comfortable in.

It is easiest to get a feeling for the house from the base of the hill, where it lies perched amid pines and other conifers. Red-hued woods and multiple windows dominate this one-story cottage. As if there wasn't enough natural light permeating these cozy spaces, skylights let in even more. It is easy to see the effect of all this glass, once guests step inside, as the same incredible ocean and mountain views we delighted in from the road, are even more dramatic from this vantage point. As we walked through the entry and emerged into the central cathedral ceiling living room, a pair of soft modern couches and chairs created a most inviting gathering space. We would have been content to relax in this room, with a crackling fire and a stereo setting the tone, while we just soaked in the views. However, the two bedrooms are equally appealing, although only one, the master bedroom, has water views. These vistas can be enjoyed from the bed, or from the patio that is accessible through the glass doors. Each bedroom does have a private bathroom, which is a pleasant convenience. Guests can cook all their meals in the fully-equipped kitchen, and enjoy them in the good-sized dining room. When it comes to breakfast though, let Chris deliver one of her bountiful baskets of healthy gourmet goodies.

She brings this basket the night before, so that guests can dip into it at their leisure. Chris laughingly told us, though, that most guests often sample many of the breakfast wares the night before because they just cannot wait until morning. She is a vegetarian and believes strongly in animal rights. Therefore, do not expect to find any meat dishes, although she does use eggs in some of her baked goods. This substantial affair usually features fresh muffins, banana breads, fresh berries and other island fruits, homemade granola, and her special apple crisp. (It is made with a secret ingredient — butterscotch pudding.) Chris will also create exotic fruit smoothies, with a splash of protein powder — and many other intriguing libations.

Exploring the property around Westwinds is always a delightful way to spend one's time. Take Bowser down to visit the miniature horses or to investigate the pond. There are woods just beyond this, and a little path that provides even more dramatic views. There is not a lot of car traffic in these parts and many guests also enjoy just meandering along the back country roads. For those who may wish to explore a little further afield, Westside Road leads to the Lime Kiln State Park, where dogs and their human friends are welcome to explore. Best of all, guests will quickly learn that Westwinds is the kind of B&B where people feel free to do their own thing, and Chris welcomes this. She is often off traveling around the world, in fact when we visited she was preparing to head off to Egypt for a month. But even when she isn't on the premises, she does have a resident innkeeper who keeps things flowing beautifully. One word of advice, Westwinds is often booked well in advance, so we recommend making reservations as far in the future as possible — to be guaranteed of sharing this little bit of paradise.

# Friday Harbor House

*P.O. Box 1385*
*130 West Street*
*Friday Harbor, Washington 98250*
*(360) 378-8455, Fax (360) 378-8453*

*Manager: Jim Skoog*
*Rooms: 19 doubles, 1 suite*
*Rates: Doubles $185 (B&B), Suite $325 (B&B)*
*Payment: AE, MC, and VISA*
*Children: Welcome*
*Dogs: Welcome with a $100 refundable deposit*
*Open: All year*

The Friday Harbor House is just one of a small group of boutique inns in this region. Its sister properties, the Inn at Langley and the BoatYard Inn, lie on Whidbey Island, while the third establishment, the Inn at Ludlow Bay, is situated on the Olympic Peninsula. All of these share one especially pleasing characteristic — idyllic waterside settings. The Friday Harbor House is perched on a bluff overlooking Friday Harbor, with fabulous water views from just about every vantage point. It was completed just over a year ago — a rather contemporary, shingled building, designed as a retreat that would complement its native environment. We thought its wood-shingled exterior blended very well, but weren't terribly impressed with the contemporary lines of the facade. However, as we stepped inside, a far more inspired setting unfolded.

The tiny lobby is fashioned with natural woods and glass, and still exudes the aroma of freshly-milled timber. We were warmly greeted by a staff member, and while waiting to see the guest rooms, sampled some of the fruit set out in a basket on a side table. Guest rooms occupy two buildings, with the most desirable of these situated in the main inn looking out toward the water. All of these well-designed chambers are spacious and bright, especially when the sun streams through the floor-to-ceiling windows and glass doors. The latter open onto tiny porches, most of which are ideal places from which to take in the views. A distinct Asian theme permeates throughout, set against a backdrop of subtle luxury. Slate blue, cream, and chestnut complement the fabrics and highlight some of the moldings. The beds rest on boxed platforms, which, in the winter months, are topped with extra thick European mattresses and duvets. Instead of headboards, the beds are backed by a creative arrangement of decorative tiles. Guests can settle into the soft cushions on the cherry wood-framed chairs and gaze into the fireplace or out across the water. Books are provided in the room, just in case guests have forgotten theirs. These chambers are also well appointed, with small refrigerators stocked with mineral water; coffee makers and all the necessities for preparing tea or coffee; and corkscrews for opening a bottle of wine. Equally well thought out are the tiled bathrooms, complete with Jacuzzi bathtubs, baskets of Lord and Mayfair toiletries, hair dryers, and thick cotton bathrobes. Each room at the Friday Harbor House is lovely; however, given a choice, we would reserve a corner room, as much for the two walls of windows as for the additional privacy.

In the morning, a Continental breakfast of scones, pastries, fresh fruit, and coffee or tea is available downstairs. We love the intimate restaurant for dinner. It feels almost subterranean, as it is tucked against the lower terrace, providing guests with lovely views of the San Juans over the adjacent rock wall. Bleached and naturally-stained woods brighten this intimate space. The management of the inn has worked hard to bring in a fine culinary talent — Greg Atkinson. While the menu is short, it does emphasize the freshest island produce, fruits, and game. Guests may wish to sample such appetizers as the Westcott Bay oysters baked with sweet red pepper butter, the thin crust pizza loaded with fresh island vegetables, or the Dungeness crab cakes with a remouláde. Entrées include a filet of wild king salmon with a sun-dried tomato butter, filet of beef with artichoke hearts, and the island seafood stew.

After dinner, we enjoy walking with our dogs, especially down the quiet back streets, which are rarely busy at night, even during the height of tourist season. Just next to the hotel is a tiny public park, which consists of no more than a couple of benches set amid a little grass and shrubbery. Many visitors and locals alike enjoy coming up here with their dogs to look out over the harbor, read, or just visit. Others like to rent a canoe and take Bowser for a trip along the protected waters leading out to some of the neighboring islands. Another popular option is to visit Jackson Beach, where furry friends are welcome to explore, while their humans, perhaps, fly a kite.

# Wharfside Bed and Breakfast

*P.O. Box 1212*
*Slip K*
*Friday Harbor, Washington 98250*
*(360) 378-5661, Fax (360) 378-4271*

*Hosts: Clyde and Bette Rice*
*Rooms: 2 doubles*
*Rates: $80-85 (B&B)*
*Payment: MC and VISA*
*Children: Welcome (cribs and high chairs are available)*
*Dogs: Welcome, with a small fee*
*Open: All year*

A stay aboard the *Jacquelyn* is such a wonderful experience that even those who profess no affinity with the sea could be tempted to come aboard for a night or two. This is a 60-foot, ketch-rigged, motorized sailing vessel owned by Bette and Clyde Rice. For 12 years, these amiable hosts have provided landlubbers and seafarers alike with a truly extraordinary B&B experience.

We always enjoy the walk to the *Jacquelyn* because we feel as though we are about to set off on a grand, sea-going adventure, even though we know we will remain at the dock for the duration of our stay. Sada, the Rice's frisky canine welcomed us aboard. (His full name is Hosada, but according to Clyde, "Ho" sounded too much like "no," so they simply call him Sada.) On this day, we found Clyde fixing something in the galley, but he gladly left this duty to reacquaint us with his floating B&B.

Very little ever changes aboard the *Jacquelyn*, and for that we are grateful. The Rices' was the first floating B&B on the West Coast, and while there are now more houseboat B&Bs on the waters around Washington state, few are as intriguing as this one. Clyde led us down to the Victorian parlor that serves as the nucleus of the ship, particularly during the cooler months. This is not a dark space, being lit naturally, with skylights and numerous portholes. This salon features plenty of comfortable, built-in spots for reading, listening to music, or even watching a video. The lustrous woodwork is the backdrop to the pair of settees, a carved wooden desk, a television, a small bar, and an abundance of knickknacks and collectibles that the Rices gathered during their world travels. A wonderful combination of Oriental rugs, Victorian antiques, nautical paraphernalia and other unusual collectibles creates an intriguing atmosphere.

There are two good-sized accommodations from which guests may choose. The more popular Aft Stateroom's white walls and ceiling highlight the gentle curves and strapping of the boat; these flowing lines are interspersed with portholes and small prints depicting seaside scenes. Guests settle into the large, cradle-like bed topped by a rich burgundy, paisley-patterned comforter and matching sheets. Guests can turn on a little music, sample one or two of the gold wrapped chocolates, and let the refreshing salt air help them drift off to sleep. Two of the reasons for this stateroom's popularity are the private head and separate entrance. Bette reminds us, though, that although the Forward Cabin does not have a private head, the adjacent parlor is rarely used by anyone except the guests staying in the Forward Cabin — which really makes the setup seem more like a suite. The Forward Cabin contains a large double berth and two seaman-size bunks that make for a cozy sleeping experience if the children are along. All the berths are covered with patchwork quilts; as with the Aft Stateroom, electric mattress pads keep seafarers warm and cozy. The tiled shower is shared, with far more elbow room and hot water than most people equate with a boat. Robes are thoughtful additions, making trips to and from the shower more pleasant.

Breakfast is a full-blown affair, with guests sitting around the semicircular table in the galley or, weather permitting, up on deck. Bette is the head chef, and produces excellent breakfasts from her efficiently appointed galley. Her specialties still include quiche or a spiced apple strudel-like dish she calls Captain's Crunch. Our breakfast started with a hollowed pineapple filled with exotic fruits, and was followed by spicy baked eggs, shell-shaped parmesan potatoes, bacon, blueberry muffins, and coffee. Guests should be sure to ask Bette how she makes this rich coffee. (Her answer surprised us.) This happened to be a wonderful and warm fall morning, and we enjoyed this splendid repast on the upper deck.

The Wharfside is appealing not only because it offers a unique B&B experience, but also because of Bette and Clyde. They go out of their way to answer questions, point out interesting sights, and provide a variety of suggestions on what to do in the area. Clyde is also a seasoned skipper, who has sailed almost around the world with the Scripps Institute in La Jolla, California. He and Bette have wonderful stories of their extensive adventures and travels. At guests' disposal is an Eddon Gig rowboat for exploring the harbor, as well as a skippered Boston Whaler. Numerous forms of wildlife, ranging from otters and seals to whales and eagles, are often spotted during a visit. In season, many a fisherperson has caught shrimp and crabs right from the dock. We can think of no better way to enjoy an island vacation than on the water. There are times, though, when Bowser will want to get his paws on a little grass or sand. The walk from the boat up the hill is an adventure unto itself. Just after hitting dry land, there is a small, shaded park where dogs are frequently found cavorting. Leisurely walks through town with a dog are also lots of fun, especially along the quieter side streets. South of Friday Harbor is a small strip of sand that dogs can run on called Jackson Beach. Another popular outing is the San Juan County Park, a waterfront campground located on the west side of the island, which dogs are also welcome to explore.

# Tucker House

*260 B Street*
*Friday Harbor, Washington 98250*
*(360) 378-2783, (360) 378-6437*

**Owners:** *Skip and Annette Metzger*
**Rooms:** *2 doubles, 3 cottages*
**Rates:** *Doubles $85 (B&B), Cottages $105-135 (B&B)*
**Payment:** *AE, DSC, MC, and VISA*
**Children:** *Welcome (high chairs, cots, and portable cribs are available)*
**Dogs:** *Welcome in the cottages, with notice and approval, for a $15 daily fee. They must be under 40 pounds and there is a maximum of two dogs per cottage*
**Open:** *All year*

The Tucker House, built in 1898 by Clarin Tucker, lies in the heart of Friday Harbor on San Juan Island. The main Victorian residence is as close to a human-sized doll house as most people will probably ever find. (This tiny house includes a front porch bedecked with potted and hanging flowering plants.) A white picket fence encircles the entire property. Hidden within are tiered flower gardens and patches of grass interspersed with mature fruit trees. This serene setting is as ideal for reading or relaxing as it is for providing a safe setting for frolicking dogs and children.

Repeat guests will be pleased to know that life at the Tucker House remains much the same as always, as the Metzgers' share the theory that "if it ain't broke, don't fix it." Thus, the overall decor, furnishings, and atmosphere remain very much intact from visit to visit. Since our last visit, though, the main house's two guest rooms have again been made available to guests, and the three cottages have been slightly updated. The cottages nestle into the garden terraces set behind the house, thus providing private enclaves that are perfect for those traveling with dogs.

One of these, the Rose Cottage, has a bedroom and a separate sitting room. The trellis lining the lower interior walls, coupled with the flowered comforter resting upon the bed, accentuate the garden cottage motif. A tiny, separate sitting room contains a sofa bed and has a wall of sliding glass doors that open to a private deck. Guests looking for a refreshing breeze need only open the glass doors and the top of the Dutch door to let the invigorating sea breezes flow through the cottage.

Just down the knoll is the Willow Cottage, the accommodation most often requested by couples. We passed through yet another Dutch door and into the kitchenette of this cottage. The high-ceilinged bedroom, complete with a wood stove, lies to the rear of this abode. The walls are bare, except for a few prints, but the king bed's fluffy comforter and oversized pillows add plenty of interest to this space. Upholstered armchairs create an inviting sitting area off to the side. Another entrance, off the bedroom, leads out to a deck.

The most private cottage of all, though, is the Lilac Cottage, which is where the Metzgers lived when they renovated the main house. It lies across from the other two cottages and is reached by passing through various decks. We entered the cottage through the double French doors, passed beyond the kitchen and bathroom, into the wonderful bedroom with loft space. (The loft is not accessible.) This dark, cozy chamber is lined with walls of bookshelves, including some within easy reach of the queen bed. There are all sorts of quirky things about this place, but what we liked most was the unusually small door, situated up another step, that opens onto a private deck behind the cottage. A pass-through window is one link between the bedroom and the kitchen. Each cottage, with or without a kitchen, does have a table that is usually pre-set for the next morning's breakfast. When new arrivals do venture out of their cottage, they might go for a dip in the hot tub, wander about the gardens, or head over to the main house. When we poked our heads inside, we met up with Chloe and Sophie, the resident Poodle and Cocker Spaniel who padded through the house with us. There is a crispness to the interior, yet the historic Victorian details are also evident, especially in the hand-carved window and door moldings. The front parlor is where guests often gather at the beginning or the end of the day. Here, they may recline in the white wicker chairs and either enjoy a good book or watch a little television. Sunlight pours through the room's bow window during the day, while at night this inviting chamber becomes all the more cozy when the blinds are drawn.

Skip's breakfast is the highlight of each morning. Guests may eat in the solarium or take their meal back to their cottage. We especially like dining in the solarium, as it overlooks the garden and is generally quite warm, even when the outside temperature is cool. Fresh fruit bowls may be complemented with a cheese soufflé, muffins, and Skip's famous cinnamon bread. Juice, tea, and excellent coffee also accompany the meal. The Metzgers are always eager to share the recipes to their more popular dishes, even going so far as to printing the recipes on small cards and sending them home with interested guests. The most requested recipes are for their cinnamon bread and baked eggs.

Guests can work off breakfast by walking the two short blocks into town where they will find art galleries, shops, restaurants, and the ferry. Just around the corner from the Tucker House is a great place to rent a moped — or to stop and let Bowser play with the owner's dog who is usually lying in the sun in front of the place. This is a doggie haven, with the local dogs leading a casual, carefree kind of life. It is easy to meet some of the local pooches in the sunken park just across from the Tucker House. This is a wonderful spot to run a dog, as there are plenty of informal grassy areas, wildflowers, and even a few shade trees. For those who want to travel further afield, the San Juan Island National Historical Park is great for picnicking — and for exploring some of the restored barracks and outbuildings used by the British and American troops during their occupation of San Juan Island in the mid-1800s. There are two sections to this park, one on the northwest side of the island, the other on the southeast end — neither one will dissapoint. At the end of the day, return for tea and cookies in the garden at the Tucker House.

# La Conner Country Inn

*107 South Second Street*
*La Conner, Washington 98257*
*(360) 466-3101, Fax (360) 466-5902*

**General Manager:** *Gary Tachiyama*
**Rooms:** *26 doubles, 2 suites*
**Rates:** *Doubles $81-102 (B&B), Suites $130 (B&B)*
**Payment:** *AE, MC, and VISA*
**Children:** *Welcome (cribs, cots, and baby-sitters are available)*
**Dogs:** *Welcome,with notice, in two rooms on the ground floor*
**Open:** *All year*

Once best known as a farming and fishing village, La Conner's brilliant springtime show of tulips and daffodils is what now draws visitors to Skagit Valley. This region is somewhat reminiscent of Holland, with dikes holding back the encroaching sea — and, when successful, leaving exceptionally fertile farmland. Those who don't happen to visit in springtime will still find quaint shops lining the Swinomish Channel. These offer everything from antiques to trendy clothes. The centrally located La Conner Country Inn is set just a block off the channel. While it is a relatively new building, the rough-hewn board and weathered-shingle facade allows it to easily blend in with the town's other historic homes.

Guests driving in under the *porte cochère* to the rear of the building will find that the overall ambiance changes markedly to that of a traditional motor inn style: two floors of accommodations, all with separate outside entrances. This is actually a bonus for anyone traveling with a dog, as it makes it easy to get in and out of the room without disturbing the other guests. We are unhappy to report, though, that since our last visit there has been some abuse of the dog privileges. Guests traveling with dogs were once allowed a full range of room choices, but now they are limited to just two ground-floor units. We checked out these two chambers and discovered they were comparable to the other accommodations offered at the inn.

The La Conner Country Inn's Victorian decor has always appealed to us because it isn't too ornate. Brass beds fill only a portion of the room, leaving plenty of floor space for guests and their dog. One of the designated canine rooms has both a queen and a twin brass bed, and both are covered with floral spreads reflecting the room's subdued burgundy and slate blue hues. The well-positioned beds face the crackling fire, which is flanked by a pair of black leather wing chairs. Off to the side is a small breakfast table that lies under a paned window. The room's decorative treatments are minimal, as loosely woven baskets are the only accents against the crisp white walls. A color television, a direct dial telephone, and a clock radio set on the oak bedside table are just a few of the additional amenities. The large bathroom has the added convenience of a second separate sink. We liked the touch of the Caswell Massey shampoos, conditioners, and soaps.

When not relaxing in their rooms, guests have a couple of options — the library and Palmers restaurant. The former is an inviting space, where a mix of traditional furnishings, including overstuffed sofas and wing chairs, all rest on an Oriental carpet covering the hardwood floor. Guests may select from a variety of newspapers and magazines set out on the coffee table, or simply put their feet up and enjoy the warmth emanating from the beachstone fireplace. Dried and fresh flowers provide some decorative interest to this cozy chamber. In the morning, a substantial Continental breakfast is also served here. Guests may choose from cinnamon buns and scones, granola, and other cold cereals, along with juice, coffee, tea, and hot chocolate.

Dinner is an entirely different experience. The intimate Palmers restaurant is not operated by the Thompsons, but by Thomas and Danielle Palmer. This cozy, multi-level eatery is housed in a cottage nestled into the hillside behind the inn. Guests may step into the English-style pub, specializing in micro brewery beers, and sip one of these libations. We love the character of this intimate chamber, as there are only four seats at the bar and just two additional tables. Up a flight of stairs, we found the equally charming restaurant with its beamed, cathedral ceilings, stained glass windows, and a fireplace. Some patrons choose to start with the pan fried oysters in a lemon caper aioli; the steamed mussels with white wine, shallots, garlic and butter; or the wilted spinach salad with smoked duck. The pasta menu is extensive, with the spinach fettuccine topped by smoked king salmon, artichokes, hearts of palm, sundried tomatoes, and roasted pistachios; or the penne with prawns, shiitake mushrooms, leeks, spinach and a pernod cream setting the tone. Entrée specialties run the gamut as well, featuring a hazelnut crusted halibut with an sherry beurre blanc; the roast duckling with fried polenta and a wild raspberry demi-glacé; or the grilled medallions of beef tenderloin with a bordelaise sauce and roasted garlic cream.

After dinner, we took the dogs for a walk downtown for a little window shopping. We always enjoy strolling along these narrow streets, up and down the hills, viewing the Victorian homes and the intriguing waterfront area. Another jaunt worth investigating is the Padilla Bay National Marine Estuary. This is a series of interpretive trails that are open to hikers and their leashed dogs. There are three trails worth exploring: one forested route, another hugging the shoreline, and a third that follows a dike. All of these walks are under three miles. However visitors choose to spend their time in and around La Conner, we recommend a visit during the quiet seasons when the town is peaceful and the pace is leisurely.

---

# Moby Dick Hotel and Oyster Farm

*Nahcotta, Washington   98673*
*(360) 665-4543, Fax (360) 665-6887*

*Owners:* Fritzi and Edward Cohen
*Rooms:* 10 doubles
*Rates:* Doubles $75-85 (B&B)
*Payment:* MC and VISA
*Children:* Welcome
*Dogs:* Welcome for a $10 nightly fee; dogs may not be left alone in the
     room and it is preferred they spend the day outdoors
*Open:* All year

Nahcotta. The name originated from a Chinook chieftain, but today, people are more likely to know this village for something else entirely — its oysters. Unlike the towns on the southern shore of Long Beach Peninsula, this tiny northern community is based more on oystering than on tourism. Oystering in Nahcotta dates back to well before the 1800s, and it is what still drives most of the business in this hamlet. So, along with the abundance of natural beauty in and around Nahcotta, visitors will also find plenty of oyster processing companies lining its shoreline. Two people who discovered this low-key place and decided to make it a part of their lives are Fritzi and Edward Cohen. Although they also own the Hotel Tabard Inn in Washington D.C. and a small organic farm in Virginia, they call the Nahcotta and Moby Dick Hotel their home.

We were cautioned to overlook the hotel's less than appealing exterior, and to focus instead on the interior spaces. After seeing the yellow stucco rectangular building, devoid of ornamentation, we heeded the warning, crossed our fingers, and ventured inside. What we found is a surprisingly expansive space that is long on character. Though it was originally built as a hotel in 1929, during

World War II it housed the Coast Guard Horse Patrol. Everyone we spoke with credits the Cohens for having the patience and foresight needed to create the distinctive 1930s decor. It is the interior decor that endears guests and locals alike to this low-key hotel, nestled upon the forested shores of Willapa Bay.

The building's overall scale is small, with the exception of the first floor, which contains two living rooms and a dining room. Guests frequently spend a good deal of time nestling into the chairs and couches set around the fireplace, after having picked out something interesting to read from the Cohen's collection of books. (By the way, the hosts own over 20 copies of *Moby Dick*, any of which guests are welcome to borrow.) Others might be more inclined to play the piano, watch television, or perhaps try to identify a distant shore bird by using the telescope. Given enough notice, there is little need to leave the hotel, as gourmet dinners can be arranged for and enjoyed in the adjacent dining room. These meals always feature fresh produce from the hotel's garden, along with a choice of fresh seafoods that might include everything from salmon and Dungeness crab to shrimp and oysters (of course). The oysters grow in beds just off shore from the hotel, raised exclusively with non-chemical methods.

After dinner, we headed upstairs to one of the small and simply furnished bedrooms. Nature, art, and literature play a big role at the hotel, and it is especially evident in these spaces. The furnishings may reflect the Art Deco period, but in each room a motif is developed — centering on, for example, the ocean, its wildlife, or a piece of literature. Most of the guest rooms contain double beds and share a bathroom. Room 11 is the only one with a private bath. Families usually need to reserve a pair of bedrooms — or request Room 8 which is outfitted with both a double and a twin bed. A downstairs bedroom is the most desirable for those traveling with a dog, as it has a separate outside entrance. Though the bedrooms are a little on the small side, we found the upstairs sitting area, naturally lit by a skylight, to be a delightful place to gather, as it was rarely used by any of the other guests.

In the morning, guests are treated to a full breakfast in the dining room. This is an ample meal that ranges from standard American fare to something a little more intriguing. Some choose to start with the homemade granola and juice, and follow it with eggs, bacon or sausage, and toast. Guests seeking something a little out of the ordinary are generally asked what they would like for their breakfast special. Oysters are usually an integral component of breakfast, whether served raw, on the half shell, or baked into an omelet. Buttermilk, banana, or berry pancakes are other options. The Cohens are advocates of garlic, and it grows abundantly in their garden. They, like many others, feel that it holds some medicinal value, so they include it in most of their recipes. (The pancakes are perhaps the only exception.)

The Cohens welcome dogs; however, they prefer that during the day dogs remain outside touring the area with their owners. This is usually not much of an imposition, as there is plenty to do nearby. The hotel rests on plenty of acreage and it is a pleasant stroll down to the water from the hotel. Nahcotta is also easy to explore on foot, whether checking out the oyster fleet or observing one of the canning operations. We recommend that guests make time, at some point, to have dinner at The Ark — a fine restaurant within walking distance of the hotel. The Ark serves oysters every which way, along with other native seafood. Kite flying, a favorite pastime here, isn't the only thing to do on the peninsula. Just up the road apiece, visitors will discover Leadbetter Point, a veritable natural preserve, with trails crossing the dunes, following the ocean, and winding around to the bay. Dogs must be leashed when they are visiting, but this helps protect the waterfowl and other wildlife who make their homes within this sanctuary. At the end of the day, guests will want to return to the hotel and head out to the sauna in the woods, where any aching muscles will be thoroughly rejuvenated.

# Puget View Guest House

*7924 61st Avenue N.E.*
*Olympia, Washington 98506*
*(360) 459-1676*

**Hosts:** *Barb and Dick Yunker*
**Rooms:** *1 cottage*
**Rates:** *$89 (B&B)*
**Payment:** *MC and VISA*
**Children:** *Welcome*
**Dogs:** *Welcome, with notice and approval*
**Open:** *All year*

We can understand why people love Washington state — especially along the coast, where the confluence of mountains and ocean is inspiring, particularly on a clear day when the sparkling blue waters and surrounding evergreens meld into a rich backdrop of color. It is on these days that the scenic inlets are meant to be explored, whether in search of a heron, bald eagle, or perhaps a frolicking sea lion. There are plenty of private homes tucked along these inlets, but few accept guests and their canine companions. So we felt fortunate to discover the Puget View Guest House, where guests have a private cottage and virtually unlimited opportunities to explore their natural surroundings.

This was our third visit to the cottage, and we followed the familiar road meandering through the forest to the Guest House. As we drew closer, the forest seemed to envelop us, but not in a claustrophobic sense — rather, in a protective way. We pulled into the Yunkers' driveway, where we found their house and cottage nestled on a bluff. Barb was puttering about, enjoying her few free moments by tending to her garden. She brought us inside her house into an inviting, beamed-ceiling room warmed by a wood stove and filled with traditional furnishings. The simple, uncluttered lines form a backdrop to the expansive views of the water through the picture window. We lingered in here for a bit before Barb, who is as energetic as she is gracious, escorted us out to the cottage.

The two-room cottage, which is surrounded by gardens of rhododendrons and lilacs set beneath a canopy of trees, is separated from the main house by a short path. With the onset of spring, the magnolias and other flowering plants create an awesome display of color across the property. The interior has not changed much since our last visit, with a master bedroom to the back of the cottage and a sitting room set toward the front. The bedroom's white spread dotted with pink flowers stands out against dove gray walls. Some framed prints and posters adorn these walls, but a look beyond them through the small windows reveals lovely views of the woods. The best views of the sound — albeit not as dramatic as those garnered from the Yunkers' living room — are through the windows in the sitting room. Braided rugs cover the bleached hardwood floors in here, and off to one end, a sofa bed and chair create a small sitting area. A small table, equally appropriate for meals or for working on a puzzle, is set up in the opposite corner. There are no formal cooking facilities, except that guests can create simple *hors d'oeuvres* with the microwave and store drinks in the small refrigerator. A barbecue on the back porch is ideal for those who wish to create their own dinners. Barb arrives at the cottage each morning with a generous Continental breakfast consisting of fruit and juice, coffee or tea, and a variety of homemade breads and pastries. The Yunkers also offer a variety of theme picnics that may be of interest to some guests.

The idea of offering picnic lunches and dinners developed because the Yunkers felt as though their guests were arriving and then "immediately jumping back into the car for dinner."

Unfortunately, in doing so, they were missing the quiet summer evenings and beautiful sunsets. The Yunkers now offer different types of picnics, which they refer to as their summer cookouts. One of these allows guests to stay at the cottage and cook their own meal. The Yunkers will furnish briquettes and all the "fixings," including hamburgers, buns, a deli salad, and potato chips and relishes. Those who prefer to dine at the beach will want to try the old-fashioned "wiener roast," where guests cook hot dogs over a campfire. These are accompanied by a deli salad, a beverage, and a dessert. Finally, there are also boat outings, where the Yunkers take guests on their boat for oystering, or simply exploring the picturesque waterways. Barb suggests that guests bring their own canoe or kayak, which may be launched from the Yunkers' beach.

A switch back trail leads down the steep hillside to this beach. It is as fun to walk along it with Bowser as it is to search for agates and sand dollars on it. Some 500 feet away is the 100-acre Tolmie State Park, which is teeming with wildlife and nature trails. This park is rarely crowded, perhaps because it is set well off the beaten path. Dogs and their human friends are welcome to explore the trails or picnic along the beach. Those with scuba equipment may wish to investigate the underwater park just offshore. A good day trip is an expedition into the Olympic National Forest for day hikes with Bowser.

---

# The Sandpiper Beach Resort

*P.O. Box A*
*Pacific Beach, Washington  98571*
*(800) 567-4737, (360) 276-4580*

*Manager: Betty Stensrud*
*Room: 30 condominium suites*
*Rates: $55-160 (EP), children between the ages of 2 and 14 are $5*
*Payment: MC and VISA*
*Children: Welcome (cribs and high chairs are available)*
*Dogs: Welcome, but they must be on a leash when on the property and*
*properly curbed. Small dogs are $10, larger dogs are $15.*
*Open: All year*

Out on the Olympic Peninsula, near the southwestern edge of the Quinault Indian Reservation, lies Pacific Beach. One of the northernmost beach towns, it begins in the heavily-touristed town of Ocean Shores and extends to the quieter hamlet of Moclips. While plenty of people flock to the easily accessible southern section of the coast, we prefer pushing further north to Pacific Beach and The Sandpiper Beach Resort.

We've received many rave reviews about the Sandpiper Beach Resort, especially from families who like to bring their dogs along on vacation. This place gives guests that warm, fuzzy feeling, and even extends it to their kids and dogs — the staff genuinely seems to like having them here. The Sandpiper is the sort of spot that can easily become a family tradition, and many guests book their accommodations a year in advance. A pair of gray-shingled buildings (known as Beach Houses I and II) comprise the bulk of the guest rooms, although a few individual cottages also dot these well-tended grounds overlooking the Pacific Ocean.

Each suite can accommodate from two to six people. In general, the largest suites occupy the top floors of the four-story Beach Houses, where cathedral ceilings add dimension to the well-designed spaces. Guests may choose from between one, two, and three-bedroom units. The kitchens may not be overly spacious, but they are well stocked for preparing just about any type of meal — from snack to gourmet. The sliding glass doors in the fireplaced living rooms open to small porches and provide lovely views of the ocean. Telephones and televisions are absent, so guests will have to resort to the old-fashioned way of entertaining themselves — conversation, puzzles, and an array of board games. Guests are generally left to themselves during their stay, unless they require more firewood, or perhaps an additional towel or extra bar of soap. We liked the extra touch in the bathrooms — electric towel warmers similar to those commonly found in England.

Most visitors don't feel too compelled to do very much here, other than take Bowser for long walks on the sandy beach, fly kites with their children, or just dig their toes into the sand. Guests may use the barbecue area in front of the Beach Houses for impromptu barbecues. A children's playground is also on the beach. Our dogs love to dig holes in the sand, so we thought it would be fun to enlist them in a clamming expedition. Afterwards, it's easy to clean off any shells or clams in a little shack at the resort. Unless guests plan to have clams as their primary staple, we advise bringing enough food and drink to last for the length of the stay; however, a few forgotten items can be picked up in the well-stocked gift shop. The shop is also well outfitted with buckets, zorries, and kites, and they also serve a pretty good cup of cappucino.

Dogs must be leashed on the property, although they have a little more freedom down on the beach. There are plenty of state parks that line these shores, beginning with Pacific Beach State Park and continuing south to Griffith's Friday State Park and Ocean City State Park. Pacific Beach encompasses nearly nine acres; as we mentioned, it's a great beach for clamming. Ocean City State Park, on the other hand, covers more than 100 acres and is a favorite among scuba divers. Guests and their canine companions will love roaming the sandy shores and, perhaps, even venturing into the water in the warmer summer months.

---

# Lake Crescent Lodge

*National Park Concessions, Inc.*
*HC 62, Box 11*
*416 Lake Crescent Road*
*Port Angeles, Washington   98362-9798*
*(360) 928-3211*

*General Manager: Garner B. Hanson*
*Rooms: 25 doubles, 33 cottages*
*Rates: Doubles $64-96 (EP), Cottages $99-124 (EP)*
*Payment: AE, DC, CB, MC, and VISA*
*Children: Welcome (cribs and cots are available)*
*Dogs: Welcome with a daily fee of $4*
*Open: April through October*

Travelers searching for simple accommodations amid spectacular natural surroundings will find the Lake Crescent Lodge to be an ideal destination. The lodge is nestled among giant fir, spruce, and hemlock trees along the shores of Lake Crescent. The renowned rain forest is further inland, while the Juan de Fuca Strait are just a short distance away. It used to be that small ferries would steam back and forth along the lake, bringing visitors to this isolated spot. Today, Highway 101 loops past the lodge, allowing easier access without encroaching too much upon this natural setting.

The main lodge was built in 1916 and was formerly known as Singer's Tavern. It remains much the same today as it was 80 years ago. New arrivals enter the rustic great hall, where the impressive stone fireplace is usually crackling and popping. Any time of day, a few guests are comfortably settled into the cushioned mission-style chairs and sofas or enjoying the warmth of the solarium. The solarium is one of our favorite places on a sunny day, as its walls of paned windows overlook the deep blue waters of Lake Crescent.

Planters filled with red geraniums, placed amid a sea of wicker chairs and tables, thrive in this tropical environment. As guests step back inside, they will see an extensive collection of Northwest Native American artifacts that are displayed on the mantel, in glass cases flanking the fireplace, and along the eaves. We were especially drawn to the miniature totem poles placed on the beams.

Interested guests can then go directly from the great hall into the dining room, where they will a find beamed ceiling and whitewashed walls, with a contemporary ambiance. The dining room is situated on the same side of the lodge as the solarium, and its plate glass windows offer equally inviting views of the lake. We visited late in the season, just a few weeks before the lodge was due to close. Even then the menu offered an array of hearty and enticing meals. Ample breakfasts start the day, with stacks of pancakes, French toast, and overstuffed omelets topping the menu. Dinner patrons may select from an array of entrées including the shrimp piquant, scallops florentine, king salmon filet, and chicken Dijonaise. Oysters and crab, when in season, are always a favorite option with the lodge's clientele. We suggest ending the meal with one of the specialties — a freshly baked piece of pie. After dinner, most head back to their cottages to give their canine companions an evening walk.

There are a number of cottage choices, although our favorites are the Roosevelt Fireplace Cottages and the Singer Tavern Cottages. The bleached wood shingles and eaves make the exterior of the Singer Tavern Cottages very appealing. These are set closest to the main lodge; although an expanse of lawn and shade trees separate them from the lakefront, their water views are largely unobstructed. The narrow porches that run the length of the cottages are bedecked with rocking chairs. The interiors are reminiscent of a motel room, with attractive peach colored walls and pairs of double beds. There is no need to worry about the children or the dogs breaking any knickknacks — there are none. Most families appreciate the preponderance of outdoor activities, without the distractions of televisions or telephones. We quickly discovered that most guests come to this resort for the assortment of recreational diversions and not for the functional accommodations.

While the Singer Tavern cottages are appealing, and probably easiest to reserve, our first choice is the four Roosevelt Fireplace Cottages. Situated directly on the lake, these cozy abodes were constructed in 1937, when Franklin Roosevelt was exploring the region to consider designating it as a national park. The bleached shingle exterior walls are interspersed with expanses of paned windows, while the interior knotty pine walls and hardwood floors set the overall homey ambiance. Simple sofas and chairs form inviting sitting areas around the beachstone fireplaces, while queen or king beds covered in white cotton spreads abut the opposite walls. Coffee makers and small refrigerators are welcome amenities, especially in these otherwise rustic surroundings. Anyone interested in making a reservation for the Roosevelt Fireplace Cottages should note that they are often booked months in advance and it is critical that guests reserve early. We were happy to learn that even though most of the resort shuts down in October, the Roosevelt Fireplace Cottages remain open year round. Guests who choose to stay here in the off season receive a Continental breakfast delivered to their cottage.

The final dog-friendly accommodation option is the Marymere Motor Lodge, whose rooms lie along the shore. From the exterior there seems little to recommend these rooms; however, the interior spaces are actually quite appealing and are similar in decor and furnishings to those in the Singer Tavern Cottages — simple, clean, and uncluttered. Most people who select the motor lodge rooms do so for their totally unobstructed lake views.

There is plenty to do at the Lake Crescent Lodge, although we are always disappointed when we remember that dogs are not allowed to set paw in the Olympic National Park (with the exception of the parking lots, the Kalaloch beach, and the Shady Lane Trail at Staircase). Guests and their leashed dogs are free to wander the expansive property, though, and the open grassy areas surrounding the lodge. Water-oriented canines can accompany their human friends on fishing expeditions for salmon, steelhead, or the crafty Beardslee trout. Those who don't want to fish can always explore the miles of lake shore, perhaps stopping for a picnic. (The lodge staff will pack box lunches). After a busy morning, some might leave their canine companion to nap on his own while they take the short hike to scenic Marymere Falls. A trip to the Lake Crescent Lodge may not be an appropriate vacation for people who want to spend their days hiking with their dogs, yet it is worthwhile for anyone willing to compromise a bit and mix a bit of dog-less hiking with all the other activities at the lodge.

# Inn at Ludlow Bay

*P.O. Box 65460*
*One Heron Road*
*Port Ludlow, Washington 98365*
*(360) 437-0411, (360) 437-0310*

*Manager: Laura Bagley*
*Rooms: 35 doubles, 2 suites*
*Rates: Doubles $165-200 (B&B), Suites $300-450 (B&B)*
*Payment: AE, MC, and VISA*
*Children: Welcome*
*Dogs: Welcome in 2 rooms*
*Open: All year*

The Inn at Ludlow Bay rests at the end of a small peninsula within the lovely resort community of Ludlow Bay. It is near, but should not be confused with, the Port Ludlow Resort. Though the inn is new, it has been built in a style reminiscent of the expansive shingled cottages lining Maine's coast. Porches add definition to the first floor, while the lines of the upper levels form interesting eaves and turrets. Equally intriguing are the expansive interior spaces lined with walls of windows overlooking beach grass and gardens, offering views that extend beyond this point of land to the water. Guests staying here usually have the sensation of being on an island.

Each of the guest rooms is well designed, and we can vouch for the fact that the dog-designated rooms are as lovely and gracious as all the other bedrooms. The guest chambers are furnished with natural cherry, Mission-style furnishings — with writing tables filling alcoves and cushioned chairs set in front of fireplaces tiled in a black and white Art Deco style. With the exception of taupe highlights, all the walls and trim are white. The down comforter, too, is covered in a white duvet and is complemented by black-and-white-checked accent pillows resting against the oversized bed pillows. The extra high king or queen bedsteads allow guests to lie in bed while enjoying the water views. Another place guests enjoy relaxing (and, surprisingly, are still able to take in the views) is in the Jacuzzi soaking tub. Though the tub is located in the bathroom, its frosted glass windows slide open in the direction of the bedroom windows. A separate and oversized, glassed-in shower is also available. After a refreshing shower or bath, guests can wrap up in the supple terry cloth robes provided. Lord and Mayfair chamomile soaps, shampoos, creams, and bath crystals, are placed in baskets set upon marble and cream colored tiles lining the tub and counters. Modern conveniences, such as a television and VCR, are concealed in the cherry armoires, while a small refrigerator, coffee maker, and basket of gourmet coffee with Stash teas are set in an unobtrusive alcove. A wine opener is included in this potpourri of goodies, as is an extensive list of wines available for purchase.

The Inn at Ludlow Bay is the sort of place where guests can make themselves comfortable in a number of areas. During a cool day, the sun room is just the place to be, while on inclement days we prefer the fireplace bar. We thoroughly enjoy settling into one of the deep couches in front of the fireplace and sampling one of the inn's many microbrews or wines. Another area popular for reclining is out on the porch, where rattan tables are positioned to take advantage of the water views and the activity at the marina. When the sun sets, though, most guests gravitate to the dining room, whose three walls of windows can be opened to allow in the breezes. We visited when the fall menu was in place. Appetizers included the mussels steamed in lemon grass, coconut milk and a cilantro broth; the roasted garlic pumpkin bisque; and the tea-smoked Guinea fowl set on a couscous salad with a walnut sherry vinaigrette. Entrées included the rack of lamb with a pomegranate lamb reduction, the free range chicken with a pecan honey mustard sauce, and the roasted pear and cherry stuffed rabbit with a rosemary cream sauce. We rarely run across a menu with so many appealing options.

After dinner, some guests might want to walk their dogs to the end of the peninsula. Out here, there are a few shade trees, but the highlight is the enormous Port Ludlow totem pole — carved out of a 720 year-old western red cedar tree that blew down in a big storm. It was erected in 1993, after being carved by local artisans. There are a few picnic tables here, but mainly, it is just a peaceful spot for an early-morning or late-evening stroll. Guests are also free to walk along the lane leading to the Port Ludlow Resort, where there are hundreds of acres and inviting paths to follow.

People pleasures include playing golf at the 27-hole Port Ludlow Golf Course or renting a boat from the marina and exploring the numerous inlets. The inn is situated on the Olympic Peninsula, and the entire northeast section of the Olympic National Forest it is available to hikers and their dogs. The best way to access it from Port Ludlow is to drive to Quilcene. Trailheads for hikes up Mount Townsend and Mount Zion are just outside of town, and plenty of other day hikes lie along the perimeter of this spectacular national forest. In the spring, the area is especially scenic as wildflowers are in full bloom.

# The Bishop Victorian Guest Suites

*714 Washington Street*
*Port Townsend, Washington   98368*
*(800) 824-4738, (360) 385-6122*

**Proprietor:** *Joseph Finnie*
**Rooms:** *13 suites*
**Rates:** *$54-98 (B&B), Children under 11 years of age are free*
**Payment:** *AE, MC, and VISA*
**Children:** *Welcome (cribs and cots are available, with prior notice)*
**Dogs:** *Welcome, with approval*
**Open:** *All year*

Port Townsend lies at the entrance to Puget Sound and has an appealing natural harbor. Residents, during the late 1800s, believed these characteristics to mean that Port Townsend would someday emerge as the Northwest's largest city. In anticipation of this potential growth, affluent people were drawn here, building elaborate Victorian homes and ornate public buildings along Water Street — thus creating an infrastructure that would support their future community. Unfortunately, the transcontinental railroad that was supposed to ensure the residents' prosperity never arrived, and the town became an isolated outpost. More recently, the city has enjoyed a resurgence after a portion of it was designated as a National Historic District.

Today, as visitors drive down Water Street, they will still see lovely brick buildings lining the waterfront. If they look up toward the bluffs, the eaves and turrets of the rambling Victorian homes come into view. The Bishop Victorian Guest Suites, formerly known as the Bishop Block Building, is a part of this history. Built in 1890 by William Bishop, this three-story brick building rests just a block off Water Street.

In some ways The Bishop is still reminiscent of a bygone era, as small shops occupy the first floor of the building, and the guest rooms lie on the top two floors. After ascending the interior stairs, we emerged into a broad space that was part hallway and part foyer. Here, we met the new owner, Joseph Finnie, along with his manager's yellow lab, Artie. The dog wiggled out from behind the front desk, hoping for lots of TLC (and of course, getting it). Sated, he then wandered off in search of more attention elsewhere.

With a change in ownership, there usually follows a change in the physical nature of an inn. In the case of The Bishop the transformation process has been a positive one. Many of the suites that once served as apartments are now updated, with their unique nooks and crannies making each a bit different from the other. Some of them boast exposed brick walls, while others offer distant water views through oversized windows. We walked into one suite with a large living room and kitchen adjoining a cozy rear bedroom. In another, two large bedrooms connect to a small sitting room and kitchenette. The decor varies as well; some bedsteads are covered in fluffy floral spreads, others in handmade quilts. Flowered cotton napkins and coordinated placemats adorn the breakfast tables. The eclectic mix of furnishings has obviously been collected through various sources over the years. Brass or carved oak headboards combine with antique oak dressers and maple end tables. These pieces may not be museum quality, but they do add personality to each of the suites. Joseph is in the process of replacing some of the furniture and all of the existing art work. He has begun adding live plants and dried flower arrangements to create a residential feeling in these chambers. Guests who want assurance that they will not be disturbed by street noise should request a suite to the rear of the building.

Each morning a light Continental repast is laid out in the foyer, where guests can select from juice, coffee, fresh fruit, and muffins. Most take this meal back to their suite. If they haven't already noticed the antique rosewood couches covered in green velvet that line the main hall, they will want to take a moment to admire them. Guests craving something a little more substantial may wish to stock their refrigerators with eggs, bacon, and other breakfast goodies, to add to this light fare.

Of course, morning is also the time when the dogs are ready for some exercise. We discovered that this is one of the best times to walk around Port Townsend, as the streets are quiet and it's mostly locals who are out and about. We found a wonderful bakery just a half block from the inn. It makes a variety of luscious breads and pastries and an excellent cup of cappucino. Water Street and the harbor are easy walks along the flats, although anyone wanting more of a workout can ascend the steep hill to the bluff. The bluff happens to be filled with quaint residential streets lined with Victorian homes. Another walking option is the 444-acre estate of Fort Worden, which is only a mile outside of town. Visitors can take tours of the restored Victorian homes and barracks, and visit the Marine Science Center. Dogs are also welcome here and can romp across the open grassy areas and through the woods. Yet another option is Marrowstone Island. Although it is a 20-mile drive from Port Townsend, the 775 acres of forests and trails make this an fine choice for both canines and their human friends.

# Lake Quinault Lodge

P.O. Box 7
*South Shore Road*
*Quinault, Washington  98575*
*(800) 562-6672 in WA, (360) 288-2571, Fax (800) 288-2415*

**Manager:** *Russell Steele*
**Rooms:** *89 doubles, 3 suites*
**Rates:** *Doubles $55-110 (EP), Suites $195-210 (EP), Children*
*under the age of 5 are free of charge, ages 5 and over are $10*
**Payment:** *AE, MC and VISA*
**Children:** *Welcome (cribs, cots, and baby-sitters are available)*
**Dogs:** *Welcome in the annex guest rooms with a $10 daily fee per pet*
**Open:** *All year*

Far from civilization, in territory still owned partly by the
Quinault Indian Reservation, stands a classic cedar lodge that has
proudly withstood the test of time. The Lake Quinault Lodge was
built in 1926 through the combined efforts of Frank McNeil and a
wealthy lumber man, Ralph Emerson. McNeil had spent his
vacations in these spectacular rain forests of the Pacific Northwest
and had fallen in love with them. He knew there would be others
who would also cherish this majestic region. McNeil and Emerson
applied to the U.S. Forest Service for a special permit enabling them
to build on the shores of Lake Quinault. The lodge they designed

was constructed in an incredible ten weeks, using the talents of many skilled craftsmen. Materials were hauled over 50 miles of dirt roads to the crews working 24-hours-a-day.

The expansive two-story, shingled lodge has also played host to many famous people over the years, including Franklin D. Roosevelt. In 1937, he was traveling through the region and was so impressed by its natural splendor that he felt moved to give it national park status in order to preserve its fragile beauty. Today's visitors will find that time has changed little in the Olympic National Forest, including the lodge.

The Lake Quinault Lodge has been beautifully maintained and much of its historic feeling is still intact. People tend to congregate in the lobby of this rambling structure, whose dozens of tiny paned windows overlook emerald-green lawns and the lapping waters of Lake Quinault. The lobby's open-beamed ceilings have been stenciled with Northwest Native American designs, while old newspaper clippings and Northwest Native American art hang from the walls, acting as reminders of its rich heritage. The day we arrived, the rain was falling steadily. (It frequently falls steadily, and anyone who doubts this should just check the totem pole outside that doubles as the rain gauge — it often shows rainfall well into the multi-foot range.) This did not seem to hamper anyone's good spirits on this day, as guests were gathered around the massive wood-burning fireplace, whiling away the hours reading or playing games. The turn-of-the-century wicker chairs looked as though they had held countless numbers of guests over the years. The warm and inviting atmosphere is equally appealing in the main dining room, known as much for its fine food and seafood specialties as it is for its scenic views. The lodge serves three excellent meals each day, but most noteworthy is dinner.

Lodge rooms have also remained relatively unchanged from the 1920s. Brass or white iron double and queen beds grace the creaky hardwood floors, along with comfortable couches and arm chairs. Old-fashioned floral wallpapers enliven these spaces. Bathrooms are a bit dated, but clean, and are outfitted with a few thoughtful amenities such as almond soaps, fragrant shampoos, and shower caps. Natural board walls add a warm, rustic quality. Those traveling with dogs are asked to stay in the equally historic one-story annex building, as each room has a separate outside entrance. The eight guest rooms have a cabin-like quality to them, especially with their paneled walls. As with the lodge rooms, these chambers are primarily equipped with brass beds and some wicker furnishings. On the other end of the lodging scale are the more contemporary lake-side guest rooms. These relatively new additions to the resort are housed in two, three-story buildings. They are decorated with pastel color schemes and are quite luxurious. (We suggest reserving these for friends or family who don't have Bowser in tow.)

An indoor heated swimming pool, Jacuzzi, and sauna are available for those who are not fond of lake swimming. There is also a game room with ping-pong, pool tables, and video games. Canoes and rowboats may be rented for fishing or exploring the lake. Fishing is one of the more popular pastimes at the lodge, and draws a fair number of guests each year. Anglers will find Dolly Varden, rainbow, and cutthroat trout abundant in these waters. (Fishing licenses must be secured from the Quinault Indian Tribe.) Croquet, badminton, and horseshoes are also available on the grounds. Those interested in exploring the rain forest should know that nearly 200 inches of rain fall on it each year, creating incredibly an ecological environment that is unique in the United States. The hiking in these parts is as beautiful as it is wet.

The rangers at the National Forest Service station will be happy to offer suggestions for extensive day and overnight hikes or lead visitors on any of its numerous interpretive excursions. For those who don't already know it: dogs cannot even set a paw in the Olympic National Park. But the lodge is not in the national park; it is in the national forest. Dogs and their human friends are welcome to explore the many trails near Lake Quinault. One of the easiest and most spectacular hikes is around the lake. This seems like one big nature trail, with markers along the way describing what people and their dogs are seeing. Another slightly more aerobic option is just off the Lake Quinault Trail, and is known as the Willaby Creek Trail. It follows Willaby Creek for a bit, and, although it never climbs above the tree line, it does offer a closer look at some of the old growth rain forests for which this area is so famous.

# Alexis Hotel

*1007 First Avenue at Madison*
*Seattle, Washington 98104*
*(800) 426-7033, (206) 624-4844, Fax (206) 621-9009*

*Manager: Stan Kott*
*Rooms: 39 doubles, 15 suites, 40 Arlington Suites*
*Rates: Doubles $170-205 (B&B), Arlington Suites $120-200 (B&B),*
*Suites $220-395 (B&B); children are free of charge when staying*
*in rooms with their parents*
*Payment: AE, CB, DC, DSC, MC, and VISA*
*Children: Welcome (cribs, cots, and baby-sitters are available)*
*Dogs: Well-behaved dogs are welcome, but their human counter-parts*
*must sign a damage waiver*
*Open: All year*

The ownership of the Alexis Hotel changed a few years ago, and it is now a part of the Kimpton group of fine hotels; however, it remains true to its original precept — a small, luxurious, service-intensive hotel. Set within the heart of Seattle's financial district, it is within easy walking distance of the famous Pike's Place Farmers' Market and Pioneer Square. The Alexis Hotel was built in 1901, but was then known as the Globe Building. Throughout the 1920s, it housed assorted specialty shops; in the 1930s it was renovated and became the Arlington Garage. Finally, in 1980, the structure was gutted so that only the exterior walls remained intact. The completed renovation — including the intricate moldings, rounded windows, and intimate alcoves — was so inspired that it won the Honor Award from the American Institute of Architects and was soon listed in the National Register of Historic Places.

We always look forward to visiting the Alexis, as it exudes a certain degree of European charm and sophistication. The lobby is intimate, with a few comfortable sitting areas separated from one another by potted plants and Oriental vases filled with flowers. Guests' privacy is highly respected, which is perhaps why the hotel attracts those who are interested in maintaining theirs. Bob Dylan, who visited with his bulldog, and Robert De Niro, who likes to travel with his canine entourage, are just two of the Alexis' more notable guests who enjoy bringing their canine companions.

Famous or not so famous, guests are often intrigued with this wonderful hotel because they can always find a room to suit their mood. Each formal space is individually decorated, with some spaces containing black-lacquered furniture set against deep rose-colored walls, while others emphasize natural woods and soothing earth tones. Guests may expect to find at least one antique, be it an armoire concealing a television, a nest of bedside tables, or a mahogany sideboard. When the Sultan of Brunei was visiting, he took over half the hotel and redid many of the rooms in rich, dark colors. Subsequent guests who stay in these spaces might feel as though they are, in some small way, privy to the royal treatment.

We did not stay in the Sultan's suite, but in another enormous space with boxed-beamed ceilings and floor-to-ceiling windows. Pinpoint lighting fell against the draperies, tapestry-covered couches, and antique armoire. The king bed was separated from the living room by a sliding Shoji screen. The next day, we peeked at some of the other rooms and ventured into one with a mahogany bed topped by a virtual mountain of oversized pillows. Another chamber was equally appealing, but not as much for the decor as for its corner location. Given the choice, we would request a corner room with windows facing the street. (The other option is a back alley — not as interesting, but it is quiet.) Another especially intriguing possibility is one of the six wood-burning fireplace suites. Regardless of room choice, guests will find their chamber appointed with well-stocked minibars containing complimentary sodas, tonics, and juices. The whirlpool baths are the focal point of the dramatic, black-tiled and marbled bathrooms that can be found in some of the suites. All guests enjoy the luxury of thick terry robes, cotton towels, sewing kits, shampoos, and an assortment of toiletries. Those who want to thoroughly indulge themselves can sample the full line of spa products available in each bedroom. In the evening, guests return to find turned-down beds and gold-wrapped chocolates placed on their down pillows.

Families who require a little more space, or business travelers who need long-term accommodations, should check into the neighboring Arlington Suites. These are in the seven-story Arlington Building (circa 1901), which was first renovated in 1982 at a cost of over $120,000 per suite. During our visit, the suites were closed for redecoration, and would remain so until the spring of 1996. The new look is an eye-catching Art Deco style. One aspect of the Arlington Suites that will not change, though, is the suite size. Each space will remain between 750 to 1,500 square feet. Guests may request kitchens, dining rooms, living rooms, and either one or two bedrooms. Our favorites: those with fireplaces and balconies, the latter of which are privy to views of Elliott Bay.

Most guests, whether they stay in the suites or main hotel, eventually end up in the Bookstore — an intimate bar by night and an equally great place to start the morning. The excellent coffee and fresh fruit, coupled with a choice of croissants, muffins, and pastries is a surprisingly substantial breakfast. Some who might skip the morning meal may find themselves here in the evening, sipping on a drink and looking through the eclectic collection of books and magazines. Others are waiting for their table at one of the city's premier restaurants, The Painted Table.

We have always liked the physical layout of The Painted Table, with its regularly changing art display and impressive collection of designer plates. Evidently, the food did not always match the ambiance, but this has all changed recently with the addition of a new chef to whom Seattle seems to be responding favorably — Chef J. Tim Kelley. His appetizers are substantial enough to be meals in themselves. We suggest the organic beef tartar with arugula and horseradish oil, the lemon grass cured salmon, or the grilled five spice quail. Entrées range from the Mongolian barbecue loin of pork served with an egg noodle and scallion cake, pea vines, and Asian slaw; the seafood risotto brimming with mussels, tiger shrimp, and bay scallops; or the pan seared salmon with potato gnocchi, tarragon and corn sauté, and an herb salad. Desserts vary with the day, but two popular choices are the mocha silk mousse gâteau, with an espresso caramel sauce, and the frozen banana soufflé, with strawberry, chocolate, and mango sauces.

Those who want to work off their culinary indulgences can utilize either of the two sports clubs that are within walking distance of the hotel, or they can head out for a jog along the waterfront. Something more rejuvenating in mind? Perhaps a session in the steam room will provide the needed remedy. Those who are fond of late night walks may wish to reconsider — we didn't feel especially safe wandering the streets at this time of the evening. During the day, though, there is the waterfront to explore, along with a small park near Pike's Place Farmers' Market. A short drive to northern Seattle brings visitors and their dogs to Green Lake. This is the area to see and be seen in. On a nice day, the city dwellers find this an easy place to come and walk, run, do in-line skating, and most importantly, walk their dogs. There is a trail that most walkers follow around the lake or through the trees. As with most popular spots, though, it is busiest in the summer months, but quite manageable during the off season.

At the end of the day, whether it was spent checking out the parks or hiking in the mountains, it is always a pleasure to return to the Alexis. The incredible attention to detail and the genuine friendliness of the staff is refreshing, especially when guests realize there is a no-tipping policy. The Alexis Hotel is probably one of the most romantic and elegant small hotels in this region, offering a bit of European grace, style, and sophistication without the corresponding price tag.

# Four Seasons Olympic Hotel

*411 University Street*
*Seattle, Washington 98101*
*(800) 332-3442/U.S., (800) 821-8106/WA,*
*(206) 621-1700, Fax (206) 682-9633*

**General Manager:** Peter Martin
**Rooms:** *178 doubles, 200 suites,*
**Rates:** *Doubles $215-290 (EP), Suites $500-1150 (EP), Children*
*under 18 are free of charge*
**Payment:** *AE, CB, DC, MC, and VISA*
**Children:** *Welcome (cribs, cots, and baby-sitter services are available)*
**Dogs:** *Welcome, but they must receive special permission if the dog*
*weighs over 70 pounds*
**Open:** *All year*

The Olympic Hotel opened in 1924 to much fanfare. This elegant and sophisticated Italian Renaissance-style building was the first of its kind in the still provincial Pacific Northwest. As spacious and ornate as the hotel was, its wide open facade and inefficient use of space turned out to be a very inappropriate design for a hotel. Not only did it not appeal to the guests, but the hotel soon began to lose business and eventually fell into disrepair. In the late 1970s there was talk of demolishing the hotel. However, the residents of Seattle felt strongly that a building with such history and unique features should be saved and restored. The Four Seasons Ltd. and the partnership of Urban Investment and Development Company were granted a lease in 1980 and began renovating the structure.

The Olympic Hotel's 60 million dollar restoration was one of the largest privately financed, historic restorations ever undertaken in the United States. Detailed plans were drawn up and executed, with as much attention devoted to the comfort of future guests as to maintaining the exquisite details. The number of guest rooms was reduced from 756 to 450, giving each chamber a more spacious configuration. Fifty percent of these bedrooms are now alcove rooms, where French doors separate the sleeping areas from the sitting rooms. All these rooms combine old-world formality and elegance with modern-day comfort and a pleasing array of amenities.

The furnishings are reproductions of fine English antiques by Henredon and Baker furniture makers, and are coupled with richly textured fabrics and hand-woven carpets. Varying shades of chocolate brown, taupe, and cream colors combine for an elegant warmth. Beds are triple-sheeted and covered with thick comforters and masses of pillows. Everything a guest would expect lies within these luxurious spaces. If, perchance, it does not, it can often be readily secured. Armoires conceal the remote-control televisions and VCRs, along with the well-stocked minibars. A basket of gourmet goodies is set on top of an end table. In addition to a secondary telephone in the bathroom, there are hair dryers, make-up mirrors, scales, and terry cloth robes. As one would expect, the hotel prides itself on first-class service, whether guests need their shoes shined, clothes laundered, or special treats for their children or dogs. Doggie visitors receive a bottle of water, along with a bowl and gourmet dog biscuits. Children, on the other hand, may request special movies, videos and board games, all of which may be accompanied by cookies and milk.

The guest rooms are lovely, but it is the public areas that are especially noteworthy, as ceilings seem to soar overhead. Ornately-carved oak highlights the cavernous two-story main lobby; however, it is not all original. During the restoration, architects discovered that segments of oak were missing from the paneling. They ultimately found matching oak in England and imported it. Craftsmen spent hundreds of hours carving and treating the wood so it would match the original. The adjacent Garden Court is especially spectacular, mainly due to the expansive floor-to-ceiling Palladian windows. This is a veritable garden of immense, fresh flower arrangements and mature ficus trees illuminated with twinkling white lights — at night the effect is especially festive. Those who come here frequently do so for lunch or cocktails; however, high tea tends to draw its share of regulars as well.

The Georgian dining room not only sounds regal — it looks regal. Lustrous, paneled walls interspersed with Palladian windows and elaborately-carved moldings, crystal chandeliers, and potted palms set the overall elegant ambiance. This is an à la carte menu, with some guests opting to start with the oyster bisque and a warm wild rice pancake, lobster and roasted forest mushrooms in a morel sauce, or the Northwest oysters on the half shell. During our visit, the Georgian Room's signature entrées included the thick cut, smoked salmon with Washington apples and apple brandy sauce, and the veal tenderloin with morel mushrooms. We thought the braised duck with caramelized orange sauce, the mountain berry spiced game hen, and the venison pepper steak sounded equally tempting. Shuckers is the hotel's popular oyster bar, and is a terrific place to grab a quick bite to eat.

Guests in search of a little exercise will enjoy the well-conceived health club with its large pool and Jacuzzi set in a huge glass atrium. Just outside the glass structure are nicely landscaped sun decks. A nearby weight room contains rowing machines, bicycles, treadmills, Stairmasters, and a Nordic Track. Best of all, guests who forget their athletic gear need not worry — they have complimentary use of swimsuits, shorts, T-shirts, athletic shoes and even shampoos, conditioners, combs and brushes. Of course, all this will appease the human guests, but not necessarily their canine companions; however, doggie guests should remain patient — there are plenty of terrific walks we can suggest.

We love the location of the Four Seasons Olympic. It is set in the heart of the city's finest shopping and strolling district, and is less than a block from the theater. We felt comfortable walking throughout this portion of the city, both day and night, as there is always plenty going on and plenty of people around. There is even a pedestrian mall just a few blocks away that city dogs will enjoy. Others may prefer to take a stroll down to the waterfront, or simply window shop along the wide streets.

Those searching for a little green space, though, should probably jump in their car and head over to the Washington Park Arboretum, situated near the University of Washington. Once here, visitors and their dogs can follow the Waterfront Trail, which is a boardwalk crossing over the marshes. There is plenty to see in the way of native flora and fauna, not to mention waterfowl. Another great outing leads people and their dogs to Seward Park on Lake Washington, just south of Seattle. There are 280 acres for walking and exploring, including some forested acreage and picturesque shoreline beaches. Two other options within the metropolitan area are the Cougar Mountain Regional Wild Land Park and the Tiger Mountain State Forest — both accessible to people and their dogs.

# The Beech Tree Manor

*1405 Queen Anne Avenue North*
*Seattle, Washington 98109*
*(206) 281-7037, Fax (208) 285-4932*

*Hostess: Virginia Lucero*
*Rooms: 1 single, 5 doubles*
*Rates: Single $45-65 (B&B), Doubles $55-75 (B&B)*
*Payment: MC and VISA*
*Children: Over 5 years of age are welcome (roll-away beds are available)*
*Dogs: Welcome with notice and approval*
*Open: All year*

Take a lovely, turn-of-the-century Victorian home, furnish it with antiques and exquisite linens, and most importantly, find a hostess who is as delightful as Virginia Lucero, and herein lies the very essence of a truly inviting B&B. The Beech Tree Manor was built in 1903, and is named for the majestic copper beech tree that dominates the front of the house. There have been only two owners in all these years — Virginia and the original builder. He and his 14-year-old Irish bride built the home and then lived here until the 1970s. The house sat on the market for five years before Virginia discovered it, bought it, and renovated it. Today, it is one of many well-preserved historic homes in this attractive Queen Anne Hill neighborhood.

Virginia is a native of Seattle, although she also spent a number of years in Washington, D.C. Her home reflects these two periods of her life; formal antiques and contemporary Northwest art comfortably meld together. Apart from Virginia's collection of massive canvases of modern artwork, lining both the circular stairway and upstairs hall, the feeling of the Beech Tree Manor is reminiscent of an English country home. The original hand-carved moldings and embossed tin wall coverings are original. The beamed-ceiling living room is often the central gathering place. It runs the length of the house and is filled with a wonderful hodgepodge of chintzes covering the overstuffed couches, armchairs, and window seat. There are pillows everywhere, and still more fabric and lace framing the windows. Against the walls, Virginia displays her collection of pottery, which she hangs from decorative ribbons. Jake, the resident bulldog, can usually be found lounging in front of the massive beachstone fireplace. In the evening, guests often congregate here to enjoy a quiet moment or two while sipping a little sherry before the fire. This combination of warmth from the sherry and the fire is quite relaxing, but once guests head up to bed, they will discover one of the best features of this enchanting B&B.

The charming guest rooms all occupy the second floor, and evoke the same homey feeling as the downstairs public areas. Brass or ebony bedsteads are covered with extra fluffy down comforters. The softness of white antique sheets and pillow cases is a marked contrast to the floral and bold-striped chintzes on many of the duvets. The linens are unlike anything most people have ever slept on. Whether appliquéed or embroidered with delicate flowers, all are exquisite. Virginia used to sell these fine linens out of the B&B, but recently has stopped doing so. Most of the bathrooms are private, and although they lack the endearing character of the bedrooms, they do contain the necessities — ivory soaps, modern showers, and soft, fluffy towels. A few of the bedrooms connect with a bathroom containing a claw-footed tub. One of the most requested rooms is set to the rear of the house, and is quite romantic with its quarter-canopy bed and antique white linen coverlet.

The morning breakfast is a full meal that is served in the formal dining room, around an antique table set for twelve. Virginia makes everything from scratch, often including hard-to-find seasonal fruit in her fruit plates and homemade muffins and breads. Depending upon her whim and the number of guests she is cooking for, there is everything from quiche and chili eggs to pancakes and baked French toast with nuts, cinnamon, and fresh cream. Those who look forward to a great cup of morning coffee will thoroughly enjoy Virginia's variety of freshly-ground coffees.

After breakfast, some like to step onto the outdoor porch, set with wicker rockers, where they can read the morning newspaper or one of the B&B's many magazines and books. From here, guests will find the extensive flower gardens that line one side of the house. Set within the midst of the gardens is a small statue of a bulldog — appropriate, given Jake's prominent position in the household. We always enjoy taking our dogs for a morning stroll about Queen Anne Hill. Two small parks are located just a few blocks down from the B&B. From either vantage point, there are scenic views of downtown Seattle and the harbor. A still more interesting adventure is a hike through Seattle's Discovery Park, just north of the city. Dogs are welcome across the 500-acre expanse of trees, bluffs, and beaches. Lush with foliage and natural beauty, the park lies directly on Puget Sound and there is usually plenty of wildlife to distract both humans and beasts. For those who would like to investigate the array of diversions in the downtown area, there are trolleys and buses that can whisk both human and beast to Seattle's center in just a little over five minutes.

---

# Pensione Nichols

*1923 First Avenue*
*Seattle, Washington 98101*
*(206) 441-7125*

*Innkeepers: Lindsay and Nancy Nichols*
*Rooms: 10 doubles, 2 suites*
*Rates: Doubles $85 (B&B), Suites $160 (EP)*
*Payment: AE, DSC, MC, and VISA*
*Children: Welcome*
*Dogs: Smaller dogs welcome, but negotiable*
*Open: All year*

We've stayed in pensione's all over Europe, because they are intimate, personal, and reasonably priced. The Pensione Nichols may lie on American shores, but it is more reminiscent of the European version. Moreover, it is ideally located in downtown Seattle, and within easy walking distance of Pike Place Market, the Kingdome, and the theater and shopping districts. Those familiar with the historic Smith Block building may know that the Pensione Nichols also shares this address; however, we had to search carefully before locating the tiny sign pointing us to the doorway.

We arrived a little early one afternoon, and had to wait a bit for someone to let us in. While this may have been a little inconvenient, we must admit, we liked the security aspect. Guests ascend two flights of stairs to reach the top floor of the pensione, where they will emerge into a bright foyer that serves as the reception area. Chloe, the 15-year-old resident dog, trotted up to say hello and then disappeared to the back of the pensione. Guests tend to gather in the foyer's small sitting area, or retreat, like Chloe, to the rear of the building. We followed Lindsay into an enormous living room with a wall of windows overlooking Elliott Bay. Some people had settled into the pair of gray sofas, deluged with late-day sunlight. Given the exposure, we knew just why the huge ficus tree in here was thriving. On the opposite side of the room, various mismatched, round wooden tables were set for the following morning's Continental breakfast.

The bedrooms are found mostly on the third floor, with a few spilling over onto the second floor. All are simply furnished, but offer all the necessities. We like the fact that unoccupied rooms are left open, so that newly arriving guests can peruse the room choices and pick the one that is most appropriate for them. The doors are propped open with whimsical little stone doorstops, in shapes ranging from a hedgehog to a cat and a dog. These rather boxy chambers are enlivened with pale yellow walls, which are brightened by the natural sunlight pouring in through the old-fashioned frosted skylights housed in the high ceilings. Simple, white cotton spreads cover the beds, while neatly folded comforters are placed at the foot. There is usually a chair or an antique oak bureau, with bath towels laid out on a rack. All these bedrooms share two bathrooms, and those who can overlook the shared WC will find them to be well appointed and quite expansive. Our favorite bathroom is sort of an Art Deco space with black and white tiles and a claw-foot tub. (There is also a separate shower.) Those who prefer real windows with views should request the largest rooms overlooking First Avenue. Travelers who would like to ensure a peaceful night's sleep might be more happy with a bedroom at the rear of the building.

Families with dogs will want to think about reserving one of the two suites on the second floor. These were completed only recently and offer far more space, amenities, and privacy than the others. We like the one facing Elliott Bay, although a fire escape ladder partially obscures the views. These chambers are long, narrow spaces, which guests enter from the back. We came upon a raised area, surrounded by a half-wall, that contained a queen bed and a sofa bed. Guests walk past the bedroom area and the full, modern kitchen to the living room. The only drawback to these spaces is that although they have one wall of windows, they do not have the benefit of the third-floor skylights — so they can be a little dark at times.

Pensione Nichols is a fine place for walking a dog during the day, but we would not have felt as comfortable wandering about during the wee hours of the night, as there are a couple of adult-oriented businesses in the area. The Pensione is centrally located, so that everything is just a short walk away (and we know Bowser will enjoy the exercise). Just outside of Seattle, there are a number of interesting areas that might appeal to people and their dogs. Carkeek Park offers a diversity of walking trails that meander throughout its 200 acres of forest and creeks. Just to the south are two more wonderful parks, known as Washington and Seward Parks. Both offer plenty of easy walks and an abundance of scenery.

# The Historic Sou'wester Lodge

*P.O. Box 102*
*Beach Access Road (38th Place)*
*Seaview, Washington  98644*
*(360) 642-2542*

**Hosts:** *Len and Miriam Atkins*
**Rooms:** *6 lodge rooms, 4 cottages, 8 trailers*
**Rates:** *Lodge Rooms $59-99 (EP), Cottages $75 (EP),*
     *Trailers $35-87 (EP)*
**Payment:** *VISA*
**Children:** *Welcome (cribs, cots, and baby-sitters are available)*
**Dogs:** *Welcome everywhere except for the main inn, but they cannot be*
     *left unattended*
**Open:** *All year*

The Long Beach Peninsula reputedly has the longest stretch of beach in the world, and at 28 miles long, we won't argue the point. We hope readers will believe us when we tell them that the peninsula also contains one of the more unique accommodations in the Northwest — the Historic Sou'wester Lodge. The name seems innocuous enough, and the location can't be beat, as it is lies at the end of a beach access road and across from high, grass-covered sand dunes. As we drove up, we first noticed the barn-board red, rambling old lodge, dwarfed by a stand of pine trees. Off to one side were four small cottages painted to match the lodge. So far, nothing out of the ordinary. That is, until we happened to glance across the way to see the vintage collection of mobile homes — their domed silver exteriors festooned with murals. But we will get back to them a little later. To understand the Historic Sou'wester, it is important to know a little about its history — and, more importantly, to understand Miriam and Len.

The Westborough House, as the Historic Sou'wester was formerly known, was built in 1892 by Oregon Senator Henry Winslow Corbett, who used it as his family's country estate. Almost 100 years later — in 1980, to be exact — Miriam and Len discovered the neglected home and decided to buy it. At the time, they were also in the process of creating a new life for themselves. For over 15 years Len had assisted Bruno Bettelheim (the noted child psychologist) at the University of Chicago. He and Miriam wanted a change, though, and drove across country thinking they would open a center for troubled children in Southern California. Fortunately, they never reached California, stopping instead in Seaview. They liked what they found and thought this would be a wonderful place to settle, especially when they learned that the old Westborough House was for sale. After buying it, they repaired the roof, rewired and repainted the interior, and filled it with all their worldly possessions. In 1981, The Historic Sou'wester Lodge was ready for business.

Guests traveling with dogs can stay in either the cabins or the refurbished trailers, but will undoubtedly gravitate to the lodge, as this tends to be the social and cultural center for the place. We entered through the glassed-in, wraparound porch and found Len, an affable, gray-bearded gentleman with a wonderful South African accent. We chatted a bit in the expansive living room, which reminded us of a scholar's library, with its beamed ceilings, tongue and groove fir walls, and built-in bookshelves flanking the fireplace. Throughout this common area we discovered an intriguing collection of the Atkins' furniture and literature, which they have acquired during their world travels. A brass chandelier casts muted lighting across the worn Oriental carpet and hardwood floors. Other than a little refurbishing, so little has been done to the place since the Corbett era that it is easy to imagine what life at the lodge must have been like over 100 years ago. Just off the living room are the three downstairs guest rooms, each quite Spartan and simply decorated. These accommodations are part of the famous Bed & (MYOD) Breakfast, which, as Len jokingly explains, means "Make Your Own Damn Breakfast." The kitchen is just around the corner and is open for guests' use. The remaining lodge guest rooms are apartments, complete with kitchenettes, which are rented for longer periods of time.

Our focus, though, is on the cottages and trailers. The cottages are simply furnished in what Len describes as "Early Salvation Army" and offer such amenities as a kitchen, one or two bedrooms, a sitting room, and a bathroom. Guests usually enter these quarters by way of the enclosed car park, which opens up into the 1950s-style kitchen. From here, the circular flow of the cottage brings guests to either a bedroom or sitting room, and then finally into the bathroom. The decorative touches consist of an assortment of Post Impressionist posters and postcards, which Miriam has placed about the rooms. Other than that, there is definitely nothing fancy, cute, or contrived about these accommodations — just clean and unpretentious guest cabins, with the pounding surf and smell of salt air drifting in through the windows. We took special notice of the tiny note in each kitchen that begins with *From your dog...* and continues by asking guests to please make a special effort to keep dog hair swept up, as it easily gets imbedded in furniture, beds, etc.

The second option for those traveling with Bowser is the Tch! Tch! RVs, which are set off to the other side of the lodge. The Atkins mockingly refer to Tch (the British equivalent of Tsk) as Trailer Classics Hodgepodge, jesting that Senator Henry Corbett and his "patrician *petit bourgeois* alliance" would surely have "perished at the thought of... having this motley, proletarian assortment of recreational vehicles" parked in their neighborhood, much less in their own backyard. In any case, the trailers are the original American classic, with true "Sears Roebuck/Montgomery Ward 1971 catalogue ambiance." They are, in fact, 1950's curved-chrome trailers that come fully furnished, complete with kitchens. Visitors can step inside to see an "Early Salvation Army" chic, with plenty of books, linens, and space. Some of the trailers are painted on the outside — similar to the many murals we now find on buildings from time to time. One sketch replicates a memorable scene from the movie *The African Queen.* Another trailer, which Len affectionately calls "The Disoriented Express," depicts a train chugging along the side of it. The ambiance is decidedly unique, but thoroughly appeals to the low-key type of guest who generally stays here.

What newcomers will soon discover, if they didn't suspect it already, is that the Long Beach Peninsula lends itself to long strolls along the beach and unhurried days. People come in the spring to dig for razor clams or fly their kite — kite flying has long been a passion among residents of these parts. The roads are also flat, making bicycling a natural diversion. The region is also renowned for other particularities, such as cranberry bogs, having one of the oldest lighthouses in the Pacific Northwest (the Cape

Disappointment Lighthouse), and being the termination point of the Lewis and Clark expedition (the Fort Canby State Park). Fort Canby, by the way, offers all sorts of recreational diversions for people and their dogs. There are nature trails, spectacular walks along the rocky shoreline, and even a forest — all of which should provide enough exercise for human and beast. For those hoping to stay closer to home, there is a secret path along the beach that is perfect for walks with Bowser. The exact location is not so secret, though, especially for those who follow the detailed map located on a wall in the entry.

A tired dog will happily sleep in the evening, giving his human friends the opportunity to steal over to the lodge for the Atkins' Fireside Evenings. These are held in the living room, where, depending on the night, guests are treated to concerts, theatrical performances, or poetry readings; or they might participate in worldly discussions. Guests and their children (because "even infants should not be denied the opportunity for cultural enrichment") are encouraged to participate, bringing with them a valued and appreciated contribution to the overall atmosphere. Visitors from all backgrounds are thus provided with a wonderful opportunity to get to know each other and to share in the informal and fun discourse. The ambiance here is truly unique, and perfect for anyone who wants to be within steps of an expansive beach and who thinks the off-beat accommodations merely add to the experience. After years of playing host, Len issues this warning: his guests either love the place or detest it. We hope our description helps our readers to decide which category they fall into.

# Simone's Groveland Cottage

*4861 Sequim Dungeness Way*
*Sequim/Dungeness, Washington 98382*
*(800) 879-8859, (360) 683-3565, Fax (360) 683-5181*

*Innkeeper: Simone Nichols*
*Rooms: 4 doubles, 1 cottage*
*Rates: Doubles $65-90 (B&B), Cottage $90*
*Payment: AE, DC, DSC, MC, and VISA*
*Children: Not appropriate for children under the age of 12*
*Dogs: Small dogs welcome in the "Secret Room"*
*Open: All year*

Sequim is one of those rare places on the Olympic Peninsula that does not get much rain. This area lies in the rain shadow of the Olympic Mountains — it is therefore a desirable destination for travelers who are tired of crossing their fingers hoping for a rain-free vacation. Fertile farmland seems to stretch for miles here, before sloping up into the foothills of the Olympics. But closer to the ocean, flat roads wend along bluffs and rural routes to all sorts of wonderful villages. One of these is Dungeness, home to the exquisite Dungeness National Wildlife Refuge. One of the lesser-known treasures in this area is Simone's Groveland Cottage, set just a half-mile from the beach and harbor.

Built at the turn of the century, the cottage was once a private home for a wealthy merchant and his family. Today, it reminds us of an English country cottage with its white picket fences, trellises, and arbors draped in roses and climbing vines. Surrounding this white clapboard and shingled house are vibrant perennial gardens, which were still in bloom when we visited, even though it was late in the season. This bucolic setting is even further enhanced by a creek that skirts the edge of the property — and by the canopy of fruit and shade trees filtering the sun in the backyard. The main house is connected to an old-fashioned general store, where sloping wood floors and unfinished walls provide plenty of character. Simone was in the process of closing the store permanently, though, so that she could finally implement what she had long been contemplating — converting it back into a Great Room. By the time guests visit again, this will be a formal space for weddings, chamber music, or simply relaxing before the substantial river rock fireplace.

The rest of the inn will remain the same — which should greatly please returning guests who are used to their well-appointed rooms and Simone's pampering. As we mentioned, the main inn is reminiscent of an English country B&B, and once inside, guests will discover that each corner is filled with an unusual antique, *object d'art*, or knickknack. We especially like the living room, with its wall of double-hung windows and its comfortable overstuffed sofas and chairs. With all the interesting collectibles in here, including china, contemporary art, and mountains of books and magazines, it is easy to overlook the lovely stained glass windows. The adjoining dining room, which overlooks the backyard, is the site for each morning's bountiful breakfast. This is quite a feast, beginning with bowls of fresh fruit and scones, accompanied by a baked egg dish or other delectables. The treats begin much earlier than this, though, as first thing each morning, a tray with coffee and a newspaper is brought to each guest's bedroom.

While there are four upstairs guest rooms in the inn, they are not really appropriate for people traveling with a dog. There is, however, a separate cottage known as the Secret Room. We found it by walking through the back of the general store and across a short path. The cottage would be our preferred space, with or without a dog, as guests staying out here enjoy the ultimate in privacy. The cottage is awash in various hues of purple, ranging from a pale lilac to a deep lavender. Naturally finished, paneled-wood walls are inset with small windows framed by lilac-hued cotton curtains. Guests sleep in a high brass bed, or may relax on the adjacent couch enlivened by a purple floral throw. Surprisingly, the best views of the backyard are garnered from the tiny windows in the kitchen. A Dutch door opens from here out into the yard — guests can open just the top and let the breezes drift through the cottage. Guests staying here also have a television with a VCR.

People stay here for a variety of reasons, but it is the birders who truly love this place. There are plenty of birds to see right on the property; however, the most popular spot from which to watch the assorted wildfowl is on the Dungeness Sand Spit. While Bowser is not allowed on this particular adventure, there is a pleasant walk that appeals to canines along the rural roads leading to the Dungeness Harbor. Once at the harbor, we recommend stopping at The Three Crabs to check out its excellent menu. Slightly further afield, at the Sequim Bay State Park, leashed dogs are allowed to explore with their human friends. Another nearby option is the Dungeness River Valley, which is one of the few areas in the Olympic Mountains that allows hikers and their dogs. Another option is the Gold Creek Trail, which happens to be located right on the way to the Dungeness River Valley. If guests plan to be out and about for the better part of the day, they may wish to ask Simone to pack them a picnic lunch.

# Juan de Fuca Cottages

*182 Marine Drive*
*Sequim, Washington   98382*
*(800) 683-4432, (360) 683-4433*

*Innkeeper: Sheila Ramus*
*Rooms: 6 cottages*
*Rates: $100-105 (EP)*
*Payment: MC and VISA*
*Children: Welcome*
*Dogs: Depending upon the dog, they are welcome with  prior notice*
*Open:  All year*

The Juan de Fuca Cottages are a secret — and it seems that longtime guests and the innkeeper want to keep it that way. When we first called to get more information on the place, the innkeeper filled us in on the details only verbally, because the inn does not have a brochure or a rate sheet. This did not discourage us; rather, it made us all the more interested in investigating the clutch of cottages set on Dungeness Bay.

The Juan de Fuca Cottages, as it turns out, lie in a quiet residential neighborhood. The houses lining the road along the windswept bluff all look overlook the Juan de Fuca Strait, and the cottages are no exception. They are arranged in a semi-circle around a beautifully-manicured central lawn and glassed-in gazebo. These appealing, blue-shingled buildings are quite endearing, with their white gingerbread trim lining the eaves, their shutters with carved seahorse motifs, and their window boxes filled with flowers. Each is also fashioned with a tiny glassed-in porch, with just enough room for a pair of chairs and a side table. While the porch is privy to some exceptional views of the water, we decided to venture inside rather than linger on the porch.

We were surprised by the interior spaces, which exhibit far more character than we were expecting. The floors are fully carpeted, and the walls paneled in a honey-colored wood. Hues of blue and pink highlight the floral spreads covering the beds. One alcove holds a queen bed, while built-in cabinets form a storage space in which to slide the other bed when it is not being used. A small sitting area lies to the front of the cottage, in front of a plate glass window that overlooks the grounds and the ocean. To the rear is a fully-equipped modern kitchen, with such amenities as a microwave, full refrigerator, and dishwasher. An oak table and matching Windsor chairs fill the area separating the kitchen from the sitting room. The bathrooms are new as well, and are brightened by skylights set over the whirlpool tubs. Bottles of Nivea creme, bath gel, and soap are thoughtful extras we don't normally expect to find in housekeeping cottages. Families with up to two children would be comfortable in most of the cottages, although they are cozy. For families with more children, the two-bedroom cottage set off by itself to the rear of the property is ideal.

Regardless of how guests decide to accommodate their group, most are sure to relish the fact that they are well removed from the rest of civilization. Once we arrived at the Juan de Fuca Cottages, we indeed felt quite separate from the commercial world (strip malls, movie theaters, fast food restaurants), and frankly had little desire to go find it. Therefore, we recommend that guests bring their own food and simply plan to use these low-key accommodations as an ideal place to unwind. Some entertainment is available in the form of television and VCRs, and there are over 250 movies that guests may borrow. Each cottage also has a library of books, should travelers have forgotten their own. Best of all, if guests do not find a book to their liking, a neighbor probably has one more to their fancy .

As we mentioned, there is plenty of grass around the cottages, and when the wind blows, which is often, the glassed-in gazebo is a convenient shelter. Walks along the bluffs are also a delightful way to exercise Bowser. Guests can follow the bluff road down the hill to Cline Spit, where many enjoy watching the sailboarders tackle the high winds. This is also a favorite spot for crabbing, and many of the locals are often busy pulling in their catch. Most days, it is easy to see all the way across the Juan de Fuca Strait to Vancouver Island. We were also able to look back toward the Dungeness National Wildlife Refuge. Unfortunately, Bowser will have to stay at home or in the car for this latter outing. This six-mile strip of land is one of the longest natural sand spits in the United States. The walk along the spit is exceptional, and for those who pick the right time of day, it can feel as if they are hundreds of miles away from home.

---

# The Salish Lodge

*P.O. Box 1109*
*Snoqualmie Falls Road (Highway 202)*
*Snoqualmie, Washington 98065*
*(800) 826-6124, (206) 888-2556, Fax (206) 888-2533*

**General Manager:** *Loy Helmley*
**Rooms:** *87 doubles, 4 suites*
**Rates:** *Doubles $165-295 (EP), Suites $500-575 (EP)*
**Payment:** *AE, CB, DC, DSC, MC, and VISA*
**Children:** *Welcome (cribs, cots, and baby-sitters are available)*
**Dogs:** *Welcome in the first-floor rooms, with a $50 non-refundable deposit*
**Open:** *All year*

There are plenty of waterfalls throughout the Pacific Northwest, but among the more famous (and therefore most visited) are the Snoqualimie Falls. We had to admit, the falls were spectacular as they dropped 268 feet to the river below. As one might imagine, the sound effects are also stupendous. Set at the top of these falls is the famous Salish Lodge which, if viewed from the bottom of the falls, appears to rise from the mist like a medieval fortress.

The architecture cleverly utilizes native woods, and stone that seems to meld with every rocky outcropping it touches. Because the lodge lies near a popular tourist destination, the gracious staff works especially hard to keep the curious public at bay. For the most part, it all works quite well, creating an interior oasis that appeals to those searching for a romantic or relaxing holiday experience. The falls can be deafening at times, but as we stepped into the interior a sense of calm settled upon us. We were again impressed with the abundant use of natural materials in evidence throughout the contemporary lodge, ranging from slate floors to finely hewn redwood beams. Where there isn't natural wood or rock, there is glass — either in the floor-to-ceiling windows or in the walls of tiny crank-out windows. Ficus trees and assorted plant life also help to create private areas where guests can sit before the fireplace and soak in the tranquil ambiance.

The Salish Lodge is reminiscent of a grand country manor, with guests feeling pampered and protected from the moment they venture inside. Hallways are accessed through locked doors; so only guests with keys are able to enter these private enclaves. We were interested primarily in the first-floor rooms, as this is where guests traveling with dogs are permitted to stay. There is a reason for this, as each of these spaces opens onto grass terraces accessed through sliding glass doors. From here, guests and their dogs step down to a path that circumnavigates the lodge. The bedrooms are huge, and resemble something out of a Ralph Lauren catalog — the masculine country version, that is. King beds appear immense when topped by fluffy down comforters and piles of oversized feather pillows. Hand-crafted furniture might include a classic, naturally-finished wicker chair, a streamlined cherry Shaker table, or an oak armoire concealing the television. Interesting lithographs and black and white photographs highlight the cream-colored walls, but the focal point is a slate fireplace that faces the bed. Amenities are equally well conceived, as a huge basket of gourmet goodies rests on one table and a refrigerator is stocked with champagne, wine, and sparkling water. Bathrooms are modern and outfitted with hair dryers, robes, and a full complement of toiletries. All contain Jacuzzi soaking tubs; in some bedrooms, these rest under frosted windows that slide open so that bathers can enjoy watching the crackling fire from their spa. There are only four suites, one of which occupies a corner of the first floor. For a truly special occasion, guests can reserve this incredible space. Most notable in here are the wall of hand-carved cherry cabinets, hiding an entertainment center, and the deep, cushioned window seats that meet in the corner of the room under two plate glass windows. The glass doors open to a patio that wraps around the suite to the separate bedroom. Both the bedroom and living room have wood burning fireplaces.

This is a hotel to which travelers come when they need to rejuvenate. The food wins rave reviews, as does the wine cellar — and guests may enjoy all of this within their rooms. However, at some point, even the most reclusive guests should make their way upstairs to either the Attic Lounge or the Salish Dining Room. We like the feeling of the Attic Lounge, whose ceiling follows the contours of the roof and gives this inviting space more interest. Guests can have a drink around one of the small tables, on the leather couches, or hidden away behind a half-wall. There is usually live music in the evenings; a few lucky ones can listen to this from a table overlooking the falls. One flight down is the equally appealing Salish Dining Room — an intimate space, which, unfortunately, has only a few tables that are privy to views of the falls. Amid this backdrop, dining patrons might select such appetizers as the smoked breast of squab with a cranberry bean stew and ginger plum compôte, the Napoleon of lobster and spinach with a light tarragon sauce, or the smoked tomato and bell pepper bisque. This could be followed by the rabbit with a porcini brioche, quail stuffed with smoked squab and a fig relish, or the pheasant stuffed with wild mushrooms. The Salish Lodge's weekend brunch has won many accolades over the years, and continues to draw guests and patrons from the Seattle area.

During the day, dogs and their human friends will find plenty to do here as well. They can walk the property, which consists of a path along the falls. There is also a one-mile trail that leads visitors and their dogs to the bottom of the falls. Those who have come to hike will enjoy the many opportunities available throughout the region. One of these begins in the Tiger Mountain State Forest, where miles of trails head off in all sorts of directions; several even climb to the top of Tiger Mountain. Mount Si is another good choice for hikers, as is the neighboring Little Si. One word of caution: Because these outdoor areas are all so close to the urban world, weekends usually draw large numbers of people. If planning a short trip, we suggest trying to visit on a Sunday and Monday, as the lodge will be quieter then, and so will the many attractions that draw visitors to the area. Some may wish to visit the St. Michelle and Columbia wineries or to peruse the many local nurseries. One of the best is Carnation Farm, with more than 1,200 acres of gardens to peruse. At the end of the day, guests can return to the lodge and totally relax in the roof-top hot tub set amid flowers and gardens.

# Cavanaugh's Inn at the Park

*West 303 North River Drive*
*Spokane, Washington 99201*
*(800) THE-INNS, (509) 326-8000, Fax (509) 325-7329*

*General Manager: Jim Burns*
*Rooms: 240 doubles, 24 suites*
*Rates: Doubles $94-142 (EP), Suites $185-500 (EP)*
*Payment: AE, DC, DSC, MC, and VISA*
*Children: Welcome (cribs, cots, and baby-sitters are available)*
*Dogs: Welcome; they must be leashed in the public areas*
*Open: All year*

In 1974, Spokane received a great deal of notoriety as the host of the World's Fair. The fair served as the impetus for revitalizing the town, creating a river front park and developing a number of fine hotels. Today, some consider it to be the most livable city in the Pacific Northwest. The 100-acre Riverfront Park is still one of the more popular gathering places, with its gardens, turn-of-the-century carousel, and paths that are great for walking dogs. At the edge of the park is Cavanaugh's Inn at the Park that seems well connected to this natural setting.

What new arrivals will discover about this large city inn is that, true to its name, it does have great views of the Riverfront Park and the Spokane River. Moreover, the design of the inn is such that the natural beauty outside has also been incorporated into its lobby. This light and airy atrium, which is filled with gardens of fresh flowers, decorative shrubs, and full-size trees, is drenched in sunlight. Within this cavernous space is the Atrium Café and Deli, where breakfast and lunch are served amid these semi-tropical surroundings. Besides the Atrium Café, there is the sophisticated Windows of the Seasons restaurant, offering equally lovely views of the park and river. The twinkling lights of the chandeliers in here reflect off the highly polished marble and lustrous wood accents, making this a fine place for an intimate dinner. The menu is Continental, with entrées that include a mesquite-grilled salmon, coquilles St. Jacques, crab-and-shrimp veal roulade, Cajun blackened New York sirloin, and the pistachio stuffed pheasant breast.

Accommodations at the Inn on the Park are fairly standard hotel rooms, utilizing earth tone color schemes and contemporary furnishings. The standard amenities are also present, including a television, telephone, individual heating and air-conditioning, and balconies overlooking the swimming pool and river area. A relatively new wing, which is geared primarily for business travelers, offers a higher level of luxury than most of the other chambers. The two- to four-bedroom suites, at the upper end of the price scale, often include such features as fireplaces, whirlpools, wet bars, and access to the rooftop pool and decks.

There are numerous recreational diversions at the Inn at the Park. Many will enjoy the fitness center, with its exercise room, whirlpool, sauna, and lap pool. There is also an indoor and outdoor swimming pool (or "lagoon"). The latter is built to resemble a grotto, with boulders stacked to support a water slide and form a waterfall. A nearby footbridge brings guests over to the Riverside Park, where there is a children's petting zoo, miniature golf, and the opera house (offering a number of children's programs during the year). Bowser would probably be a little more intrigued with the Riverside State Park, which boasts over 7,000 acres for exploration. The Centennial Trail also offers miles of trails, where visitors can even view petroglyphs along the river. The Dishman Hills Natural area is a preserve in Spokane Valley, which also has an intriguing trail network to explore. Outside of Spokane, there are two wilderness areas known as Goose Butte and the Fishtrap Lake area — both are good choices for day trips with dogs.

Spokane is a great destination for people and their dogs, because there are an abundance of outdoor diversions. This is not the sort of city where it is difficult to find green space; it seems to be everywhere — a fact appreciated by both dogs and their friends.

# Circle H Holiday Ranch

*810 Watt Canyon Road*
*Thorp, Washington 98946*
*(509) 964-2000*

**Hosts:** *Betsy and Jamie Ogden*
**Rooms:** *5 cabins*
**Rates:** *$65-75/person, summer (MAP); $110/cabin, winter (B&B);*
*Children under 2 are free, ages 3-12 are $30-35 (MAP)*
**Payment:** *MC and VISA*
**Children:** *Welcome (baby-sitters are available)*
**Dogs:** *Welcome*
**Open:** *All year*

If the mention of Washington state conjures up only images of pine-studded, snow-capped mountains, deep blue waters surrounding lush islands, and plenty of rainfall, then we recommend venturing east over the Cascades into central Washington. Here, vivid blue skies, wide open spaces, and drier terrain predominate. A pleasant one-and-a-half-hour drive from Seattle leads visitors to the foothill ranch lands, where white fences and horses are more abundant than people. The Circle H Holiday Ranch is nestled into these foothills, overlooking the Kittitas Valley. A short jog off the highway and up a country road leads visitors to the Circle H. Our arrival was announced by the Ogdens' two friendly dogs, who reacquainted us with the place. The ranch itself is low-key and intimate, although the area around it is expansive — some 100,000 acres of the LT Murray Wildlife Recreation Area.

The ranch's busiest season is from Memorial Day through Labor Day, when extended families and their canine companions are in abundance. No wonder they like it — they get their own cabin, fabulous views, and a true taste of ranch living. While many choose this spot so they can spend their time riding, there are all sorts of other recreational outlets. The informal children's play area, along with horseshoes and tether ball, is always a popular diversion with the younger set. Hot summer days are usually spent near the tree-lined swimming pond. But it is the stables and lovable farm animals that are still the perennial favorites. Children often rise early to go off and help the ranch hands feed the horses. There are also ducks, goats, sheep, llamas, and a pig — a menagerie that reminded us of the cast of creatures from *Charlotte's Web*. A "baby-sitting" horse is gentle enough for the little ones to ride, or kids can create their own amusement by jumping in a haystack or two. Our only word of warning is to be sure that visiting dogs are kept under close supervision when they're busy checking out the barn animals, especially the ducks. This is about the only restriction we can think of, as for the most part, dogs have seemingly endless amounts of terrain to explore.

Besides bringing their own dog, many guests also BYOH (horse). The Ogdens have facilities to accommodate horses, and for a small fee, they also provide the feed and hay. Guests may also enjoy either a guided or unguided trail ride. The saddlebag lunch should keep most people happily sated until their return, when another ample repast awaits. The food is varied, with hearty steaks and barbecued chicken topping off the list of the most popular dishes, while hamburgers and hot dogs are two of the perennial favorites for the kids. The vegetables are simply prepared, but fresh — as is the bread. Guests might find an occasional casserole or lasagna slipping onto the menu as well. Kids of all ages will want to save room for dessert, which includes freshly-baked fruit pies or strawberry shortcake.

After dinner during the high season, there are sometimes square dances, campfires, or hayrides. During quieter times of year, guests might gravitate to the ranch house to watch a movie on the wide screen television before heading back to the cabin for the night. We prefer a trip to the sauna to work out any muscle strains from the day, then heading back to the cabin for some much-deserved sleep. A short walk from the ranch house leads to the cabins. These "rustic antique-filled cabin suites" originally housed the ranch hands, but are nicely refurbished with Betsy's collection of western memorabilia.

We liked the Lone Ranger and Tonto cabins, connected by a door that allows them to become one big suite. The bleached knotty pine walls, slatted ceilings, and painted floors provide the framework for an eclectic assortment of furnishings. Accents are bright red, whether in the curtains at the windows, the colorful carpets covering the floors, or the thickly woven wool blankets topping the bedsteads. After a day on the trails, the wonderful beds built with substantial logs and branches are a welcome sight. Small shelves placed over the windows hold western memorabilia, such as miniature totem poles and pictures of high mountain lakes set in rustic wood frames. The kitchen, complete with a microwave and a refrigerator, has a day bed set alongside it that gives guests additional room to spread out. We thought that hanging wooden fruit crates along the walls was a clever way to store china and glassware.

Another popular room combination is Dale Evans and Roy Rogers. Roy Rogers faces down the valley and has unobstructed views through the small paned windows. Guests who are looking for a good deal of privacy might consider staying in Gene Autry. Here, the sitting room is enhanced by a freestanding fireplace. The master bedroom has a colorful quilt on the bed, and there is a smaller room toward the rear fashioned with a day bed. This boasts one of the larger kitchens. Few people do much cooking in-season, though, as breakfast is delivered to each cabin the night before and only needs heating in the morning. Although Gene Autry is slightly more contemporary than the rest of the cabins, all are, thankfully, without modern distractions, such as televisions or telephones.

Few guests and their dogs find a need to leave the ranch or its immediate environs, as there are great hiking opportunities in the L.T. Murray Wildlife Recreation Area. A short drive, though, just past the town of Cle Elum, leads to two good hiking trails that allow dogs. The first is the West Fork of the Teanaway River, which is reached off Route 903. Hikers and their dogs will discover a trail lined with ample river crossings and plenty of open space for enjoying the scenic vistas. The second option is the Yellow Hill/ Elbow Peak trail, located near the West Fork of the Teanaway River trailhead. Besides the lovely views of the Teanaway Valley, hikers will also find magnificent panoramas of Mount Rainier and its majestic neighbors.

# Mio Amore Pensione

*P.O. Box 208*
*Trout Lake, Washington 98650*
*(509) 395-2264*

*Hosts: Jill and Tom Westbrook*
*Rooms: 3 doubles, 1 suite, 1 cottage*
*Rates: Doubles $80-95 (B&B), Suite $135 (B&B),*
*Cottage $60-100 (B&B)*
*Payment: MC and VISA*
*Children: Over 15 years of age are welcome*
*Dogs: Small to medium dogs welcome with approval in the Vesta*
*Room; must be leashed when on the property*
*Open: All year, except the month of November*

The tiny hamlet of Trout Lake lies at the base of Mount Adams amid farmlands and rolling hills. It takes a while to get here, as visitors must follow 23 miles of wending mountain roads that begin at the Columbia River. The scenery is beautiful, though, and worth the extra effort. Mio Amore Pensione rests just outside of Trout Lake on six forested acres. The highlight is a charming, two-story clapboard Victorian, built in 1904, which contains a few guest rooms and, more importantly, a wonderful Italian restaurant. From the moment guests enter they will find that the B&B exudes a strong European flavor — a flavor that especially appeals to Tom, who spent five happy years in Italy.

Many residents and first-time guests frequent the Mio Amore Pensione primarily for the food; to these folks, the guest rooms are considered almost secondary. The evening affair begins in the comfortable living room, where a collection of delicious *hors d'oeuvres* are presented to awaiting dinner guests. A crackling fire and classical music set the mood for the meal that follows. Out of a dozen or so entrée selections, just one is prepared each night. The entrée is chosen by the first person to make a reservation for that particular evening. Some of the more popular dishes include shrimp sautéed in olive oil, garlic, butter and flamed in orange brandy; grilled lobster tail with herb butter; filet mignon in a cognac peppercorn sauce; or the chicken breast prepared with garlic, basil, vermouth, white wine and lemon. An appetizer, sorbet, and a dessert are also included in the fixed-price meal.

After dinner, some guests like to settle in before the fireplace, while others prefer to venture outdoors for a nice walk with Bowser before everyone retires for the evening. Guests with dogs are asked to stay in the most historic house on the property — a small, stone ice house built in 1894. This rustic building has been lovingly named the Vesta Room, or, translated, Goddess of the Home. This inviting stone and mustard-colored clapboard abode is set off to the right of the main house, a stone's throw from the Trout Lake creek. A rack of antlers is fashioned above the front door. As guests step inside, they will emerge into the cozy, first-floor sitting area. A pair of single beds are found to the rear of this chamber, while a log ladder leads up to the loft, which is bedecked with a double bed covered with a colorful, handmade quilt. We think the mirror, set into an old ox yolk, is an especially creative touch. Guests can open the small window in the loft; the refreshing breezes and melodious sounds emanating from the creek will set a peaceful tone for a restful night's sleep. While there is no running water in the cottage, guests may use the facilities in the main house. Quite frankly, we found the setting to be so charming and invitingly unique, the lack of running water really did not matter to us at all.

In the morning, guests dine on an ample breakfast of fresh fruit, juice, and coffee or tea, along with a variety of homemade muffins, cakes, tortes, and breads. Afterwards, we suggest that guests ask the Westbrooks to pack them a picnic lunch so they can head out for a full day of adventures with Bowser. This area offers an array of fishing, hiking, and rafting opportunities. The rafting options range from Nature Floats and three-hour, white-water rafting excursions to the more adventuresome white-water jet boat trips. People who love to hike, though, will find a virtually endless number of trails to explore with a dog throughout the Gifford Pinchot National Forest. For pure, natural beauty and a nice hike, guests should consider climbing the Sleeping Beauty Peak trail. Those who want to stay closer to home should think about day hikes up the Snipes Mountain trail, which wends along Gotchen Creek and through old lava fields; the Buck Creek trail, which parallels the White Salmon River; or the Cold Springs trail, which offers incredible views of Mount Adams. For more details, visitors can check with the Mount Adams Ranger Station in Trout Lake. Any of these adventures will certainly help guests work up an appetite; no doubt they will want to return to Mio Amore Pensione in the evening to sample all the delectable edibles that Tom and Jill have created during the day for them.

---

# Inn of the White Salmon

*P.O. Box 1549*
*172 West Jewett*
*White Salmon, Washington  98672*
*(800) 972-5226, (509) 493-2335*

*Innkeepers: Janet and Roger Holen*
*Rooms: 13 doubles, 3 suites*
*Rates: Doubles $89 (B&B), Suites $99-115 (B&B),*
*Payment: AE, DSC, DC, MC, and VISA*
*Children: Welcome*
*Dogs: Welcome in some rooms*
*Open: All year*

While Hood River, Oregon and its famous Columbia Gorge still draw plenty of sightseers and sail boarders, just across the river, its sister community of White Salmon does not enjoy the same notoriety. Sure, when the winds begin to blow, both sides of the river become launching points for sailboarders, who view this as one of the few nearly perfect Windsurfing spots in the United States. But when these winds dissipate, life becomes quiet here, more reminiscent of the days when the timber industry, not tourism, reigned.

White Salmon may not be as easily accessible as Hood River, but it exudes almost as much character. To get to White Salmon, visitors must pay a toll in Hood River and cross a narrow metal bridge that leads over to the hamlet of Bingen. There isn't much reason to stop in Bingen, and most just continue up the hill a mile or so to the village of White Salmon. Here, the storefronts are reminiscent of something out of the Swiss Alps. Though the plain brick facade of the inn (which dates back to 1937) is not very alluring, guests will be pleasantly pleased with what they find inside.

We stepped into the foyer and were greeted with the most divine smells emanating from somewhere deep in the inn. As if to tempt us, a glass jar filled with freshly baked peanut butter cookies beckoned interested raiders. Meandering further into the inn, we expected the decor to resemble the rather bland exterior. Instead, we discovered a strong Victorian theme predominating, with a few antiques, marble-topped tables, and historic pictures lining the long, straight hallways. At the end of one hall, we found a charming parlor, where classical music was playing. This is a large space, dominated by an antique sideboard set in the midst of comfortable couches, armchairs, and still more Victorian antiques. There is a television in here, but guests are more likely to be reading from the inn's assortment of magazines and books, or playing one of the many board games. Although the views are not of the gorge, they are nonetheless endearing, with expanses of glass revealing a neatly planted hillside of grass and flowers. Guests step out through a pair of glass doors to find the ever popular hot tub. When not relaxing in these common areas, most head up to their comfortable bedrooms.

Once again, we were delightfully surprised. These spaces may not have intriguing nooks and crannies, but they more than make up for this with high ceilings and a scattering of antiques. Floral comforters cover the brass or carved wood, framed beds. The muted green and rose tones reflect the Victorian period, with old-fashioned lamps with fringed shades casting a subdued light. Area rugs dampen footsteps across the hardwood floors, and amenities include televisions, air conditioning, and private bathrooms. The corner rooms are some of the most popular chambers, as they offer a few more windows and a little additional space. After a good night's sleep, guests awaken to an aroma of baked breakfast breads that is so strong it permeates every corner of the inn.

Following one's nose is the easiest way to find the breakfast room. Guests dine at small tables covered with lovely white lace overlays and are served on old-fashioned china that reminded us of our trips to Germany's small guest houses. The food that follows is also more reminiscent of Europe than America, especially the pastries that almost defy description. Guests may start with a small bowl of fresh fruit and, perhaps, a French tart, chocolate raspberry cheesecake, baklava, or cinnamon roll. (This is only a sampling of the 20 or more pastries available each day.) The main courses are equally international, and include such options as a frittata, quiche, chile relleno, or Hungarian flauf. (Flauf consists of eggs baked with ham, Swiss cheese, scallions, and caraway.)

There are no excuses not to get a little exercise after a breakfast of this magnitude. It is almost imperative to walk, hike, stroll — anything to get the legs moving before giving in to the strong urge to retreat back to bed for a midmorning nap. Fortunately, there are plenty of things to do here, without leaving this side of the river. As one might imagine, our curiosity was piqued when we learned about the nearby Dog Mountain, just west of the Bingen. Here, there is a nice hike that begins at the Gorge and heads up to the summit, through mountain meadows and forests. Those who want to venture further north toward Trout Lake can have their pick of day hikes. Cool mornings are an ideal time to climb Little Huckleberry Mountain, where fabulous views can be enjoyed from the summit. Of course, visitors and their dogs can also limit themselves to leisurely walks around White Salmon. Many of the steep hills here provide a good workout — as much as some may want when on vacation.

# British Columbia

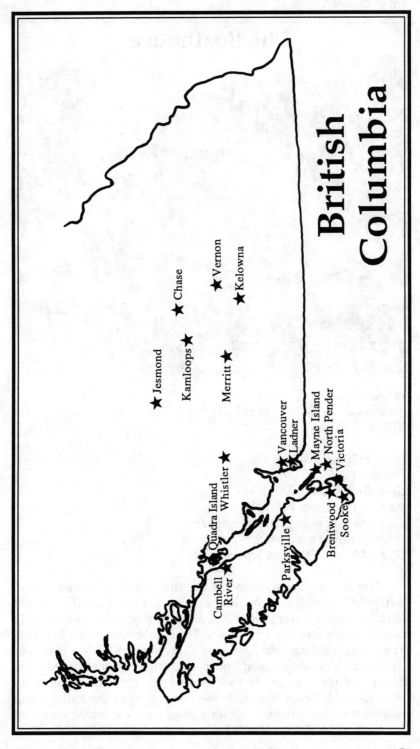

British Columbia

Jesmond

Kamloops

Chase

Merritt

Vernon

Kelowna

Vancouver
Ladner

Mayne Island
North Pender
Victoria

Whistler

Brentwood
Sooke

Quadra Island

Parksville

Cambell
River

# The Boathouse

*746 Sea Drive*
*Brentwood Bay, B.C., Canada V8M 1B1*
*(604) 652-9370*

**Hosts:** *Harvey and Jean Merritt*
**Rooms:** *1 cottage*
**Canadian Rates:** *$120 (B&B)*
**Payment:** *MC and VISA*
**Children:** *Not appropriate for children*
**Dogs:** *Welcome with notice*
**Open:** *March 15 through September 30*

Brentwood Bay is famous for the Butchart Gardens and Butterfly World. While memories of flowers and butterflies might fade, guests' impressions of The Boathouse will undoubtedly remain firmly fixed in their minds. The Boathouse was built in 1927 as a summer cottage, but for the past eleven years the Merritts have used it as a waterside Bed and Breakfast. The sense of isolation here is complete, as guests walk down a steep hillside of stairs and pass through dense woods before emerging at the cottage and bathhouse. The cottage is set on pilings over the water, and once guests step inside, they begin to lose all sense of the land, focusing instead on the surrounding water and wildlife that thrives here.

We really liked the character of this place, with its red fir floors and white-washed board walls. Its fresh crisp feeling is accentuated by the sheer white tab curtains and the robin-egg blue cabinetry. Though this is only a one-room cottage, it actually feels quite spacious. Neatly displayed on the open shelves are wine glasses, china, and clay pots filled with coffee, sugar, etc. The cottage is also equipped with a toaster, tea kettle, coffee maker, and a barbecue. A refrigerator keeps things cool — especially the breakfasts, which are brought down the night before and placed in here so they will be ready for guests at whatever time they may decide to arise. After making a cup of coffee and spreading a little fresh blackberry jam on the homemade muffins, we were content to relax and enjoy the lovely vistas visible through the walls of windows. Freshly-squeezed orange juice and a fruit salad complete this repast, which may be taken at the small breakfast table set under a window or out on the porch.

If the day turns inclement, comfortable armchairs and a couch (which opens to a sofa bed) are just the place to play games, read a book, or stretch out for a nap. The adjacent bathhouse contains a private bathroom and shower. Even if the hour is late, guests often enjoy the short stroll to the bathhouse under moon and starlit skies. The early-morning hours are the best time to catch the harbor seals and otters playing on and around the rocks, or to watch the great blue herons and kingfishers swooping over the water in search of food. Bald eagles have also been spotted here. With the dock and a dinghy available for guests to use, it is fun to load up Bowser and head out for a little harbor tour, following it up with an exploration of the island across the way.

Many people like to row over to the world-famous Butchart Gardens (unfortunately, dogs are not permitted), thereby avoiding the usual traffic. Few can claim to arrive here by water, but guests staying at the Boathouse will have no problem doing so. These gardens lie on the Tod Inlet on what was formerly an old limestone quarry. The Butcharts built their home here at the turn of the century, and imported many of the exotic plants visitors will find here today. The gardens are spectacular, and there are always special programs, seminars, and other interesting horticultural events taking place here. In the summer months, Butchart Gardens puts on a fireworks' display which is visible from the Boathouse. Another favorite destination, especially for those looking for a peaceful picnic site, is the lovely white shell beach, situated just a little further down Tod Inlet.

The streets near the B&B are great for walking and are fairly quiet, as this is mostly a residential area. People love it here, and wax poetic about the serenity and calm that permeate the place. Many plan their trip around Butchart Gardens, but as the time passes, they are content to spend their vacation inside the cottage and out exploring the many inlets and eddies throughout the area. This is the place where, as Ralph Waldo Emerson put it, "A little warmth, a little food, and an immense quiet" go a long way.

---

# Strathcona Park Lodge

*P.O. Box 2160*
*Campbell River, B.C. Canada  V9W 5C9*
*(604) 286-8206 or 3122, Fax (604) 286-6010*

*Owners: The Boulding Family*
*Rooms: 15 lodge rooms, 14 cabins, Seale House (sleeps 20),*
*        College Building (sleeps 35)*
*Canadian Rates: Lodge $60-135 (EP), Cabins $80-135 (EP),*
*        Seale House $495 (EP), College Building $650 (EP)*
*Payment: MC and VISA*
*Children: Welcome*
*Dogs: Welcome in the cabins only*
*Open: All year*

The Strathcona Park Lodge is a privately owned lodge set within British Columbia's oldest park, Strathcona Provincial Park. This is a spectacular region, which extends from the ocean up to majestic mountain peaks that stand over 6,000 feet. It also contains one of the world's highest waterfalls — the Della Falls — which cascades through the forest in three separate tiers. Hikers will relish the trails that wend through either ancient forests of Douglas fir and western red cedar, or through alpine meadows brimming with delicate flora and fauna. It is in this park, nestled against the shores of Campbell Lake, that the Boulding Family has operated their lodge for the last 36 years.

This place is far more than a simple mountain retreat; it is also renowned as an outdoor education center. Some visitors use the lodge as a base camp for exploring the wilderness on their own, or they come to participate in one of the 20 wilderness out-trips available through the center. During the quieter spring and fall months, most people staying here take part in the supervised programs, which could include a family adventure week, an Elderhostel, or one of the leadership courses — known as W.Y.L.D.

(Wilderness Youth Leadership Development) or C.O.L.T. (Canadian Outdoor Leadership Training Center). During the summer months, guests usually take advantage of the experienced guides, who organize age-appropriate outdoor activities. Even those who don't take part in these formal programs will be amazed by the list of activities and diversions they can choose from while staying at the lodge. Some of the more popular options include hiking with a naturalist, participating in a ropes challenge course, or going rock climbing, canoeing, or sailing.

This place draws all types of visitors, ranging from the very young to the very old — all of whom have come to gain a better appreciation of the area's many natural wonders. It may seem that this is only a place for the high-energy type, but an equal share of the guests also come here for the relaxed mood and the lakefront lodgings. The accommodations range from log and timber chalets to lakefront housekeeping cabins. The cabins are set on a hill overlooking the lake, and all of them welcome dogs. Those looking for direct lakefront access should request the ivy-covered Baikei Cabin, which overlooks a sandy peninsula and is situated next to one of the paddling and swimming areas. Some want not only to be located near the water's edge, but also to have a little more privacy. These guests should inquire about Cabins 22-24, as they are situated in the woods on the opposite end of the property. Others, who like to be centrally located, will discover that Cabins 1-3 are ideal for their needs — close to both the Waterfront Center and a paddling pool.

Some of the smaller cabins are tucked into the woods near rock walls lined with wildflowers; others are set alongside orchards. For a more bucolic setting, some guests choose either Whiskey Jack or the two-story Nancy's cabin. Whichever accommodations visitors select, the overall ambiance is just one step above camping. The cabins have natural board walls, twin bedsteads, and sometimes a sleeping loft. Some of these lodgings are fashioned with minimally-appointed kitchens; we would recommend stocking up, as there isn't a store for miles. While the cabins may not appeal to those who are looking for a frilly inn or a charming B&B, they will offer just the right ambiance for guests who are interested in low-key, budget lodgings amid picturesque surroundings.

All three meals are served up in the main dining room, in a building that rests at the top of the hill. Hearty, home-cooked foods are served buffet-style, in a manner that is reminiscent of being at camp. The entrées include options such as the native-style barbecued salmon, roast chicken, roast beef, ham, and barbecued spare ribs. Diners may also select from side dishes such as potatoes, lasagna, spaghetti, or rice; a wide variety of salads; and trays brimming with an assortment of cheeses, vegetables, and fruit. In the summer months, much of the produce and fruit is picked right from the gardens and orchards on the property. Best of all are the extensive dessert options, which include such mainstays as carrot cake, cheese cake, an array of berry pies, and an assortment of cookies and pastries.

The Strathcona Park Lodge is as appealing for dogs as it is for people. All the trails in Strathcona Park are open to dogs. For ease of access, we recommend trying out those surrounding the lodge first. These range from old logging roads to trails wending along bluffs. From the lodge, hikers and their dogs can follow the Raven Trail — and get a closer look at the guests who are testing their ropes skills over on the bluffs. Another option is the Deer Trail, which leads to a scenic lookout over Campbell Lake. One other popular lakeside trail is the Eagle Point Trail, which parallels the water's edge. All of these nearby trails make for great introductory hikes and will prepare dogs and their human friends for more strenuous outings throughout the rest of the Strathcona Park.

---

# Quaaout Lodge

*P.O. Box 1215*
*Chase, B.C., Canada  V0E 1M0*
*(800) 663-4303, (604) 679-3090, Fax (604) 679-3039*

*General Manager: Brian Turnbull*
*Rooms: 68 doubles, 4 suites*
*Canadian Rates: Doubles $79-103 (EP), Suites $135 (EP)*
*Payment: AE, DSC, MC, and VISA*
*Children: Welcome; children under 16 are free of charge*
*Dogs: Welcome with a $5 fee*
*Open: All year*

A Kekuli is the winter shelter for the Shuswap Indians. Although rarely used anymore, these round dwellings were constructed with a wood shell that was covered with cedar mats and then packed with soil for insulation. An opening at the top of the shell served two purposes — it allowed the smoke from the cook fire to escape, and also provided an additional entrance and egress. Another opening at ground level was typically used as an escape tunnel. Woven mats were used for just about everything, although the tribespeople did sleep on mattresses made of animal skins stuffed with cedar frawns, feathers, or bunches of grass. The contemporary Quaaout Lodge's gently flowing lines are similar to those of a huge Kekuli. Although guests won't be sleeping on animal skin furs or cooking over a fire, they will be able to appreciate the history and beauty of this space. We did not enter this Kekuli from the roof, but through pairs of massive wooden doors. The first pair of doors was fashioned with a pair of hand-carved bear head handles, while the second set was outfitted with carved wolf head handles. This Kekuli's domed ceiling and central fireplace are authentic, but instead of mud-matted walls, guests will find plate glass windows revealing views of the woods and beyond to Little Lake Shuswap. An extension of the main Kekuli forms a glassed-in dining room, while another wing contains the guest bedrooms.

As we looked around, we noticed some guests were lounging about and enjoying hot chocolate before the fire, while others were out walking along the lake. Off to the edge of the property, there are a few teepees that guests may reserve in the summer months. Camping in teepees is a novel experience that our kids would surely love, but we rather preferred the bedrooms on this visit. The bedroom wing's exterior design resembles an accordion of sorts. The unusual jagged pattern allows each of the guest rooms to have a nice view of the water. The decor consists of brightly-colored Shuswap patterns found on the quilted spreads and at curtains framing the windows. Most of the spaces have just enough room for the bedsteads, a small table with two chairs, and a long bureau with a television, a coffee maker, and some other goodies. Bathrooms are modern, tiled, and well appointed. The suites offer the best views and the most amenities. These chambers are exceptionally large and have king beds set in front of fireplaces and near Jacuzzi tubs. Light the candles, enjoy a soak, and then wrap up in a terry robe afterwards.

The food at the lodge's restaurant is excellent, and should appeal to most guests. Against the backdrop of the lake, patrons can peruse this seasonally changing menu. Some might opt to start with pasta tossed in a basil cream sauce; the rabbit and chicken ragoût with fiddlehead greens; or the platter of smoked and poached local fish. Entrées include honey glazed baby back ribs; pork loin with a cranberry honey jus; and an herb crusted salmon. Apple crisp, berry bannock with maple cream, and a chocolate mousse terrine served with a berry coulis are several of the dessert options.

Bowser will love it at the Quaaout Lodge. The property has jogging and hiking trails, as well as plenty of grass. There is a sandy beach (almost a half-mile long) that children will love, along with a good-sized playground. We especially like the see-saw of carefully balanced logs. Horseshoes, volleyballs, and Frisbees can be secured from the front desk. There is an indoor exercise room; however, during the summer months most of the exercise equipment is brought out to an open-air gazebo overlooking the lake. After an invigorating workout, many enjoy relaxing in the sauna or hot tub, or cooling off in the attractive indoor pool. The staff can advise on nearby cross-country and downhill skiing options, or arrange for canoe, sailboat, or houseboat rentals. Many come here in October to observe the famous sockeye salmon run in the nearby Adams River. People can walk along platforms and easily observe this impressive natural phenomenon. One of the best viewing points, according to the staff at the lodge, is from the Roderick Haig-Brown Provincial Park. When the salmon are not running, there are over 2,500 acres of trails for hiking with a dog. Another lake (slightly more isolated than Little Lake Shuswap) is Adams Lake, where leashed dogs are welcome.

# Circle H Mountain Lodge

*Summer: P.O. Box 7*
*Jesmond, Clinton, B.C., Canada   V0K 1K0*
*Telephone/Fax (604) 459-2565*
*Winter: 3086 Babich Street*
*Abbotsford, B.C., Canada   V2S 5H7*
*Telephone/Fax (604) 850-1873*

*Owners: Mitch, Daphne, Kerry, and Trevor Henselwood*
*Rooms: 5 doubles, 4 cabins*
*Canadian Rates: Daily — Adults $106 (AP), Children $82 (AP),*
*                  Weekly — Adults $640 (AP), Children $497 (AP),*
*                  Children under 6 years of age are free of charge*
*Payment: Personal checks*
*Children: Most appropriate for children 6 years of age and older*
*          (baby-sitting is available)*
*Dogs: Welcome in the cabins*
*Open: May through October*

If horses, mountains, and wild open spaces spur your imagination, then head north to British Columbia's Cariboo region, where the Fraser River still steadily carves out portions of this magnificent terrain. Traveling along these isolated back roads, it doesn't take much to imagine what life here must have been like during the 1850s — a time when gold drew prospectors to this region. Soon after the discovery of gold, a north/south stagecoach route was established that started in Lilloet (at Mile 0) and worked its way north to Cariboo. Along the way, roadhouses were built to offer food, drink, and overnight accommodations to travelers. At the time, the roadhouses were commonly referred to by the mile marker they were located nearest to along the route. Today, visitors will still run across hamlets known simply as 70, 100, and 108 Mile Houses. Clinton was the site of one such "mile house," and still contains many of the historic buildings from the turn of the century.

Unlike the desert climate further south, the area around Clinton and Jesmond is verdant and dotted with trees, ponds, and lakes. Settlers have built their ranches here, erected miles of fences, and set their horses out to graze amid the expansive pastures. Clinton is the last real town travelers come to before making the final 25-mile push up a dirt road leading to Jesmond. The Henselwoods warn first-time visitors to trust their directions, because usually, just when new arrivals think they are hopelessly lost, they come upon the Circle H Mountain Lodge. The effort is well worth it.

The lodge is set in a high valley surrounded by beautiful limestone mountains, and the even more spectacular Mount Bowman. The lodge is nestled in the midst of it all, giving guests a sense of isolation that isn't easy to find these days. The friendly nature of the Henselwoods and casual feeling of the ranch have long drawn guests to the Circle H Mountain Lodge. Over 160 acres of green meadows, stands of mixed wood trees, and a creek surround the ranch, which consists of the old-fashioned log lodge, a guest wing, and four sleeping cabins. The entire ranch can accommodate only 16 guests at a time. Five bedrooms lie in the guest wing, which is fashioned with two shared bathrooms and a shower room. The bathroom facilities are also used by those staying in the rustic log cabins. Guests with dogs will reside in the cabins, which can accommodate from two to four people and are a perfectly pleasant place to bed down for the night.

Many come here to ride. The Henselwoods once leased their horses; however, they are now raising their own herd. Over the last year, they purchased enough horses to accommodate all of their guests. These horses, along with some newborn colts, are now theirs to train and care for year round. Two rides are offered each day — either a morning and an afternoon ride or a morning ride with a long midday break before the early-evening ride. Twice a week guests can also go out on the full-day ride, which consists of traversing the high country meadows and passing through the deep cool forests. The guides leading these rides bring people into some beautiful back country, where wild horses still run and exotic wildflowers grow in abundance. When not riding, some take their dogs and head off on a fishing expedition or a leisurely canoe ride on Kelly Lake. Hiking through this country with a dog is just as appealing as horseback riding. Along the way the dogs might track down upland birds, deer, or moose, while their human friends search for wild strawberries, onions, and rose hips. As the day winds to a close, most look forward to their return to the ranch, perhaps to go for a swim in the pool or relax in the sauna before enjoying a home-cooked meal around the wood stove.

The ranch is situated at an altitude of over 5,000 feet, and something about the elevation and fresh air causes appetites to spiral out of control. (The fabulous food might also have something to do with it.) Daphne is in charge of these feasts, which are complemented with freshly-baked breads. All of the food is cooked in, or on, a huge wood stove. Guests settle down at the long dining room table, which is covered with an oil-skin cloth and lined with pitchers of wildflowers. Platters of cheese and bread, bowls filled with fresh fruit, and salads are all served family style. If a guest catches some trout, Daphne will prepare them for dinner. Daphne is British, and will sometimes present an old-fashioned English meal of roast beef, Yorkshire pudding, potatoes with mushroom gravy, and a strawberry trifle. Should guests like an alcoholic libation to accompany their dinner, they need to bring their own. The hosts also recommend bringing a few extra goodies for children, to satisfy any between-meal cravings.

After dinner, most like to hang out on the covered porch that runs the length of the lodge. This is the quiet time of the evening when the adults put up their boots, the children play, and Bowser snoozes — just another great day at the Circle H Mountain Lodge.

# Lac Le Jeune Resort
# Woody Life Village

*650 Victoria Street*
*Kamloops, B.C., Canada V2C 2B4*
*(800) 561-5253, (604) 372-2722, Fax (604) 374-9997*

*Owner:* Derick McDonald
*Rooms:* Lac Le Jeune — 6 cabins, Woody Life — 30 cabins
*Canadian Rates:* Lac Le Jeune — $77-97 (EP),
　　　　　　　　　Woody Life — $85-115 (EP)
*Payment:* AE, DC, MC, and VISA
*Children:* Welcome
*Dogs:* Welcome in the cabins
*Open:* April - October

Fish Lake is not exactly a name that inspires people to visit — unless, of course, they are avid fishermen. The name Lac Le Jeune, on the other hand, is far more intriguing. However, it still is not a natural destination for most people, unless they happen to be headed between Calgary and Vancouver via tour bus. We discovered this little known fact on the day we visited, as this tiny resort frequently books tour groups. When we arrived, though, it was absolutely deserted. This is the way it is most of the time, as the buses (usually two) generally arrive late in the day and depart early the next morning. This allows those who book independently of the tours to have the entire place to themselves for most of the day.

There are two distinct parts to the resort. Lac Le Jeune Resort has been around for more than 20 years. Just down the road lies its sister resort, the Woody Life, built in 1990. Given a choice, we prefer the old-fashioned look and feel of Lac Le Jeune, and especially its lovely lakeside setting. The main lodge and cabins are built of dark timbers, but inside they are a pleasing combination of contemporary decor and traditional design. The cabins are set beyond the lodge, on a grassy knoll above the lake. We were pleasantly surprised by the cabins' interiors, which are fashioned with natural wood walls, contemporary furniture, and pretty peach and green floral fabrics. The dark green accents are carried through to the kitchenette's countertops as well. Guests have a small living room with a fireplace, and generally one or two bedrooms. Sofas and rocking chairs are comfortable places for passing the time inside. Or guests can step outside to the small porch. The smell of the surrounding woods and views of the lake are most invigorating.

Guests are free to cook in their cabin kitchens, or they may dine in either one of the resort's restaurants. Both dining rooms offer good home cooking, topped off by a variety of fresh trout dishes. We prefer the intimate feeling at the Lac Le Jeune Resort's restaurant, as much for the big, old-fashioned stone fireplace as for the views of the lake through the plate glass windows. While the restaurant does not serve to the general public, the staff appreciates knowing ahead of time if cabin guests are planning on dining with them that evening.

Just down the road is the Woody Life Village, with its huge log chalets topped by light green-colored roofs. These chalets generally contain two sets of housekeeping accommodations, fashioned with queen beds, a living room space, modern kitchens, and private bathrooms. The decor is attractive, but simple, and the units are spotless. Although they are situated near the water, they don't have the same lake views as the cabins back at Lac Le Jeune. This is, however, an ideal spot for families who want to be close to the indoor swimming pool complex, which comes complete with a slide, a whirlpool, exercise and weight rooms, and saunas. There is even a fitness trail that wends through the property, for those who are looking for a fun outing that includes their canine cohort. Guests staying at the Woody Life Village gather for meals in the main lodge, which is a larger version of the housekeeping chalets. The honey-colored log walls are exposed; in one corner is a stone fireplace. Although the place can get busy, the small, naturally finished oak tables surrounded by Windsor chairs give patrons a sense of intimacy. While this section of the resort is new, well established beds of flowers and newly planted trees will soon lend a sense of timelessness to the grounds.

As we mentioned, the days around here are mostly quiet — and perfect for relaxing. Dogs love to be walked along the lake, and there are plenty of hiking trails criss-crossing the region. Guests may also wish to take a stroll across the street to the primitive log store, where dinghies and canoes are rented. Bowser may wish to accompany his human friends on an exploration of the lake. This is an ideal spot to test out fly fishing skills, and it is well known for its good-sized fish. Lac Le Jeune is part of a provincial park that is only 60 acres but offers plenty of diversions in this small space — including an archeological site.

# The Grand Okanagan

*1310 Water Street*
*Kelowna, B.C., Canada V1Y 9P3*
*(800) 465-4651, (604) 763-4500, Fax (604) 763-4565*

**General Manager:** *Frank Faigauf*
**Rooms:** *150 doubles, 25 suites, 30 homes*
**Canadian Rates:** *Doubles $115-220 (EP), Suites $189-230(EP),*
  *Homes $265-325(EP)*
**Payment:** *AE, DC, JCB, MC, and VISA*
**Children:** *Welcome (cribs, cots, and high chairs are available)*
**Dogs:** *Welcome*
**Open:** *All year*

An ancient legend still circulates along the shores of Okanagan Lake that a mythical monster, Ogopogo, lives somewhere in its depths. This whimsical sea serpent is depicted in a statue set along the lakefront in Kelowna. While the fables about Ogopogo date back centuries, The Grand Okanagan Resort does not.

This is a first-class resort, which combines a contemporary hotel with time-share vacation homes and condominiums to form an expansive enclave encompassing 25 acres of park land and beach. It is built in a Mediterranean style. (Although Kelowna is far from the sea, the area's temperate climate does lend itself to this form of architecture.) The designers kept the interior spaces light by incorporating two massive Palladian windows that mirror one another. We walked through one framing the hotel's main entrance, and after emerging into the cavernous tiled lobby, found another one overlooking the water side of the hotel. In the midst of the lobby is a massive statue of a black dolphin and its calf, which seem to be leaping from a huge fountain.

As we walked over to the main desk to inquire about the guest rooms, we stopped to greet a pair of terriers strolling with their owners. The main portion of the hotel is surrounded by three-story wings containing the more expansive two-bedroom suites. Most of the guest rooms in the adjacent buildings are preferable for those traveling with dogs, as they have easy outside access to the lakefront boardwalk. Unfortunately, many of these are also time-share units that can only be reserved 48-hours in advance. Anyone planning a last minute trip to Kelowna might want to check out this option.

All of the rooms are attractive, though, and are decorated in pale peach, ecru, and sea-foam green color schemes. Beds have thickly quilted floral spreads and dust ruffles that are coordinated with the full-length draperies and valances. Bleached woods in the contemporary furnishings lighten these spaces even more. Brass sconces and bedside table lamps provide crisp contrasts to the colorful paintings, potted plants, and decorative flower arrangements. The amenities are just what we would expect of a four-star hotel, with televisions concealed in small cabinets, direct-dial telephones, and modern bathrooms fashioned with an array of toiletries.

We especially liked the larger suites, as they offered a more varied list of amenities, and usually better water views. Some have tiled Jacuzzi tubs nestled into the corner of the rooms, fireplaces in separate living rooms, and even small kitchens. The two-bedroom suites are perfect for families traveling with a dog, as they are outfitted with a central living room, a kitchen, and a bedroom off to either side. All of these suites also have private patios or balconies. Those who do not require as much space, but enjoy many of the aforementioned luxuries may wish to inquire about the Grand Club rooms, where wet bars, bathrobes, newspapers, and a complimentary breakfast are *de rigeur*.

Water seems to be a reccurring theme at the Grand Okanagan, in evidence whether dining at Dolphins overlooking the lagoon, sitting in the lobby and listening to the water splash from the fountain, or relaxing in a guest room overlooking the lake or the swimming pool. The heated pool is very inviting, and is set in one of the hotel's courtyards overlooking the lake. Those who don't want to get their exercise by swimming laps can use the exercise room, equipped with free weights and an assortment of cardiovascular equipment, as well as baby-sitting services.

The hotel's intimate restaurant is Dolphins, where the views are as fine as the cuisine. Guests may wish to start with an appetizer of spicy prawns sautéed with tomatoes, lime, red chili, and garlic; oysters on the half shell; or the smoked yellowfin tuna. When we were there, entrées included the jasmine smoked duck breast with a mango purée; rack of lamb with garlic, rosemary, and Pommerey mustard; or the halibut poached in a Grand Marnier sauce. The Sunday brunch is as popular among guests as it is with locals. Children have their own mini-buffet table, while adults may sample from a lavish assortment of foods that include everything from a custom omelet station and a carving trolley to an extensive assortment of unique desserts. The stipend for young children is hard to beat — $1 for each year of the child's age.

While there is plenty of grass at the resort, the place most appropriate for walking dogs is along the boardwalk. Just next to the resort there is also an open, lawn that is great for exercising

Bowser. Guests and their canines can also walk into town along the water, and continue along the lake for miles. Unfortunately, the major waterfront park in town is off-limits to dogs, but there are plenty of other great walks and hikes to be enjoyed in the surrounding area. Wild Horse Canyon has a fun hike that can be reached by following Lake Shore Road 16 km to the south. A parking area is situated off to the right and the trail is just beyond it. The Crawford Hiking Trails, located off June Springs Road, are also quite popular. To reach them, travelers follow the Bellevue Creek Forest Service road. Parking is available above Bellevue Creek Canyon. Bear Creek Provincial Park also has plenty of hiking trails that allow dogs. One of the best is found by following Highway 97 south to Westside Road, then turning onto Beach Creek Road. A vacation to the Okanagan Valley is not complete without visiting the wineries or golfing at some of the 39 regional courses. Hot-air ballooning, float plane adventures, boating on the area's lakes, and even tours of the apple farms and North America's largest alpaca farm should also be on guests' short list of things to do.

---

# Idabel Lake Resort

*S. 13E, C.2, R.R. #5*
*Kelowna, B.C., Canada  V1X 4K4*
*(604) 868-2722*

*Owners: Vivien and Paul Burridge and Lesley and Doug Johnson*
*Rooms: 10 rooms, 6 cabins*
*Canadian Rates: $105-195 (EP), Cabins $120 (EP)*
*Payment: MC and VISA*
*Children: Welcome*
*Dogs: Welcome in the cottages with a small charge, but they must be*
*leashed when on the grounds*
*Open: All year*

The Idabel Lake Resort is not one of those resorts guests just stumble on; even with directions it is not easy to locate. However, once we arrived, we knew it had been worth every twist and turn on the logging roads that led us here. The little resort is not in Kelowna — it's actually 55 km up in the mountains, past the turnoff to the Big White Ski Resort. A two-lane highway took us most of the way, before we turned off onto the logging roads. These wide, dirt highways are the domain of the logging companies and their massive rumbling trucks. People unfamiliar with these types of roads need to keep only two things in mind — stay to the right, and pay attention. The trucks seem to appear out of nowhere and take up the majority of the road. They are in radio contact with each other, though, so once they spot a visiting vehicle, they will often relay information about its whereabouts to other truckers heading in that direction.

The Idabel Lake Resort is set in a small mountainous valley right on the edge of the lake. There are some houses around the lake, but guests of the resort generally have the lake to themselves. The mile-and-a-half-long Idabel Lake is unusual in that it is actually swimmable; most of the mountain lakes in this region contain leeches, making them less than desirable for humans or dogs. The resort is comprised of an old-fashioned main lodge, a few outbuildings, and the cabins. The main lodge is a rustic, dark wood edifice, with interiors naturally brightened by three walls of windows overlooking the water. As we climbed the stairs, we heard wind chimes blowing in the breeze. Sisters Vivien and Lesley have owned the resort with their husbands for the past six years. The sisters are from England, and have enchanting British accents. Best of all, they have brought an assortment of memorabilia from their homeland. Pictures of the English countryside and its cottages are displayed against one wall in the lodge, while the menu in their restaurant reflects some of Great Britain's more intriguing dishes.

The Idabel offers guests everything they could possibly desire in a tranquil mountain vacation. While some guests stay in the lodge rooms, we prefer the cabins that are nestled behind some boulders on a bluff overlooking the water. The unusual, rounded shape of the cabins' green roofs is modeled after the work of an architect by the name of Steiner, who designed his buildings to blend in with their natural surroundings. The interiors are far more common in appearance, with knotty pine walls, beamed ceilings, and an open floor plan that focuses on the lake views. These are minimally-furnished affairs, but relatively new; they were built less than ten years ago. The kitchens contain electric appliances and all the basics needed for preparing meals. A central living room is furnished with some chairs and a sofa bed, and upstairs is an open loft with two futon beds set upon platforms. It is also upstairs where guests can appreciate the rounded curves of the roof line. Navy blue floral cotton prints frame the windows and cover the futon cushions. Other than this decorative touch, the furnishings are fairly basic. What we, and most others, focus on are the nice views of the lake that are visible through a pair of picture windows and a Palladian window set above them.

While the cabins are a good place to gather at night, there is so much to do in the daytime that few spend much time indoors. The lake encompasses more than 10 acres, but guests tend to stay in the waters near the lodge. Here, they can swim from the 60-foot dock or take a dinghy out for some fishing. Children love this place, especially in the summer months, when they can play on the cleverly-designed adventure playgrounds or head out to the Jolly Roger pirate ship on the lake. The former consists of a small log cabin that serves as a playhouse, an 80-foot slide, and plenty of logs and things to climb upon. Mother Nature also supplies all sorts of big rocks — which make for equally fine climbing. More organized activities might include horseshoes, baseball, and volleyball.

The resort also has a reputation for its well-trained horses. The stables are within walking distance of the lodge. Guests can go out for an hour, for a dinner ride, or overnight adventure. Others may prefer to do their riding on mountain bikes — either their own or the resort's. There are miles of trails and roads throughout this region. Even in winter, the resort is a hub of activity, with a lighted skating rink on the lake, miles of cross-country ski trails, and guided snowmobile rides. Although dogs are required to be leashed on the property, they have unlimited trails to explore, a lake to swim in, and more walks along back country roads than they could ever take advantage of during their stay.

If the weather is not cooperating on a particular day, then some guests enjoy heading indoors to the game room where there are table tennis and video games. The pool table is another popular outlet and is found in the lounge near the small restaurant. While the cottages have cooking facilities, we rather like the atmosphere in the dining room, with its dried flowers, small cluster of tables, and fabulous lake views. The menu is a hearty one, topped by an English favorite — cottage pie (a British version of shepherds pie). Guests may also dine on steak and kidney pie with a hint of rosemary and thyme; a chicken and mushroom pie; or beef bourguignonne. The garlic mushroom fettucini, beef stroganoff, and the seafood linguine are also perennial favorites.

We were very pleased to discover the Idabel Lake Resort. It is a special kind of lodge that offers personalized attention, a variety of diversions, and loads of character. Guests who stay here once are likely to find it to be one of those places that will easily become an annual tradition.

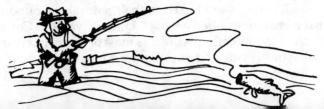

# River Run Cottages

*4551 River Road West*
*Ladner, B.C., Canada  V4K 1R9*
*(604) 946-7778, Fax (604) 940-1970*

**Hosts:** *Bill and Janice Harkley,* **Innkeeper:** *Karen Bond*
**Rooms:** *4 cottages*
**Canadian Rates:** *$85-150 (B&B)*
**Payment:** *MC and VISA*
**Children:** *Welcome*
**Dogs:** *Welcome with notice*
**Open:** *All year*

The Harkley's found a passage in Mary Emmerling's *Cottages* that they feel aptly describes their four riverside cottages. "All cottages are small, but small size does not preclude richness of form. The cottage floor plan permits a generosity of movement, a minimum of doors and corridors, and a central space, with nooks around it for conversation, intimacy, meditation and contemplation of nature. All cottages are linked to their natural surroundings in ways that mere houses often are not." Life at River Run Cottages is about as close to Emmerling's ideal as most of us are likely to find.

A swing of the gate and guests enter a magical world of color, form, and texture. Multicolored flowers and greenery are found throughout, from the hanging baskets and window boxes to the decorative wine casks. Grape vines entwine a pergola overhead. A wooden walkway leads to each of the cottages, whether they are floating, set high on the river banks, or tucked somewhere in between. Regardless of one's ultimate choice, guests will be in for a treat.

Waterlily is an intriguing cottage that floats on a wooden platform. White exterior walls are merely the backdrop to the blazing red, pink, and yellow flowers overflowing from the planters. Off to the side, softer hues of color emanate from the cottage's stained glass windows. Once inside, a glowing union of lustrous teak, mahogany, and bird's eye maple combine in the fine cabinetry. Pale blue, lavender, and rose chintz fabric covers the thick cushions lining the built-in sofa. Guests who arrive at night will find that the lights have been turned on, soft music is playing, and a fire is ready to be lit in the wood stove. A kitchenette has a refrigerator, two burners, and glasses and china neatly lining the shelves. The queen-bedded loft is a cozy place to settle into for a night (or two, or three). In the morning, guests can walk out to their private deck containing captain's chairs and a table, drink their coffee, and watch the ducks paddle about and the birds soar overhead.

Another intimate space is the Net Loft, which is named for the fishermen who, years ago, mended their nets here. This two-level suite is connected by a spiral staircase. At the top of the stairs is the bedroom, with its four-poster log bed. Guests can settle in here, or perhaps on the huge white sofa in the living room, and enjoy the river views. There is a fresh look to this entire space, as terra cotta floors nicely combine with light oak and wicker accents. At night, this spacious abode becomes even cozier, when the fire is lit and the shades are drawn. French doors open to a private deck, complete with a Japanese soaking tub.

The Farmer's Cottage is set out from the banks of the river, complete with a deck from which to enjoy the view. Guests walk through French doors onto hardwood floors that lead to a full kitchen, then beyond to a cozy sitting room, complete with an antique wood stove. Guests may relax on the sofa or in the chintz-covered armchair. Regardless of choice, the views are great. The separate bedroom contains a queen bed, and next to it is the tiled bathroom with a Jacuzzi for two.

The River Room is the newest addition. It was built to accommodate all those potential guests the hosts were forced to turn away for lack of space. This studio is situated in a corner of the Harkley's house, and even shares their bathroom. Cranberry and hunter green colors lend a warmth to this cozy chamber, complete with a pull-out queen bed, wood burning fireplace, and views of the water through a greenhouse window. The dock is just outside the doors, and guests will find chairs and a hammock for lounging, as well as various water craft for launching.

All guests are welcome to borrow the rowboat, double kayak, or canoe. They may also use the cottage bicycles and ride the flat roads around Ladner. An easy 20-minute ride from River Run brings guests to the ferry that runs over to the Vancouver Island. Some may want to take Bowser and a rowboat out to one of the small islands near the inn for a picnic.

Bill is a runner and jogs throughout the area. He is happy to have guests and their dogs tag along, as he shows them some of the more intriguing points of interest along the way. One of his favorites he has dubbed Eagle Park, because he once counted 30 eagles in the trees of this little oasis. (Another woman counted 80.) The eagles seem to come in at dusk, so this is the best time to head out to look for them. Other birds that are fun to watch are the cormorants, loons, swans, and ducks. Another popular outing is to take Bowser for a leisurely stroll along the dike into Ladner.

There are a number of fine restaurants in the area for dinner, but diners shoud save a little room because the next morning's breakfast is an extravaganza. Breakfast menus are left in the cottages each evening. The fare varies with the day, but guests can always look forward to their "appetizer" of French press coffee, orange juice, and fresh fruit. Homemade baked goodies are presented just before the main portion of the meal arrives. On any given day this includes such options as Eggs Benedict with hollandaise and fresh chives, a fresh salmon and leek quiche, thick French toast with maple syrup, or Bill's famous River Run Eggs. The now not-so-secret recipe recently appeared in the cottages' newsletter. The trick is the homemade salsa, which smothers the two eggs on English muffins. If that isn't enough to start the day, then guests can also have some cereal, porridge, toast, or yogurt. Whether they take this hearty affair on the deck or in the privacy of the cottage, it is a meal not soon forgotten — and neither is a stay at the River Run Cottages.

# Fernhill Lodge

*C-4, R.R. 1*
*610 Fernhill Road*
*Mayne Island, B.C., Canada V0N 2J0*
*(604) 539-2544*

*Hosts: Brian and Mary Crumblehulme*
*Rooms: 7 doubles*
*Canadian Rates: $95-140 (B&B)*
*Payment: MC and VISA*
*Children: Welcome; under the age of 5 are free of charge*
*Dogs: Welcome with approval*
*Open: All year*

Mayne Island has a rich history that dates back to the mid-1800s. Miners from Vancouver Island, who were trying to head north to join the Fraser River Valley's gold rush, would come together on Mayne Island before attempting to row across the Georgia Strait. As a result, there are plenty of historic enclaves on the island. One of the most interesting is Miners' Bay. First-time visitors will find everything from intriguing antique buildings and a lovely old church to the town's original jail. This hamlet isn't just for history buffs, though, as there are an assortment of outdoor opportunities to take advantage of as well. Bennet Bay Beach is one of the more popular destinations for a leisurely outing, while Mount Parke might be a little more appealing for those who want to take their canines on a hiking adventure. Nearby Campbell Bay has a scenic trail that leads to a beautiful swimming beach and some sandstone caves that are fun to explore. Most visitors, however, come to Mayne Island to relax amid the quiet surroundings.

Fernhill Lodge is one of the more intriguing places to unwind. It is situated on five hilltop acres surrounded by manicured gardens and dense forests. Guests and their well-mannered dogs are welcome to explore this acreage, where arbutus trees and conifers create a veritable park-like setting. The grounds are somewhat reminiscent of traditional English gardens, where arbors are draped with vines, trellises are dripping with fragrant flowers, and benches are set in private hideaways. Those yearning for a place for quiet contemplation may wish to follow a path down to the cliff, where there is a bench that looks out over the water. Guests who visit during the summer months will be surrounded by the aromatic fragrances emanating from the rose and herb gardens. These gardens are well known to those in horticultural circles, but even novices can appreciate the lovely combination of texture and color. Brian uses many of the plants he grows in the array of authentic international dishes he prepares several nights a week. Guests who study the books in the Crumblehulme's library are certain to pick up on Brian and Mary's wide range of interests — especially history and food.

Brian has gathered a number of intriguing recipes from the Roman, Medieval, and Renaissance periods, which guests can enjoy by making dinner reservations in advance. The theme is usually set by the first person to make a reservation. If the above food categories are not of interest, then Brian can prepare one of his native West Coast or all-encompassing international meals. One of the more popular dishes from the Medieval era is the game hen tart sprinkled with fresh herbs. A favorite entrée from the Roman era is lamb marinated in a coriander wine sauce. One of the assistant chefs also prepares authentic Japanese meals on occasion. Breakfast, on the other hand, usually begins with fresh juice, fruit muffins, and scones. This is often followed by light pancakes, herbed omelets, and other assorted dishes adorned with edible flowers. Eggs are provided by the lodge's "happy hens." When not eating, guests may relax in the sun out on one of the decks, or inside in the library. They can read, play a game of Medieval skittles, or perhaps the piano — this is the place to completely relax amid the tranquil surroundings.

With all this history floating around the place, guests might think they're staying in an antique house; however, it is a far more contemporary cottage with weathered shingles and paned windows. Each guest room has a private entrance, making the rooms especially desirable for traveling dogs. Each room also has its own motif. The guest room themes often feature furnishings or accent pieces from a particular period. The chambers include such decorative themes as Asian, Jacobean, French, Victorian, Moroccan, and Indian. Some might think the rooms are a little on the dark side, but we thought this an inherent part of their appeal. Even without knowing the specific theme of the room, guests usually recognize the general gist of the chamber. All are filled with a delightful and eclectic mix of furnishings. The Asian is fashioned with traditional tatami mats, Japanese screens, and a low queen bedstead, while the Edwardian is furnished with a 17th-century, four-poster oak bed surrounded by a blue and white color scheme and assorted pewter knickknacks. A third chamber, the Moroccan, also has a four-poster bed, but it is surrounded by dark, ornately carved woods. All have private baths. The newer additions, East Indian and Moroccan, offer private decks and hot tubs.

The Crumblehulme's know Mayne Island very well and can recommend all sorts of activities for guests and their canines to investigate. There are interesting coves to explore and wonderful hiking trails that meander through dense forests. The wildlife on the island ranges from deer and raccoons to sea otter, seals, and king fishers. Bicycling is as popular as boating, and the hosts can suggest places to rent a kayak or canoe; or they can explain where to secure a sailboat or fishing charter to further take advantage of the surrounding waters. At the end of the day, though, most enjoy returning to Fernhill Lodge, where they can relax in the sauna out in the woods, soak in their private hot tub, or perhaps sip a cup of tea out on the deck.

# Corbett Lake Country Inn

*Box 327*
*Merritt, B.C., Canada  V0K 2B0*
*(604) 378-4334*

*Innkeeper Peter McVey*
*Rooms: 3 doubles, 10 cabins*
*Canadian Rates: Doubles $55-65 per person (MAP), Cabins $47-89*
*                          per person (includes dinner)*
*Payment: Personal checks*
*Children: Welcome; children under 9 years of age are half price*
*Dogs: Welcome if leashed on the property*
*Open: May-October*

The Corbett Inn lies along a spectacular stretch of highway known as the Coquihalla, which traverses the high mountain plateaus between Peachland and Merritt. The inn is only three hours from Vancouver, yet it feels far more removed from civilization than that. These are the high, dry foothills of the Cascades, and it is here that the lodge rests on what was originally part of the Duke of Portland's ranch. Peter McVey now owns 305 of these acres, to which guests return to experience its unpretentious surroundings, superb fly fishing, and gourmet meals. Peter is from England, where he trained in the kitchens of the Lord Mayor of London. He brings his flair for food and his passion for fly fishing to the wilds of British Columbia.

We drove in from the Okanagan valley, and were so busy admiring the scenery that we almost missed the lodge, which is set well off the road behind stands of pines and aspen trees. We first came across the gray cedar lodge, but could also spy the cedar-shingled cabins in the woods. The lodge is just as we imagined it — dark wood walls, hardwood floors worn with years of use, and rooms brimming with treasured fishing paraphernalia. Along the hall, leading to the dining room, delicate hand-tied flies are framed and displayed like miniature trophies. The dining room, appropriately enough, is the largest chamber in the lodge, with views of the forest and lake framed in two walls of windows. This room is reminiscent of an old-fashioned hunting lodge, with animal skins and antlers decorating its walls. In July and August, cabin guests are left to their own culinary devices, but during the remaining months of operation, dinner is included in the tariff. Guests will find it is worth every penny.

Peter serves a four-course meal each evening and there are no choices. Guests are treated to whatever is fresh and whatever inspires him. In this way, most feel less like *guests*, and more like personal friends of the innkeeper. This meal might begin with consommé or a rich creamy soup, followed by a delicate smoked salmon or hearty Caesar salad. The entrée of the evening could range from rack of lamb or chateaubriand to beef Wellington or trout. The dessert  might feature a fresh fruit cobbler, or Peter's specialty — cheesecake. Even the wine list is interesting. Most people let Peter do the selecting.

During the day, guests are left to their own devices, although Peter is usually available to give some advice on the finer points of fly fishing. Anglers may fish in Corbett and Courtney lakes either from the shore or from a rowboat. The truly passionate fisherman can arrange to fly fish on two other private lakes located on the Douglas Lake Ranch. Peter has spent years restoring the natural balance of these two lakes and restocking them with trout. He even has his own stocking farm. Corbett Lake is also blessed with a small, deep water swimming area where people can take a dip on very hot summer days.

Like the lodge, the authentic, rustic feeling has been well preserved in the cabins. A couple of these are in the pine groves near the lake shore, but most are situated off the lake on a bluff overlooking the distant mountains. These gray cedar cabins look festive with their cherry red doors and window trim. Hardwood floors lining these informal interiors are sometimes brightened by an Oriental or braided rug, but in general, guests can expect an eclectic grouping of mismatched furniture and bedsteads. We liked the crisp red and white gingham curtains framing a kitchen window in one cabin, and the old-fashioned easy chair in another. Most of the cabins have some type of kitchen, a living room, a separate bedroom, and a private bath. Guests may sleep in a twin, fold-out, or a double bedstead, and a lucky few will get a fireplace. All of the cabins are as immaculate as they are appealing.

While dogs must be leashed around the cabins, some guests prefer heading off across the bluff to let their dogs run. The property has enough acreage to keep most dogs and their human friends happily occupied for hours, although guests shouldn't expect many deep forests. The trees are fairly spread out and the terrain rocky. Some of the more popular day trips include venturing south on 5A to the Kentucky-Alleyne Provincial Park, where there are wilderness areas, hiking trails, and an assortment of fishing and swimming options to investigate. Also south of the inn is Allison Lake, a park where people and dogs can spend time near the water or hiking around it.

# Cliffside Inn

*Box 50*
*North Pender Island, B.C., Canada  V0N 2M0*
*(604) 629-6691*

*Innkeeper: Penny Tomlin*
*Rooms: 2 doubles, 2 suites, 1 cottage*
*Canadian Rates: Doubles $135-145 (B&B), Suites $145-185 (B&B),*
*Cottage $165 (B&B)*
*Payment: MC and VISA*
*Children: Not appropriate for children under 16 years of age*
*Dogs: Welcome in the Edgewater Cottage and in the Rosehip Room,*
*with approval*
*Open: All year*

North and South Pender Islands have the same climate as most of the other Gulf Islands — sub-Mediterranean. The "Penders," as they are often referred to, are joined by a bridge, so visitors can double their fun by exploring both islands. These islands have been called "the islands of hidden coves and beaches" and "the friendly islands." Most who stay here would agree that these are accurate descriptions. Not only can people and their dogs explore the hidden coves and walk along the picturesque paths, but they can also bicycle along the gently sloping hills. There are few towns here, and even fewer tourists — making these islands an ideal getaway for those seeking a little solitude. Driving from the ferry to the Cliffside Inn, guests are likely to be tempted by the roadside vegetable stands and small art galleries; but these stops can be saved for later, as more surprises await at the inn. The Cliffside Inn is located on three secluded oceanfront acres, which have been in Penny's family for nearly a century.

More recently, Penny Tomlin created a private retreat for adults (and their well-mannered dogs). Guests can come for the exquisite breakfasts, distinctive rooms, old-fashioned pampering, or for the complete privacy. The lush landscape surrounding the inn is a mixture of huge shade trees, forests, and lawns framed by split rail fences. This is merely the backdrop, though, for the most impressive views are overlooking the channel and Mount Baker. Each room offers some view of the water; however, only two of these welcome dogs — so we will focus on these chambers.

Guests who stay in the Rosehip Room are treated to all the privileges of the inn. This private abode offers a wall of sliding glass doors that opens out to a patio and beyond to the gardens. Many also enjoy watching the birds and wildlife frolic — right from the brass bed, which is covered with a feather comforter. There is a private bathroom, but the adjacent fireside sitting room is shared. Those staying here are also treated to a gourmet breakfast in the solarium each morning. Many of the omelets, breads, and other delectable edibles are created with ingredients from Penny's extensive herb, vegetable, and berry gardens.

Edgewater Cottage offers a completely different vacation experience. This board and batten cedar house is set just 20 feet from the cliff's edge. It, too, is decorated in a casual country-style, but it is a little more rustic and lacks the ruffles and knickknacks that characterize some of the inn rooms. Penny has intermixed comfortable furnishings with some of the antiques from her family's home. Two bedrooms contain double beds, and in the living room there is an air-tight wood stove. Guests have a full kitchen, which is stocked with all the breakfast provisions they might need — and more. Eggs, fruit, ham, bread, croissants, and juice provide plenty of options for this morning meal. The television is a modern convenience, but we much preferred the expansive deck, which offers some of the finest water views on the property.

Most dogs are completely at home here, as there is plenty of acreage and privacy. Descend the long staircase to the sandstone beach, where dogs and their friends can walk for awhile before reaching its end. Penny knows of other interesting outings as well; guests can just tell her approximately what they have in mind and she will come up with some great suggestions. The Prior Centennial Provincial Park is on North Pender Island and is brimming with 40 acres of deep forests set below Lively Peak. Some prefer to meander about Medicine Beach on Bedwell Harbor. Over on South Pender, there is Mount Norman, and dogs and their owners are invited to hike up this peak, as well. One of the best things about returning after a long day of exploring this region is the chance to soak a while in the hot tub, which is set on cliff-hanger deck. Even if guests have not left the premises all day, we recommend an evening visit out here, where the deep and dark starry nights are sure to make a lasting impression.

---

# Tigh-Na-Mara

*1095 East Island Highway*
*Parksville, B.C., Canada V9P 2E5*
*(800) 663-7373, (604) 248-2072, Fax (6040 248-4140*

*Managers: Joe and Jackie Hirsch*
*Rooms: 110 doubles, 37 cottages*
*Canadian Rates: Doubles $89-164 (EP), Cottages $104-169 (EP)*
*Payment: AE, DSC, MC, and VISA*
*Children: Welcome (cribs, cots, high chairs, and baby-sitters*
*        are available)*
*Dogs: Welcome in the cottages, except during July and August*
*Open: All year*

Warm water and soft sand beaches are not normally what people associate with British Columbia's coastline. Scenic and rugged — yes. Swimmable water — rarely. The Tigh-Na-Mara lies along Vancouver Island's longest stretch of sandy beach; a beach that also happens to come and go with the tide. When the tide is out, miles of sand flats extend out into the Strait of Georgia. In the summertime, the sun warms the exposed sand and it, in turn, warms the incoming water and makes it swimmable. As one might imagine, these ideal conditions draw a large summer crowd to the resort. Unfortunately, Bowser is not a preferred guest during this time of year, but that is probably for the best, as it would be just too chaotic for most canines. Our hosts are actually doing us a favor by restricting the dog-visiting season, since the ideal time to be here is after the crowds are gone and a sense of calm returns to the resort.

The Tigh-Na-Mara lies well off the main route, under a canopy of Douglas firs and arbutus trees. The log cabins and lodge are fixtures within this forest, and though the condominiums are new, they are tucked unobtrusively into the wooded shoreline. Guests traveling with their dogs may request cabins situated near the shore, the children's play areas, or along an edge of the resort. The one-bedroom cabins are just right for couples and their dogs, while families may want to reserve a two-bedroom unit. The log exteriors still look rather new; and the natural knotty-pine paneled walls make each cabin homey. Vaulted ceilings inset with skylights and plenty of paned windows let in a surprising amount of sunlight. Mauve and gray tones predominate, whether in the good quality carpet, sofas, or armchairs. A fieldstone fireplace warms the living room, dining area, and kitchen. Fully-stocked kitchens include coffee makers, along with a small supply of coffee and tea. Linens and towels are furnished, and even though these are housekeeping cottages, we were pleasantly surprised to find a nice complement of shampoos, soaps, and other toiletries. The separate bedrooms are just large enough to hold a twin or queen bed, which is covered with a simple cotton spread. The butcher block dining room table is large enough for everyone to have a sit-down meal together, although we thought it was equally fun to barbecue out on the grill and eat at the picnic table on the little patio. The cottages are very private, and maids will not even visit unless specifically asked.

Guests may also take any of their meals in the resort's fine restaurant. The chef, who is British, has cooked at restaurants all over the world. It is difficult to decide where to sit here, whether in front of the massive stone fireplace or out on a glassed-in porch. This restaurant is extremely popular, but guests who visit in the off-season will find reservations much more easily secured. The cuisine is Continental; the fall menu offered such appetizers as a pumpkin and hazelnut soup, steamed mussels, and a game pâté with a fall chutney. Main courses included the pheasant breast with a wild mushroom brandy sauce; the steamed halibut with pink peppercorns and a rosé butter; and a lemon pepper pasta with shrimp, salmon, scallops, and snapper.

After dinner, it is often nice to stretch our collective legs. This is the best time of day to head down to the shore for a leisurely evening stroll. This place is great for families, as there are two well-designed playgrounds set up in different parts of the resort. They offer substantial wooden jungle gyms, slides, and even trampolines. Children of all ages will find something appealing about these play areas. There is also a tennis court, swimming pool, spa, and exercise room. Nature trails wend throughout the resort, although most people and their dogs eventually find themselves on the beach or flats.

It was a gray day when we visited and the beach was quite deserted — just the way we like it. A stairway and path lead down to the wide swath of pristine beach with its gentle sandy shoreline — much of which is covered with knotty driftwood. The tide was out, and a few people were out walking on the flats with their dogs. Anyone who runs out of things to do here can set off to investigate any of the lovely provincial parks in the area. One of the best is Englishman River Falls Provincial Park, which has lush woods, plenty of water, and fine hiking trails that allow dogs. Another popular option, situated a short distance from the resort, is Rathtrevor Provincial Park. Dogs are welcome here, and there are plenty of beachside trails that turn into woodland trails. Swimming is also available.

---

# April Point
## Lodge and Fishing Resort

*P.O. Box 1*
*Quadra Island, Campbell River, B.C., Canada  V9W 4Z9*
*(604) 285-2222, Fax (604) 285-2411*

*Innkeepers: The Peterson Family*
*Rooms: 37 rooms, suites, houses*
*Canadian Rates: Rooms $99-229 (EP), Suites $395 (EP),*
*                Houses $395 (EP)*
*Payment: AE, DC, MC, and VISA*
*Children: Welcome, children under 16 years of age are free of charge*
*Dogs: Welcome in some of the accommodations*
*Open: All year*

If the words Tyee, Coho, and Chinook set your heart a racing, then we would like to recommend an exclusive vacation retreat. This is the consummate fisherman's ultimate destination, with a combination of rustic and well-appointed accommodations, a complete flotilla of Boston Whalers, and enough black labs to keep Bowser in doggie heaven for years to come. We were greeted by Max, a handsome Black Labrador, along with Katie, Katie, and Katie, three of his black lab friends. Max and Katie are Eric's dogs — Eric is one of the owners of the place — the rest belong to longtime guests, and all happen to be named Katie.

We spent most of our time with Eric and his black labs. He is a gracious man, whose keen knowledge and love of Quadra Island stem back to his childhood. When he was a young boy, his father and mother moved the entire family here from San Francisco. When they first arrived at April Point, there were seven fishing shacks — and nothing else. As Eric describes it, first there were seven shacks, and then there were none; it seems the local anglers did not appreciate the rambunctious children who interrupted their solitude. Though it was not an easy life, it was an interesting one, with Eric's dad rowing the children to a neighboring cove for school each day.

With the exception of Eric's father, who passed away years ago, the family is still a tight-knit team. Mrs. P. still cooks the fruit pies that guests have come to love. Eric watches over the lodge, and is a food and wine connoisseur — which helps in developing an intriguing menu and extensive wine list. He also owns a farm on the south end of the island and spends a great deal of time there tending to his livestock and gardens. Eric's brother Warren handles corporate clients; when he is not doing that, he is often out in search of the ultimate fishing spot. On any given day, Warren, or one of the excellent guides, will know just where to go in search of fish.

Getting here by car requires a little tenacity, as most visitors need to take two ferries to get to the island. During the season, though, guests frequently arrive by seaplane or private boat. For anyone arriving by land, April Point is located down a narrow, twisting road that eventually ends at the point. Actually, this is not a natural point of land, but rather, a shellfish depository. For hundreds of years, the inhabitants would gather here and break open their oysters and shellfish, tossing the shells aside when they were done. Over the years, it built up to such a level that it formed a point of land; the point is now considered historic and cannot be altered beyond what the Petersons have done to it.

Guests will find a series of accommodations available to them and their dogs. Four cabins sit nestled in the woods overlooking Discovery Passage — these would be our first choices. Next to these abodes are the Passage View Rooms (#36-38). These are surprisingly modern inside, being attractively decorated with Northwest art and complemented by bright patterned spreads on the pairs of queen bedsteads. Modern bathrooms, some with Jacuzzi tubs, are as welcome a sight as the freestanding fireplaces. The remaining rooms are tucked into the rocky crags all around the resort, forming private enclaves. These include the laid back boathouse suites (#4-7), that are the most rustic accommodations, and are perched over the harbor. Each of these offers two bedrooms, a living room with a fireplace, and a private bathroom. What endears guests to the April Point Lodge, though, is not the rooms or the amenities, it is their feeling of oneness with the wilderness around them and the other guests.We felt like part of the lodge's extended family.

Whether admiring a bald eagle perched on a piling or looking out past the pool to the grass jetty — and beyond to Discovery Passage — the scenery is truly out of this world. We loved the "pool," which is simply a rocky indentation that fills up with water when the tide comes in. It also effectively separates the lodge from the rock and grass jetty. Out on this jetty, Eric often prepares authentic Pacific coast native feasts for his guests, using bentwood boxes. He steams the salmon, crabs, mussels, shrimp, and vegetables in these boxes, using skunk cabbage as the lining. Eric is now an expert, having gained his experience through the teachings of local anthropologists and writers who are familiar with these techniques. When not dining on the spit, guests eat in the lodge. The atmosphere in here is especially restful at night, with candlelight flickering off the wall of windows overlooking the water.

During the day, however, the focus is on fishing. April Point has some of the best guides available anywhere and they know these waters well. If there are salmon to catch, the guides will find them. During the season, there are fishing competitions and derbies. We loved listening to all the stories about the fish that did — or didn't — get away. Unfortunately, on the day we went out, the big one never materialized; however, we did pull in a couple of smaller salmon. After we came in off the water, Max, his entourage of Katies, and our guide's dog Shadow, were on hand to greet us. It was the day before Thanksgiving, and everyone was heading into the lodge to carve the pumpkins that would eventually be used for making April Point's famous pumpkin soup (served in the pumpkin shell, no less). Unfortunately, we could not stay for the festivities, and had to catch the next ferry off the island.

Dogs have a fine time here, and are treated like members of the family. This is a heavily wooded peninsula, with little to no car traffic, so guests and their canines should thoroughly enjoy quiet walks along the water. Quadra Island is huge, with mountains to climb and forests to explore. One good picnic spot is the Rebecca Spit Provincial Park, just off Heriot Bay Rd. Here, visitors can picnic, swim if they like, or simply explore the wooded spit with their dog. Three hiking trails that we can recommend lie in the middle of the island. One of these, the Morte Lake Trail, is a moderately difficult hike up to the lake. The Chinese Mountain Trail is adjacent to this and offers similar terrain. Just up the road, visitors will find the last of the three trails — the Old Growth Trail — via Nugedzi Lake. This is the most difficult of the bunch, and is perfect for energetic dogs and their human counterparts.

April Point is truly a family affair, with generations of people returning year after year. Eric told us of one fellow from Argentina who, at 86 years old, has made the annual pilgrimage back to April

Point for years. He recently called Eric with the sad news that he might not be able to make it this year. Eric told us that he was thinking of flying down and bringing the man back up with him, so that this gentleman wouldn't miss a year. After spending a comparatively short amount of time at the April Point Lodge, it is easy to understand why this old-fashioned fishing resort has such a dedicated following.

# Tsa-Kwa-Luten Lodge

*P.O. Box 460*
*The Resort at Cape Mudge*
*Quadra Island, Quathiaski Cove, B.C., Canada V0P 1N0*
*(800) 665—7745, (604) 285-2042, Fax (604) 285-2532*

*Owners: Cape Mudge Kwakiutl Band*
*Rooms: 32 suites, 43 cabins, 1 guest house*
*Canadian Rates: Suites $80-150 (EP), Cabins $230 (EP),*
*                 Guest House $460 (EP)*
*Payment: AE, DC, MC, and VISA*
*Children: Welcome*
*Dogs: Medium-sized dogs are welcome in the cabins, with approval*
*Open: April 5 to October 15*

At the southern end of Quadra Island lies an 1,100-acre evergreen forest that belongs to the Kwakiutl tribe. It was on this land that Captain Vancouver first set foot in 1792 and visited the Kwakiutl village. For years, this part of the island was better known for its shipwrecks than for its native tribe; however, with the completion of the Tsa-Kwa-Luten Lodge, this appears to be changing. People now have a chance to learn more about the Kwakiutl culture, as well as their traditions and native foods.

We drove along narrow roads toward the famous Cape Mudge Lighthouse before turning down a dirt road leading to the lodge. A dense canopy of trees formed what seemed like a tunnel through the forest, a passage from which we didn't emerge until we reached the lodge. The Tsa-Kwa-Luten Lodge is built along the waters at the edge of this forest. The main building is constructed out of Douglas Fir in the tradition of the Kwakiutl tribe's "big house." Its interior is truly spectacular, with massive logs and carved beams supporting the 50-foot high vaulted ceilings. One end of this "big house," is fashioned with huge plate glass windows that extend from the floor to the peak of the roof — revealing spectacular vistas of the forest and water. A small collection of carved ceremonial masks and screens, along with petroglyph rubbings, are other highlights of this expansive chamber. On some evenings, members of the tribe will put on these masks and robes and perform traditional Kwakiutl dances. Guests can observe these performances and then enjoy salmon being baked over open fires — just as the tribe's forebearers would have done.

Set just off the main lodge are two wings of guest suites, both of which face the water. Just down from the lodge, and concealed in a stand of pines, are four guest houses set on the beach. Dogs are welcome to bring their human friends and stay here, if they can vouch for them. These are especially appropriate spaces for canine travelers, as they offer much more space than the standard guest rooms and are far more secluded. These accommodations, like the main lodge, are also contemporary structures built of Douglas Fir. They feature plenty of windows offering panoramic views of Discovery Passage, where killer whales swim, seals frolic, and birds soar. These cabins are also ideal for families, and are actually quite reasonable for two couples who are considering splitting the lodging fees. The interiors are comprised of two bedrooms, a living room, a full kitchen, and a bathroom. The rooms are decorated around simple pine furnishings and accents and utilize earth-tone color schemes. Northwest and native Kwakiutl artwork hang on the walls, which adds interest to these otherwise immaculate spaces. The most luxurious cabin is the four-bedroom and three-bath guest house, which is equipped with both a private Jacuzzi and a fireplace. Most guests don't have a private Jacuzzi and instead visit the fitness facility, which offers an outdoor hot tub and a sauna. Whichever cabin guests stay in, they will have access to all the same amenities as those staying up in the lodge, including daily maid service.

Anyone who likes the outdoors will love it at the Tsa-Kwa-Luten Lodge. The lodge is surrounded by more than a thousand acres for human and beast to explore. All sorts of nature trails lead through the forests. From the lodge it is also an easy walk out to the Cape Mudge Lighthouse. Along the way, some might spot a peregrine falcon or snowy owl, but are probably more likely to see kingfishers, great blue herons, ospreys, and cormorants. Just north of the lodge, the Haskin Farm Trail or the Old Community Hall Trail offer moderate hikes ranging from 45 minutes to one and a half hours. The lodge supplies just about anything guests might have forgotten. They will rent mountain bikes and kayaks or provide the boat, tackle, bait, and all-weather gear for salmon fishing expeditions. Golf can also be arranged on a nearby course. For those interested in learning a little more about the Kwakiutl culture, we recommend visiting the Cape Mudge village, where there is a museum and an extensive collection of Potlatch artifacts, masks, ceremonial items, and authentic petroglyphs.

# Sooke Harbour House

*1528 Whiffen Spit Road, R.R. 4*
*Sooke B.C. Canada VOS 1NO*
*(604) 642-3421, (604) 642-6988*

*Innkeepers: Fredrica and Sinclair Philip*
*Rooms: 13 doubles*
*Canadian Rates: $250-295 (breakfast and lunch included)*
*Payment: AE, MC, and VISA*
*Children: Welcome*
*Dogs: Welcome*
*Open: All year*

Fifteen years ago, Fredrica and Sinclair Philip bought a small, white clapboard farmhouse overlooking the sea. They originally wanted to open a restaurant here, specializing in native island foods, but what they created was a little bit of paradise for anyone needing a total escape from reality. Fredrica tells us the inn is a work in progress, but as with all great artists, she and Sinclair are continually adjusting and fine tuning. It isn't really necessary though, as most visitors feel the Philips have already created their masterpiece.

Theirs is an oasis of sorts, protected by mature trees and plantings and surrounded by an incredible array of impressive flower, herb, and vegetable gardens. Some of these lie in raised beds, while others line the walks; everywhere one looks there is a delicious palate of color. This artful display is carried into the inn. Most of what is grown in the gardens is eaten — including the flowers. In many of the rooms guests will find lovely dried flowers hanging from the beams and fresh flowers filling decorative vases. Some of the guest rooms reflect their horticultural ties, including the Edible Blossom Room, The Herb Garden Room, and the Underwater Orchard.

Guests may reserve rooms in either the Old House or the New House. We stayed in the Blue Heron Room, which is fashioned with a wall of French doors and windows that reveal mesmerizing colors of the sea, mountains, and sky. From just about any angle, whether in the Jacuzzi soaking tub, in front of the fire, or on the deck, we could relax and still enjoy these lovely views. A wet bar is convenient, as is the small refrigerator containing coffee and other items for an early- morning treat. (Breakfast is delivered to the room a little later.) As with all of the other guest rooms, in here little personal touches appear; for example, a tiny wood box filled with treasures from the ocean, dried flower wreaths, or books on romance by the sea.

The Blue Heron may be one of the more luxurious spaces, but each room boasts a beauty all its own. Stark white walls make the vivid, sometimes impressionistic art all the more riveting. Bedsteads are covered with thick down comforters, soft linens, and layers of pillows. Guests may warm themselves under the down or by the fireplace, but more often, they are drawn to the oversized French doors that reveal views of the gardens and water. A small tray holds fruit, homemade cookies, and a decanter of port. Dogs are treated with equal consideration; a pair of dog bowls are set out on a mat, along with a blanket or bedding, should they be needed.

The intimate dining room has little alcoves and walls of windows, where climbing vines frame vistas of the Juan de Fuca Strait. This is a place for quiet contemplation — and fine food. Actually, it was food that originally drew the Philips to the inn. They wanted to start a restaurant that specialized in native ingredients. It turned out they couldn't always get what they needed, so they ended up growing most of the ingredients right on the premises. The preparation and presentation of the food is truly impressive.

In the afternoon, we walked by the back door of the kitchen and found, discreetly hidden from view by more lush plantings, a sort of outdoor kitchen, with breads left out on racks to cool. There are few steadfast recipes here, just a wish to combine the most interesting flavors to create the most appealing foods. Instead of selecting specific courses, we asked the chef to use his imagination. He created multiple courses that were as visually unforgettable as they were gastronomically memorable. Our salads arrived looking more like miniature flower arrangements — far too lovely to eat, but we managed. A lightly-smoked trout served with a baby red potato salad, golden tomatoes, and a smoked-apple horseradish sauce; herb-crusted oysters with a curry spice yogurt sauce; and grilled local prawns were fabulously presented. Entrées could have included sole stuffed with salmon, ginger, and Vietnamese coriander mousse on a bisque of Dungeness crab; halibut with a red and black currant, Japanese plum wine, and lemon thyme butter glaze; or a cracked Dungeness crab. Organic meats are also available, including the Malahat Farm veal short ribs with a wild mushroom, sun-dried tomato, roast garlic and rosemary sauce. The sauces add far more than taste — they are a visual backdrop for the artistic presentation. With each course, we sampled a different wine from British Columbia. Philip is a wine connoisseur, and had just returned from a buying trip to the Province's wineries. His passion for wine, especially for British Columbia wine, is contagious.

Afterwards, we sat on the huge sofa and enjoyed a sweet after-dinner wine before the fire. Most people do linger here after their meal, enjoying a little coffee and the overall ambiance. Others might go for a moonlight walk along the mile-long Whiffen Spit, just below the inn. This is also a wonderful place to stroll with Bowser during the day. We found seals playing in the water and a bald eagle circling overhead, as well as plenty of intriguing waterfowl. Along the way, we met another Golden Retriever, three Collies, two Dachshunds, a Scottish Terrier, and a Cocker Spaniel — this is indeed doggie heaven. Those wanting a longer outing may wish to take the Galloping Goose Trail or pick up another mountain trail that parallels the water. Whatever recreational outlet guests choose, they will find that the attention the Phillips give to their suites and their fine food is most impressive — as is their genuine desire to make their guests and their dogs completely comfortable in this enchanting inn by the sea.

---

# Fossil Bay Resort

*1603 West Coat Road, R.R. 2*
*Sooke, B.C., Canada V0S 1N0*
*(604) 646-2073, Fax (604) 646-2121*

*Host: Gerhard Wild*
*Rooms: 6 cottages*
*Canadian Rates: $135-160 (EP)*
*Payment: MC and VISA*
*Children: Not suitable for children, as the resort is close to cliffs*
*Dogs: Welcome in two cottages*
*Open: All year*

The Fossil Bay Resort is one of the newer additions to Sooke's oceanside cottage resort community. Of the four that we mention, Fossil Bay is the westernmost, and consequently, has the feeling of being the most remote. When we asked some of the locals in Sooke about the Fossil Bay Resort, they just shook their heads in puzzlement, because they couldn't visualize where it was located. We found it, though, just five miles from the scenic Juan de Fuca Marine Trail — one of the better places to hike with a dog along this section of Vancouver Island.

Dense forests line the road up to Fossil Bay, and at various points a clearing reveals water views. As we neared the resort, it appeared that some clear cutting had occurred fairly recently. Whoever was responsible for it left just enough pine trees to conceal the resort from the road. We drove down a dirt lane toward the water, then turned into a little parking area across from the main lodge — a contemporary log house edged by woods. We could just make out the rooftops of the cottages set along the cliffs below.

We met Gerhard, who has owned the property for the past seven years. It wasn't until just recently, however, that he was able to build the cottages and open them to guests. The lodge and the cottages are quite separate, giving guests the feeling of privacy. We followed a path from the lodge down to the cottages that line the cliff, some 30 feet above the water. These contemporary clapboard buildings reveal little from the outside, but once inside, the light and airy interiors have almost a Caribbean feeling to them.

We stepped across terra cotta tiles to the center of the pale peach-colored room. To the rear is an alcove containing a king bed backed by a handsome oak headboard with wildflowers carved into it. A white cotton spread covers the bed, which is flanked by draped bedside tables. The room's lines are clean, the place is spotless, yet there is still plenty of character. We loved the small fireplace, with its decorative brickwork. Set on the mantel are knick-knacks from the sea — intriguing shells, pieces of unusually shaped driftwood, or smooth stones. The only other collectibles are duck decoys and baskets of dried flowers. The bathrooms and kitchen are both outfitted with the same white, raised-panel cabinets and green Corian countertops. Guests will discover that they have just about everything they will need to create meals; they will just have to stock up in Sooke, as there are no stores for miles. This is a very romantic spot, which seems ideal for couples (and their dogs) who need to unwind. Whether lying in bed, sitting in front of the fire, or eating dinner by candlelight, guests can always look through the windows to the ocean. At times, the water seems close enough to touch, especially when rejuvenating in the hot tub on one's private deck. Those who cannot seem to relax without a television will find that each cottage has a remote controlled television and a VCR.

Hiking trails abound throughout Sooke. As we mentioned, the extensive Juan de Fuca Marine Trail is only five miles from the resort. By following the West Coast Road, visitors and their dogs will also find three oceanside provincial parks — Whiffen Spit,

French Beach, and Jordan River. These places are as wonderful for walks along the beach as they are for serious hiking. Another outing that we enjoyed entailed walking a quarter mile through China Beach's rain forest before we emerged at a sandy beach. Other beaches worth investigating are Mystic Beach and Sombrio Beach, which are also situated along West Coast Road. Those interested in heading further afield may wish to venture up the coast to Port Renfrew. From here, a gravel road leads to Fairy Lake, Lizard Lake, and Lake Cowichan — providing more than enough swimming and hiking adventures for a canine companion.

# Ocean Wilderness

*109 West Coast Rd., R.R. #2*
*Sooke, B.C., Canada V0S 1N0*
*(800) 323-2116, (604) 646-2116*

*Innkeeper: Marion Rolston*
*Rooms: 9 doubles, 1 cottage*
*Canadian Rates: Doubles $85-175 (B&B), Cottage $225 (B&B)*
*Payment: MC and VISA*
*Children: Welcome (high chairs, cots, and baby-sitters are available)*
*Dogs: Welcome with a $7 nightly fee*
*Open: All year*

Rugged, mountainous beauty combines with a gently curving shoreline to make Vancouver Island's west coast memorable. Sooke lies along this stretch of coastline, with the urban charms of Victoria less than an hour away. It is easily accessible from Victoria, and even from Vancouver, yet Sooke feels remote. It would be silly to come all this way and not stay at an inn on the water, which is one of the many reasons we liked the Ocean Wilderness. It lies just steps from the beach amid five acres of old growth rain forest. Ocean Wilderness is a delightful Bed and Breakfast, and one with a good deal of pizzazz. The centerpiece is an authentic log cabin that was built in the 1930s by a local Norwegian logger. Surprisingly, Marion is only the second owner in all these years. During her tenure, she has made several changes to the property by building a guest wing (of rough hewn cedar, not logs) and a Japanese teahouse — and by clearing various paths across the property.

As guests enter the guest wing, they will find hardwood floors often covered with Oriental carpets or braided rugs. Marion's diverse antique collection, from the world over, also fills these spaces. She might have an antique side table from France, a settee from England, or an Oriental urn that serves as a lamp. Guests sleep in canopied beds with heavy down comforters, and can choose rooms with soaking tubs for two that also have unobstructed views of the ocean, mountains, and wilderness. Candlelight often flickers in these windows at night, setting a romantic tone for couples. The Mate's Room and Rainforest Room offer skylights for stargazing and forest views, while the Captain's Quarters and Pacific Panorama are fashioned with soaking tubs set in front of windows that overlook the Strait. Sheringham and Carmanah, on the other hand, lie on the first floor and guests staying here feel as though they are surrounded by dense woods. Wilderness, the only guest room located in the log house, is a little cozier than the others, and feels more rustic, primarily due to the log walls. Bathrooms are well appointed in all the rooms — including bathrobes. About a half-hour before breakfast, Marion, or one of her staff, will deliver coffee or tea on a silver tray decorated with flowers — a most civilized way to start the day. Afterwards, most enjoy taking their dogs for a walk about the property before heading over to the log house for breakfast. Ocean Wilderness works especially well for guests and their dogs, because every room but one has a private outside entrance.

The log house, too, is filled with Marion's Victorian antiques, especially in the dining room. A long table draped with a linen tablecloth is set up in front of a plate glass window. China, silver, and crystal, along with vases filled with fresh flowers, are the backdrop for the lavish repast to follow. The morning meal begins with homemade cinnamon rolls and melt-in-your-mouth biscuits that guests often smother with homemade jams and jellies. Farm fresh eggs are used for creating the various baked dishes that follow. Most are surprised to discover that the dining room isn't used only for breakfast. Marion has also used it for everything from putting on plays to hosting a clairvoyant. In the summer months, she has wonderful cookouts on the beach. On Thursdays and Sundays, guests come down to the shore to enjoy salmon, crab, prawns, halibut, shrimp, and clams, along with corn on the cob, cobblers, and other delectable edibles. As guests sip wine and sample the various wares, otters and seals often frolic just offshore. While Bowser should probably forego the cookout, he will find there are plenty of other things in the area to make a dog leap for joy.

During the day, guests and their canines can follow the trail to the inn's beach and private cove. Just up the road, there are all sorts of hiking trails to take advantage of — one of the more popular is the ever growing Juan de Fuca Marine Trail. Almost all trails in the area offer varied terrain, as well as unparalleled views of the ocean and mountains. At the end of the day, let Bowser nap in the room while you navigate the stone path to the miniature Japanese teahouse for a soak in the private hot tub. There is also a wonderful massage therapist available, who will undoubtedly be able to massage away muscle fatigue or tension. Whether it be a rejuvenating massage or a therapeutic soak, we can think of no better way to end a day on the western shore of Vancouver Island.

# Point-No-Point Resort

*1505 West Coast Road, R.R. 2*
*Sooke, B.C., Canada V0S 1N0*
*(604) 646-2020*

*Managers:* Sharon and Stuart Soderberg
*Rooms:* 20 cottages
*Canadian Rates:* $80-150 (B&B), Additional person $8
*Payment:* VISA
*Children:* Welcome (cribs and high chairs are available)
*Dogs:* Small dogs welcome in cabins 3 and 4
*Open:* All year

The Point-No-Point Resort has been *quietly* attracting visitors since 1952 — and no wonder; once people discover this place they want to keep it a secret. It lies just north of Sooke, along a mile of oceanfront. There are 40 acres surrounding the resort — a mixture of deep forest and shrubbery. Footpaths that weave along the craggy hillside and down 75 feet to the ocean make for fine nature walks with a canine companion. But many guests feel the most captivating feature is the serene, yet breathtaking, view. We could see the bay — and beyond to the Olympics — from just about anywhere on the property, whether from the rustic, hillside cabins or from the intimate restaurant.

The restaurant is nestled on the top of this craggy hillside and serves fine food. While we waited to be seated, we relaxed in comfortable couches and armchairs set in front of the fieldstone fireplace. Although it was late in the day, the glassed-in summer porch was filled with a number of people enjoying high tea. There are only six tables in here, but the lucky ones who garner a spot feel as though little is separating them from the ocean and wildlife. From this perch, patrons can often watch eagles soaring, or perhaps see a pod of grey whales making their way along the coast.

The restaurant serves all three meals, and each one is innovative. During our visit, lunch consisted of a creamy seafood chowder with cornbread, a warm salad of mixed greens topped with grilled scallops and a pesto vinaigrette, and an herbed fettucine with smoked chicken, mushrooms, and sun-dried cranberries in a white wine cream sauce. But it is the sunset dinners that are most memorable. Appetizers might include a seafood gratinée with scallops, prawns, and red onions in a fish velouté or the Thai spinach appetizer. The latter is a combination of onion, ginger, spinach, coconut, and peanuts baked in filo, then topped with blackberry coulis on a bed of spinach chiffonade. Some of the more popular entrées were the barbecued salmon, marinated and grilled to order, the pork tenderloin with an apricot-raisin glaze, or the breast of chicken stuffed with a ricotta cheese and mushroom duxelle.

After dinner, guests need only walk a short distance to get to their cabins. While there are cabins situated all over this craggy hillside, only two of them allow dogs. These are set into the woods, with dark wood exteriors that cause them to blend in with their surroundings. When we stepped inside it was so dark we could barely make out the shapes in the room. But as soon as we opened the draperies, the sunlight flooded in through the plate glass windows revealing log walls and ceilings. Guests will discover there is more than enough space, as there is a living room, a small bedroom, a kitchenette, and a private bathroom. Two day beds in the living room double as sofas, and are positioned to equally maximize the warmth from the fire and the views of the ocean. For the most part, these simply decorated and furnished chambers are enhanced with pretty quilts covering the beds and braided rugs topping the linoleum floors. Guests have linens, daily maid service, and even a little coffee maker in the kitchen. For a substantial breakfast, most prefer the restaurant's five-grain granola, fruit salad, pancakes, and assortment of omelets.

From this high perch, bird watchers frequently spot unusual winged creatures. The resort has even developed its own detailed list of birds that guests have seen over the years. We cannot claim any expertise in this field; however, we would be curious to know what a Rufous-sided Towhee, Red-Necked Grebe, Northern Phalarope, or Water Pipit all look like. Bowser would probably be far more interested in checking out the local hiking trails. The Juan de Fuca Marine trail is in the process of being expanded, but in its present form, it still makes for a great oceanside outing with Bowser. The Galloping Goose Trail is another fun hiking option, that also happens to be located in Sooke.

Best of all, there are dozens of pullouts along the road, and often paths that lead to wilderness beaches. One of the most beautiful (and underutilized) of these is the 146-acre French Beach Provincial Park. Here, visitors and their dogs can walk for miles along the rugged beach and look for treasures that have washed ashore, or just observe the river otters, sea lions, and bald eagles in their natural state. The second growth forest here is also pleasant for extensive walks, and the views of the Olympics are fabulous.

# Four Seasons Hotel

*791 West Georgia Street*
*Vancouver, B.C., Canada  V6C 2T4*
*(800) 268-6282, (604) 689-9333, Fax (604) 684-4555*

**General Manager:** *Ruy Paes-Braga*
**Rooms:** *274 doubles, 111 suites*
**Canadian Rates:** *Doubles $285-335 (EP), Suites $335-900 (EP)*
**Payment:** *AE, DC, MC, and VISA*
**Children:** *Welcome — extensive children's amenities are available;*
       *children are free of charge when sharing a room with*
       *their parents*
**Dogs:** *Welcome, extensive doggie amenities are available*
**Open:** *All year*

If people wanted to take their dog on a first-class trip through parts of western British Columbia, where both human and beast would be thoroughly pampered, it would be easy — all they'd have to do is start in Vancouver at the Four Seasons Hotel, then move on to The Empress in Victoria, and finally to the Sooke Harbor House in Sooke. All three of these places know just how to cater to canines and their human friends, in royal style. There are plenty of fabulous hotels in Vancouver, but only one truly rolls out the red carpet for Bowser — The Four Seasons Hotel.

This luxurious hotel is set behind an unassuming contemporary facade, but as we took the escalator up from street level, its elegant interiors began to unfold. Dark wood walls, subdued lighting, and impressive antiques give the lobby a warm, residential quality. In true Four Seasons tradition, huge vases filled with lavish flower arrangements are placed upon highly polished antique tables. The lobby is merely the centerpiece for the various restaurants and small gift shops encircling it. Two of the more notable restaurants are the intimate Chartwell restaurant, and the equally inviting Garden Terrace. While the former is fashioned with paneled walls and old-world sophistication, the terrace is a veritable rain forest of potted plants and ficus trees that thrive under natural light. In addition to the light and airy garden setting, this chamber is also bedecked with an exquisite handmade Inuit rug draped across one wall. Guests may relax here for cocktails, or sample the elaborate brunch that is served each Sunday.

The Four Seasons rises 28 floors above the city of Vancouver. As one might imagine, there is an ongoing renovation program in

British Columbia

place to maintain the fresh and sophisticated look of both the common areas and the guest chambers. This building was once filled with apartments, and although it was converted to a hotel years ago, there is still a residential quality about the guest bedrooms. There are many types of rooms available to travelers and their canine companions. Some of the smaller rooms are outfitted with oversized writing desks and intimate sitting areas; the corner deluxe chambers are fashioned with separate sitting rooms and floor-to-ceiling windows; and the executive suites are furnished with mirrored French doors that can be closed to separate the bedroom from the spacious living room.

The color schemes also vary with the room, and while some have sophisticated black and white coordinated fabrics, others are festooned in equally lovely shades of russet or celadon green. Sitting rooms often contain overstuffed sofas and armchairs, as well as inlaid mahogany reproductions of English antiques. In many of the rooms, Chippendale chairs surround Queen Anne coffee tables, while drop leaf end tables are usually topped with Oriental vase lamps. Even the artwork is noteworthy, incorporating black and white sketches of the English countryside or a notable scene of the Northwest. The amenities, both human and doggie, are also extensive. Beds are covered in fine linen, and fluffy down comforters. Down pillows are also available, as are foam pillows for those who are allergic to feathers. Armoires contain well-stocked private bars and a televisions. VCRs are standard features in the suites. Bathrooms include hair dryers, scales, lighted mirrors, and trays filled with every convenience — including European soaps, conditioners, cotton balls and swabs, lotions, and bath gels. Telephones are found in the bathrooms, as well as in the sitting areas and bedrooms.

Dogs may not think much of the human amenities, but they will certainly appreciate the gourmet biscuits that await their arrival in the room (a recipe card for these biscuits is provided). These are placed in two handmade pottery bowls, alongside a large bottle of Evian water on a silver tray. Should Bowser require a few additional services, guests need only ask on his behalf. In addition to providing a special dog-oriented menu or a comfy dog bed, the staff will walk Bowser for guests who might be otherwise occupied at walking time.

While Bowser is dining on gourmet kibble, guests might want to slip downstairs to Chartwell. Dark, wood-paneled walls create a sense of warmth in this intimate space, enhanced only by the flickering fireplace. A hand-painted mural and other original works of art make this chamber seem more like a private dining room, rather than just another hotel restaurant. Guests dine at small linen-covered tables set with fine china and cobalt blue goblets. The service is impeccable, and patrons enjoy the feeling of being thoroughly pampered. Some might choose to start their meal with the smoked candied salmon loin, accented with a horseradish crème fraîche and onion and dill bannock; the Dungeness crab cake with dandelion and saffron aioli; or the charred lamb loin carpaccio with a sharp mustard and oregano sauce. The open-faced vegetarian lasagna was intriguing, with a smoked tomato oil and truffle pesto; as was the pheasant breast filled with homemade ricotta and grilled leeks. Patrons might also want to order the pepper seared beef tenderloin with a goat cheese crust, crispy elephant garlic, and a red wine sauce; the Maine lobster; the Pacific salmon; or the Fraser Valley vegetables baked in a delicate crust.

We would recommend limiting after-dinner walks with Bowser to the immediate area and saving longer strolls for the daylight hours. The Four Seasons is in the center of Vancouver's financial and shopping districts, within easy walking distance of just about any attraction. The hotel is situated across the street from the Vancouver Art Gallery, just above the Pacific Centre Mall, which has more than 200 shops, restaurants, and clubs.

Dogs who feel comfortable in the city will very much enjoy Vancouver, as there are fine walks to the waterfront, the botanical gardens, and an assortment of lush city parks nearby the hotel. The general rule of thumb for dogs and parks is that they are welcome, provided they remain leashed. The park closest to the hotel is situated between Nelson and Comox streets. Those who are looking forward to a longer outing can visit the 1,200-acre Stanley Park, which is absolutely spectacular. One of our favorite strolls here is along the Seawall Promenade, which edges the circumference of this park. In downtown Vancouver, it is possible to find a number of other small green grassy areas, but these are generally off limits to dogs in the summer months.

After a long walk, Bowser will undoubtedly be a little tired. During his nap, guests may wish to visit the hotel's health club, where, in addition to a full complement of weights, rowing machines, and Lifecycles, there is an indoor whirlpool, a sauna, and a 60-foot-long pool, all of which should provide just the right combination of passive therapy to rejuvenate the entire body.

All in all, we felt the Four Seasons provided just about everything we and our canine companions could ever want or hope for in a wonderful, city-side vacation.

# Hotel Vancouver

*900 West Georgia Street*
*Vancouver, B.C., Canada V6C 2W6*
*(800) 441-1414, (604) 684-3131, Fax (604) 662-1937*

**General Manager:** Michael Lambert
**Rooms:** 550 doubles and suites
**Canadian Rates:** $175-315 (EP)
**Payment:** AE, CB, DC, DSC, JCB, MC and VISA
**Children:** Welcome; under 18 are free of charge when sharing
         room with parents
**Dogs:** Welcome
**Open:** Open

The Hotel Vancouver looks like an old world palace, with its steeply-pitched copper roofs and magnificent sandstone facade rising high into the city's skyscape. It was built in 1939, but in a 16th-century style reminiscent of a French Renaissance château, complete with stone carvings of Greek mythological figures. Artisans were hired to create the intricate statues of native West Coast and Central Plains' chieftains, along with more Classical and Gothic subjects that still guard the facade today.

The history of the hotel is an interesting one, especially when considering that this particular Hotel Vancouver is the third hotel in a series to bear the same name. It all started in 1887, when the Canadian Pacific Railroad built a four-story, wooden hotel at this location. It was replaced in 1916 with a far grander hotel, but its beauty was short-lived, as the building fell into complete disarray within 20 years of its completion, and eventually had to be torn down. At this point, the Canadian National Railroad stepped in and began construction of the majestic hotel that we now know as the Hotel Vancouver. Surprisingly, the railroad ran out of money midway through the project. This hotel would have also gone by the wayside had it not been for the Canadian Pacific Railroad, which offered its financial support in 1937. By 1939 the hotel was completed. Ever since then, the Canadian Pacific Railroad has had a sporadic interest in the hotel. Finally, in 1987 it took over permanent management of it. The seemingly unending restoration process continues, but throughout it all, the historic beauty of the hotel survives. The lobby is the most recent project. Although we have not seen the final result, we hope the existing, prefabricated 1970s look will soon be replaced by a new decor more in keeping with the old-world style of the rest of the hotel.

The former lobby is just one example of renovations run amuck over the years. One person who saw the value in preserving the past, though, was Ethel Ferguson. She was a housekeeper who worked at the hotel for more than 20 years. In the 1960s, someone tried to eradicate the hotel's historic character in favor of bright lights and dizzying geometric patterns. Ethel had the chutzpah to take a large number of the antique furnishings and hide them. For 15 years she kept her secret, and when the management finally came to its senses and returned to an interior design more befitting that of this grand dame, she brought forward enough furniture from her secret stash to decorate 35 rooms. Those who want to take a look at some of these original pieces should ask for one of the 12th-floor guest rooms, which are decorated with many of these furnishings.

Each floor of bedrooms is different from the others. We saw a number of them and were impressed with their strong traditional English decor. Some are graced with lovely mahogany pieces, while others have a more contemporary twist that features slightly more brass and glass. Most are accented with ceiling moldings, original thick wood doors, and brass fixtures. Chintzes cover the quilted spreads and tailored dust ruffles, while coordinated draperies frame the double hung windows. Colors range from a pale blue with white and yellow accents to a burgundy coupled with subtle green hues. The windows open, but unless guests are on the uppermost floors, they will want to keep them closed — it can be noisy. The first seven floors have been renovated recently. Some of the thoughtful extras are down comforters, chocolates, vases of fresh flowers, and minibars set in armoires alongside cable televisions. Even the bathrooms have been beautifully refurbished, and all are stocked with an array of toiletries. Our favorite chambers are the corner rooms. We like them as much for their impressive views as for the abundance of sunshine that permeates them.

One of the newer additions to the hotel is the award-winning spa, located on the third floor. The huge atrium pool is surrounded by outdoor gardens filled with potted trees and flowers. The health club has everything guests could want, including a full complement of exercise equipment. The spa will loan Walkmans, or guests may watch television while they workout. During our visit, we also noticed plenty of people either heading out to or coming back from power walks and jogs with their dogs.

Those who are looking for a nearby outing will find a small grassy park just down the street from the hotel. Here they can visit anytime but in the summer months. To get to Stanley Park, guests walk down Georgia Street five or six blocks. Once in the park, it is great fun to follow the paths that lead through the forested setting.

Just a block from the hotel is the trendy Robson Street with its many boutiques and sidewalk cafés. Some may want to stop for a cappucino in one of these outdoor cafés. Bowser will probably be able to persuade either his human companion or some of the other patrons to part with a few delectable treats. Sunset Beach is another option, situated on the other side of Vancouver. North Vancouver is just one bridge away, and visitors and their canines will discover even more outdoor diversions there. One of the more popular options is to head up Grouse Mountain by tram. At the top, there are great hiking trails, paved paths, and fabulous views looking back over to Vancouver.

After a busy day, guests will enjoy returning to the comfortable confines of the hotel, where they may enjoy a memorable meal. For years, the Vancouver Hotel's rooftop restaurant was the place for romantic dining and dancing. It rests on the 14th floor and anyone who has been here knows about the spectacular city views. The formal restaurant still attracts patrons who want a romantic dining experience with a view, but this intimate space has been somewhat modernized. The ambiance might not be the same as in the original, but guests can still dine on fine food. They might wish to start with an appetizer such as the lobster bisque, a warm seafood salad, or escargot. Dungeness crab meat crèpes, prime rib with Yorkshire pudding, and medallions of venison with grilled polenta and fall vegetables were a few of the selections that topped the fall menu. Guests come here for the views and fine cuisine; but they head downstairs to Griffins for unabashed fun.

The hotel's formal mascot is a griffin, and it has been incorporated into this convivial restaurant bearing the same name. This high-ceilinged chamber's walls are painted a lemon yellow, while black and white checked tiles and large square columns of mahogany provide decorative accents. The floor-to-ceiling windows allow plenty of natural light to permeate this space. We came for the buffet (as most people do). It had been highly recommended — and sure enough, it delivered. Children will love the kiddy buffet, where they are able make their own pancakes, pour their own cereal, and create their own ice cream concoctions. An array of sweet and colorful toppings and side dishes await the younger patrons on a side table. Festive plates, napkins, and plastic cutlery complete this delightful experience. This place is fun, for both children and adults. Now if only the management could devise a special eatery geared for dogs, then everyone would be able to enjoy this place.

# Metropolitan Hotel Vancouver

*645 Howe Street*
*Vancouver, B.C., Canada V6C 2Y9*
*(800) 667-2300, (604) 687-1122, Fax (604) 689-7044*

*General Manager: Brian Young*
*Rooms: 197 doubles, 18 suites*
*Canadian Rates: Doubles $145-205 (EP), Suites $215-525 (EP)*
*Payment: AE, DC, MC, and VISA*
*Children: Welcome*
*Dogs: Welcome with notice*
*Open: All year*

We have always loved the boutique hotels in New York City, as they provide visitors (and, very often, their dogs) with a residential feeling. While Vancouver does not claim to be anything like New York City, it is a bustling place. At the end of the day, there is nothing better than walking into a small hotel like the Metropolitan, where guests instantly feel enveloped in the luxurious surroundings. The Metropolitan Hotel Vancouver was originally built in 1985 as a Mandarin Oriental Hotel, and it still reflects a good deal of its Asian heritage (even though the Delta Hotel chain owned and operated it from 1987 to 1995). A privately owned company out of Hong Kong, the Liverton Hotels International, bought the hotel in the fall of 1995 and has reestablished the gracious traditions that the Mandarin began a decade ago.

The Metropolitan is a work in progress, and there is now talk of establishing an elegant restaurant to match its exquisite five-star guest rooms. We were impressed with what was already in place — if it is only going to get better, then dining patrons should be in for a real treat. We walked into the hotel's intimate lobby, with its central sitting area, unobtrusive reception desk, and a pair of elevators that whisk guests to the upper levels. The physical space seems to flow, with curving hallways that lead to charming alcoves. We stepped into elegantly appointed bedrooms accented with soothing taupe and cream color schemes. The guest chambers are not overly large, but they are well designed. One illuminated nook might contain a small bronze statue, while another has a figure carved in stone. When guests settle in for the night under their European duvets, they probably will not need to get up again — the lights, the stereo, and the television can all be controlled by pushing a few buttons on their bedside table's console. The marble bathrooms are filled with a full complement of Swiss botanical shampoos, soaps, and lotions. The terry robes are not found in the bathroom, though, but in the closets, where there are also a small iron and ironing board for touching up wrinkled garments. The bedrooms are totally soundproof; however, guests can open the sliding door to the tiny terrace and let the refreshing breezes drift in off the water. Guests who are here to work can use the writing desks, while those who have come for relaxation can sample some of the gourmet offerings in the fully stocked minibar.

For more elaborate offerings, Le Café is located just downstairs. We understand that the space it presently occupies may be converted to meeting rooms and the restaurant moved downstairs. But until then, guests will dine in an atrium setting, where the bright and distinctive art on the walls is as notable as the fine food. The hotel's health spa is one of the best in the city. Although not as elaborate as the one at the Pan Pacific, it is state-of-the-art and outfitted with every exercise machine imaginable, not to mention squash courts. The spa also offers an indoor swimming pool, whirlpools, saunas, and massage therapy. Guests can even watch television as they work out, which might help pass the time during particularly strenuous reps.

The Metropolitan Hotel Vancouver is conveniently located halfway between the waterfront and the shopping and financial districts. From here, guests can walk a few blocks up to the trendy Robson Street, or down to the waterfront area. Bowser may be included in all these outings, as there are grassy areas to enjoy along the way. There are also plenty of parks in Vancouver — 174, at last count. Those who want to venture a little further afield may wish to visit the Mount Seymour Provincial Park. This is a semi-wilderness park with incredible views looking out to the Gulf and San Juan Islands. Dogs and their friends can hike up Mount Seymour, or follow the easier Flower Loop Trail that is also in the same vicinity. Another option is the Goldie Lake Loop Trail. Guests can bring a picnic and enjoy the day in this picturesque setting, knowing that in the evening, they can return to the more urban adventures awaiting in the city.

# Pan Pacific Hotel Vancouver

*300-999 Canada Place*
*Vancouver, B.C., Canada V6C 3B5*
*(800) 6632-8111, (604) 662-8111, Fax (604) 662-3815*

*General Manager: Martin Astengo*
*Rooms: 467 doubles, 39 suites*
*Canadian Rates: Doubles $195-375 (EP), Suites $375-1,200 (EP)*
*Payment: AE, DC, MC, and VISA*
*Children: Welcome (cribs, cots, high chairs, and baby-sitters available)*
*Dogs: Welcome — they've had all sizes*
*Open: All year*

The Pan Pacific Hotel seems more like a small city than a hotel; but then again, it needs to be big, since it sits atop Canada Place, which houses Vancouver's Convention Center. The complex was built in 1986 for the World's Fair, but it still attracts plenty of attention. From Burrard Inlet, the entire building appears to float on the water, with its five massive white sails appearing poised to pull the buildings away from the shore. Cruise ships tie up here before heading further north, and just about all visitors to Vancouver find their way to the hotel sometime during their stay.

Since the World's Fair, the Pan Pacific Hotel Vancouver continues to attract countless accolades, visiting dignitaries, and celebrities. Bill Clinton and Boris Yeltsin met here for their presidential summit in 1993. HRH, the Sultan of Brunei, stayed here, as did His Highness The Aga Khan IV. The parade of princesses and princes seems too great to mention here, but has included royalty from the Netherlands, Japan, Thailand, and Tongo. Guests over the years have spotted such celebrities as Sean Connery, Bob Hope, and George Burns, along with sports notables Wayne Gretzky and Stefan Edberg. Robert De Niro holed up here for months with his dogs, but was left pretty much to his own devices. Five diamonds have been awarded to the hotel, and the readers of Condé Nast's *Traveler* voted it one of the 25 best foreign hotels in the world. We wondered if the Canadian Pacific Vancouver could live up to all the positive press.

Anyone looking for intimacy and luxury had better steer clear of the Pan Pacific, and instead reserve a room at the Metropolitan Hotel Vancouver or the Waterfront Centre. But those looking for accessibility, fabulous water views, and the best athletic facilities in town should consider the Pan Pacific Hotel Vancouver. As visitors enter the building their eyes are immediately drawn upwards. The ceiling towers overhead some eight stories above the atrium. We rode up a series of escalators just to reach the main lobby. Once we arrived, we spent some time trying to take in every nuance of this cavernous space. The combination of falling water echoing off the marble floors and lush greenery made it seem almost tropical. Natural light pours into the lobby through 40-foot-high windows that seem to wrap themselves around this chamber. Anyone who wants to watch the activity on the docked cruise ships below, or get a closer look at those massive sails, need only step out past these windows to the observation deck.

There is no need to worry about noisy children or dogs in the public areas, as this place is so big that no one would ever notice a dog's yip or a child's enthusiastic banter. The upper floors are carpeted and quieter, but do seem to stretch on forever. The bedrooms are well appointed and are decorated in subdued color schemes with an Asian twist. The bedspreads have a bamboo pattern that nicely complements the grass wallpaper. The furnishings are quite streamlined and constructed of lightly-stained wood. The bedrooms have all the usual amenities, such as clock radios, fully-stocked minibars, and remote controlled televisions with a full complement of movie channels. The marble bathrooms are fully outfitted with toiletries and other conveniences. Guests may request same-day laundry and valet, use of the safety deposit boxes, complimentary shoeshine, and baby-sitting services. While the standard guest rooms are fine, they are not especially noteworthy, except for the views. From the upper levels, guests feel as though they are sitting in the crow's nest, with miles of unobstructed views. The suites are far more elaborate, and are designed for extended stays. Some of the most elaborate have private steam rooms, saunas, and whirlpools, along with kitchens and separate living rooms.

Some guests come to the Canadian Pacific Hotel and never have to leave, not even to exercise. The health club and spa attract professional and weekend athletes who come to play racquetball, squash, or paddle tennis; run on the indoor track; take aerobics classes — and then spend some time in the sauna, steam room, or with a massage therapist. Tanning salons make guests look healthy — even when the sun has been hidden for days. Just in case the sun does come out, the eighth-floor sun deck is available to those who want to take advantage of the 50-foot outdoor heated pool, the chaise lounges, and the Jacuzzi.

The hotel has restaurants to suit just about any palate and price level. For those in search of an elegant dining experience, the Five Sails is probably the best bet. Vancouver has an inordinate number of fine restaurants, and many of these are within easy walking distance of the hotel. Dogs will really enjoy cruising the docks around the property. There are also a series of tiered terraces and fountains just across from the hotel; these make a pleasant area for walks with Bowser. The expansive Stanley Park is also within walking distance. Guests can easily get their car out from the 750-car parking lot under the hotel — and head off on short adventures across the city's bridges to other notable parks. West Vancouver offers the Cypress Provincial Park, where the views of the Georgia Strait are inspiring. From the downtown area, it is only seven miles to the Lions Gate Bridge, which leads into the park. Once here, visitors can hike around the 7,000 acres of park land and wilderness. Two of the more intriguing trails here are the Howe Sound Crest Trail and the Baden-Powell Centennial '71 Trail. The park's forests contain trees that are over 1,000 years old, as well as low-lying ferns, false azaleas, and heather. In the winter months, visitors and their canine cohorts may wish to bring their cross-country skiing paraphernalia along as well.

---

# Waterfront Centre Hotel

*900 Canada Place Way*
*Vancouver, B.C., Canada  V6C 3L5*
*(800) 268-9411, (604) 691-1991, Fax (604) 691-1999*

*General Manager: Michael Kaile*
*Rooms: 429 doubles, 26 suites*
*Canadian Rates: Doubles $330-420 (EP), Suites $465-1,700 (EP)*
*Payment: AE, CB, DSC, DC, JCB, MC, and VISA*
*Children: Welcome; under 18 are free of charge*
*Dogs: Welcome if "knee level or below"*
*Open: All year*

Vancouver is a spectacular city, especially when visitors can see the sun and clouds reflected off the deep blue water and the mountains looming off in the distance. The best place to capture this vivid panorama is down along the waterfront, as the views further up the hill are often obscured by tall buildings. There are not too many options in the noteworthy "waterfront hotel" category, but fortunately, one of the best of these welcomes guests with "knee-high" dogs. The Waterfront Centre Hotel is one of the newer additions to the group of luxury hotels owned by Canadian Pacific. Even from a distance this building is striking. It rises 23 stories in a crescent of blue reflective glass set against a white framework. Surrounding it are well-designed terraces and fountains edged by beautifully-tended flower gardens. This place is huge, yet once inside, the feeling is far more personal and private than initial impressions would lead one to believe.

A single wall of glass seems to wrap itself around the lobby, letting in an abundance of natural light that falls across the sandstone-colored marble floors. Deep, overstuffed sofas — the type people sink into and have difficulty climbing out of — create private sitting areas that are nestled behind towering columns. We were drawn, as most are, to what appears to be a massive antique map set against one wall. Upon closer inspection, we noticed this was really a contemporary piece of art, entitled *Voyage of Discovery*. This chart tracks George Vancouver's trip to the Northwest in 1790. We thought he would be quite surprised to see all of the changes to this once wild territory.

With most of the guest rooms providing stunning vistas, we had difficulty choosing from among the many available views, which included views of the harbor, views across the water toward Stanley Park, or over the cityscape. Others who are stumped by the array of vistas should keep in mind that nearly 300 guest rooms offer views of the water. Regardless of one's ultimate decision, all of the chambers are decorated in soft earth tones, ranging from pale peach and ivory to ecru and dove gray. As new arrivals enter their room, they will find music playing, quilted bedspreads turned down, and baskets of edibles, as well as trays of mints and bottled water — all waiting to refresh them. The entire effect is designed to be soothing, and it succeeds. At night, guests can open their windows and let the refreshing breezes drift in from the water. Of course, there are plenty of other amenities, such as minibars and remote controlled televisions set in the armoire, clock radios placed upon bedside tables, and bathrooms outfitted with just about every imaginable toiletry. In the morning, coffee is set out on each floor and interested guests may help themselves. Those who want to settle under a down duvet at night — and have the convenience of a continental breakfast in the morning — may wish to reserve the Concierge Level Rooms, where, in addition to breakfast, guests are also offered complimentary cocktails and *hors' d'oeuvres* in the evenings.

The hotel offers guests the use of a full-service health club, which is outfitted with a steam room, a whirlpool, workout equipment, and a masseuse. But it is the outdoor swimming pool, set on the a third-story roof deck, that usually gets the most attention. From the pool, we had a great view of the mountains, harbor, and city. The pool is on one end of the roof deck, while the remainder of the deck is comprised of a little park of shade trees and extensive herb gardens. The chef at Herons Restaurant, just downstairs, picks most of his herbs from these gardens and uses them to create his inspiring menu. The physical layout of Herons is equally eye-catching, with walls of glass, hand-crafted wrought iron, and an atrium setting — all of which are worth visiting on the basis of visual appeal alone. The restaurant specializes in food and wine indigenous to British Columbia, ranging from organic fruits and vegetables to local meats and game. The extensive wine list contains some of the best wines that British Columbia has to offer.

We were anxious to get out and explore some of the more verdant sections of the city. Stanley Park allows dogs on all the trails in the park, but they cannot go into the Children's Zoo. Another walk takes visitors and their dogs to Brockton Point and the lighthouse. Along the way, they will pass the Royal Vancouver Yacht Club and Hallelujah Point, where an extensive collection of totem poles is found. A car is needed to visit some of the other intriguing parks near Vancouver. We suggest crossing the Burrard Bridge. Once across, both human and beast will be able to roam freely at Vanier Park, the Vancouver Museum, the Planetarium, and the Maritime Museum. Jericho Park is another viable option; it is comprised of more than 125 acres of grass, trees, and gardens.

---

# Laburnam Cottage

*1388 Terrace Avenue*
*North Vancouver, B.C., Canada V7R 1B4*
*(604) 988-4877*

**Hostess:** *Delphine Masterton*
**Rooms:** *4 doubles, 2 cottages*
**Canadian Rates:** *Doubles $120 (B&B), Cottages $150 (B&B)*
**Payment:** *MC and VISA*
**Children:** *Welcome in the cottages*
**Dogs:** *Welcome with approval*
**Open:** *Open*

The Laburnum Cottage is only 15 minutes from downtown Vancouver, but once here, guests might as well be in the English countryside. Don't misunderstand us; the Laburnam Cottage lies in a residential area with houses all around it, but somehow, Delphine Masterton has created a lovely enclave for her guests. We found this Tudor-style cottage at the bottom of a cobblestone driveway. Gardens aside, the house also resembles something out of England, with its leaded glass windows, dark wood trim, and multiple-peaked roof line that seems to ramble off in every direction. While it appears quite historic, we soon discovered that it wasn't built until the 1940s. The outside was so appealing, we could hardly wait to see the interior.

We rang the bell and Delphine answered. As we stepped into the sunny foyer, we could hear sounds of laughter coming from the kitchen. It was Thanksgiving and Delphine's family was visiting, yet she graciously welcomed us and invited us into her warm and cozy country kitchen. One of her daughters was chopping, another was pulling pies out of the immense Aga stove, and the rest of the famil was having a fine time chatting around the table. We were tempted to join them, until we caught sight of Delphine's gardens. It was fall, and even though the growing season was almost over, the gardens were still remarkable.

In fact, the gardens alone often attract many guests to the Laburnum Cottage, which resembles something out of a fine gardening coffee-table book. Narrow stone paths lead to all corners of the property, and eventually to a small footbridge that crosses a creek. Huge trees, including one fine old willow, create a canopy for the mix of shade-loving rhododendrons and azaleas. Roses were still blooming around the patio, offering the last bits of color visitors would see until springtime. This place must be spectacular in the height of the growing season, when bulbs are popping from the earth, delicate perennials are in full bloom, and dogwoods are flashing their pink and white flowers.

Set invitingly amid these gardens is our favorite chamber, the Summer House. This is a separate cottage, which seems as if it once could have been a large potting shed. Now it is a storybook cottage covered with wisteria, and an ideal place for a couple and their dog. The wood walls are painted out white, and little paned windows catch the sun as it pours in during the afternoon. A brass bed covered with a handmade quilt combines with antique wicker chairs and tables to set the overall decorative tone. Original watercolors provide a splash of color. Guests out here are totally self-sufficient, with a kitchenette, a small television, and a fireplace.

The rest of the bedrooms are in the main house and the adjacent cottage, just off the kitchen. All the bedrooms overlook these magnificent gardens; three are situated on the upper floors and one downstairs. The beds are made of brass and covered with soft cotton sheets and puffy down comforters. We felt surrounded at times by pale pinks and yellows reminiscent of a Monet watercolor. Lustrous hardwood floors are covered with Oriental rugs, while floral chintzes and silks line the armchairs and sofas and frame the windows. This traditional look is accentuated by the patina emanating from the English and French antiques. Delphine is a collector of things, and she displays her porcelains, china, and crystal throughout the house.

If the main house seems, for small children, like a disaster waiting to happen, guests should keep in mind that Delphine raised a large family here and has a keen appreciation for what it is like traveling with young ones. She recently completed a separate cottage suite; this is ideal for families and is located through the back door of the kitchen. We stepped out onto a little courtyard before entering an expansive suite. This space is fashioned with a master bedroom, along with a loft area for the children. They can bring their sleeping bags and have a fine time sleeping up here on comfy mats. Guests will also appreciate the full kitchen, stereo, and television, as well as the ambiance of a fireplace.

Regardless of room choice, all guests are treated to a full breakfast in the morning. Delphine creates fabulous meals, which most enjoy in the separate breakfast room overlooking the gardens. The terra cotta tiles on the floors, coupled with large windows, make this chamber seem almost like an atrium. Guests are treated to a full English breakfast with a continental twist, starting with fresh fruit, orange juice, and coffee or tea. Baskets of freshly baked scones, muffins, or cinnamon buns are set out for all to enjoy, while guests wait for, perhaps, blueberry or strawberry pancakes, French toast, crèpes, or omelets. Bacon and sausage also accompany this hearty repast.

Afterwards, Bowser should be all too eager to take a walk. The neighborhood is quiet and there are plenty of streets that are ideal for leisurely strolls with a dog. It is also easy to access the seemingly unlimited number of hiking trails in North Vancouver. Within minutes, visitors can be on their way to walking up the steep mountain trails, crossing suspension bridges, or simply driving to a spot to enjoy the remarkable views. The Capilano Suspension Bridge and Park is a popular destination for visitors, although dogs might get a bit nervous on the suspension bridge; it stretches 450 feet across a canyon floor that is 220 feet below. Also within the park are a number of grassy areas and nature trails that Bowser will enjoy investigating. Lynn Canyon Park has a number of trails, as well as a suspension bridge. (People are not charged a fee to walk across it.) Grouse Mountain has a gondola that can bring people and their canines up to the top of the mountain, where they can access trails along the West Coast Mountain Range. At the end of the day, though, most like to return to the Laburnum Cottage for a civilized cup of tea and scones amid the peaceful garden setting.

# The Maria Rose B&B

*8083 Aspen Road*
*Site 11, Comp. 156, R.R. #3*
*Vernon, B.C., Canada V1T 6L6*
*Telephone and Fax: (604) 549-4773*

*Innkeepers: Ruth-Maria Cushing, Peter Filas*
*Rooms: 4 doubles*
*Canadian Rates: $60-75 (B&B)*
*Payment: VISA*
*Children: Welcome*
*Dogs: Welcome, for a small fee*
*Open: All year*

Vernon lies at the northern end of the Okanagan Valley — a region known for everything from apples to emus. Farms dot the landscape beginning in Vernon and reaching as far south as Penticon. Throughout this valley, vintners, orchardists, and farmers grow grains, grapes, and even bananas; some specialize in raising emus, llamas, and bees. While the climate is temperate all year, a short trip up Silver Star Mountain will generally yield cold, dry mountain air and a good deal of snow. We visited in the fall, when the valley was still warm, but as we climbed the steep, winding switchbacks toward the mountain top, snow began to fall. The views along the way were magnificent, and as night fell, the lights of Vernon twinkled below.

Halfway up the mountain, the twinkling lights on a delicate hand-carved sign pointed us toward the Maria Rose B&B. Its lovely old-world name was matched only by our gracious hosts, Maria and Peter. Both are originally from Germany and are well versed in European hospitality. We felt as though we had stumbled upon an intimate European pensione, and had to keep reminding ourselves that we were still on North American soil. The personal touches abound, yet nothing is contrived.

When we arrived it was getting late and we were both exhausted. Thus, our hosts escorted us over to a converted garage called the Royal Coach House, where the B&B guest rooms are located. Maria told us that when she bought the property, this seemed like the ideal space to convert into bedrooms. As with most simple projects, this one had its share of complications; however, the end result seems to justify all their effort — four lovely guest chambers named King, Queen, Prince, and Princess. On this particular evening, we needed — and received — the royal treatment. Peter led us to the Princess Room, which is painted a pale pink with bright floral accents. He took the coverlet off the bed, fluffed the down comforter and pillows, and gave us a rejuvenating gel for the bath. He then left us to take a hot bath and sink into the soft cotton sheets.

A sense of solitude and utter quiet made for a wonderful night's sleep. By the next morning, we were ready to learn more about the B&B. Our room and the Prince's Room connect and also share a bathroom, making these an ideal choice for a family. Ours was the more feminine of the two spaces, with lots of lace and bright floral fabrics. A grouping of tiny pictures lined one wall, along with a heart-shaped wreath. A small, mirrored dressing table was adorned with a tray and two glasses, all of which were hand-painted with wildflowers. Even our pillowcases had delicate pink and blue flowers embroidered along the edges. The Prince's Room is fashioned in darker greens, but also has lace accents framing the windows. There is a double bed in here, along with a small sitting area. The entry to each bedroom is tiled, and brass hooks line the wall for hanging up one's outer garments. These spaces were so immaculate that we felt compelled to take off our shoes. The King's and Queen's Rooms are located on the first floor. Both have private bathrooms and small sitting areas. The King's Room is dominated by a king-size bed covered with a down comforter and a turquoise coverlet. Modern amenities include a television and small refrigerator. The Queen's Room is substantially larger than the Princess's Room, but utilizes the same basic color schemes. We liked the added touch of a little stuffed toy dog placed on each of the beds, as well as the little rose on our room key.

Both the main house and the guest house rest on seven forested acres. In the morning, the views to the valley are spectacular, if not dizzying. As we walked to the house, we noticed the resident cat happily snoozing on a rooftop. Breakfast is served in the main house, and guests generally enjoy this in the downstairs dining room. This cozy chamber is warmed by a wood stove. On this day, though, we were the only guests, and we enjoyed breakfast in the formal upstairs dining room off the kitchen. Maria is a collector, and displayed throughout her house is fine china, crystal, and silver. Everything about their home is European, including the breakfast. We started with strong coffee, coffee cake, and a light fruit salad. This was followed by delicate crèpes filled with homemade applesauce. During this hearty repast, we learned that Maria lived in Toronto for years before coming to Vernon. She traveled extensively with her dog throughout Canada, and frequently, south to Cape Cod. It was always difficult for her to find places to stay that welcomed dogs, which is why she and Peter decided to accept well-mannered pets at their B&B.

While there are plenty of things to do in the area, guests might find themselves content just to explore the property or read on the patio. Within easy driving distance, there is horseback riding, golf, swimming, boating, fishing and plenty of hiking and biking trails. The best place to take Bowser is to the top of Silver Star Mountain. This is a part of the Silver Star Provincial Park. Up here, visitors and their canines can hike the area throughout the summer and fall, and in the winter, try a little skiing instead. At the end of the day, guests are usually ready to head back to the B&B for a therapeutic sauna. We would have liked to spend a long weekend here, but unfortunately had to move on the next day. As we were leaving, Maria gave us a little goodie bag for our journey, filled with all sorts of tasty treats.

---

# Silver Lode Inn

*P.O. Box 5*
*Silver Star Mountain Resort*
*Vernon, B.C., Canada  V0E 1G0*
*(604) 549-5105, Fax (604) 549-5101 (For reservations call collect)*

*Hosts: Max Schlaepfer and Trudy Amstutz*
*Rooms: 16 doubles, 6 suites*
*Canadian Rates: Doubles $68-146 (EP), Suites $114-183 (EP)*
*Payment: AE, MC, and VISA*
*Children: Welcome*
*Dogs: Welcome*
*Open: All year*

The Silver Lode Inn is set on top of Silver Star Mountain. We knew this was the second largest ski resort in British Columbia; however, what we found at the top of the hill was unlike anything we had ever seen in a ski resort — outside of, perhaps, Vail, Colorado. Silver Star, like Vail, was built around a theme. The powers behind this area created a Victorian community that borders on being almost too cute, but stops just short of it. It would be difficult to tell what is renovated and what is original, but it is all colorful and looks authentic.

The Victorian theme village is the centerpiece, with an array of Victorian homes with vibrant facades lining the hills. The entire resort comprises a few square miles at the most, which makes it an ideal area for visitors and their canines to explore on foot. We had a fine time investigating the surrounding neighborhoods, and looking at the assortment of house styles, both large and small. Some are rambling Victorian-style ski houses, with porches, turrets, and decorative shingles. A few are painted hunter green with mustard yellow and burgundy highlights. Others are a slate blue with crimson red and green accents. Still other buildings resemble the Victorian row houses that line the hills in San Francisco. Their bright facades are especially spectacular when contrasted against the whiteness of the snow. Most of these houses are found in an area called The Knoll. Along with private residences, many of these dwellings are rented to skiers (and sometimes their dogs).

The highlight, though, is the town center, with its boardwalks and vibrant facades that consist of a few hotels and restaurants, a saloon, and an assortment of shops. Cars are left in outlying lots, and most visitors generally walk to the village from there. Set in the midst of it all is the Silver Lode Inn. Although it was built in 1986, the inn looks as though it was here long before the village grew up around it. The inn is known for its fine Swiss food. Although we were visiting during the off season, the restaurant was quite busy. We asked for a window table, then spent the better part of the evening dipping into the fondue, sipping wine, and watching the activity in the village below. Actually, the menu is far more extensive than just fondue. We were most intrigued with a few of the Swiss specialties, such as raclette, which is a crispy wedge of cheese accompanied by jacket potatoes, onions, gherkins, tomatoes, or mushrooms. More familiar dishes were the veal cordon bleu and the wiener schnitzel — both are light and delicious. All meals are served with vegetables and a choice of potatoes. Two of the more popular potato dishes are the roesti potatoes and the special Silver Lode potatoes. After dinner, we gravitated to the fireside lounge for a hot toddy before retiring. During the summer months, most guests love to sit out on the deck and enjoy their food amid planters overflowing with flowers.

While dogs are welcome in the guest rooms, they do need to steer clear of the dining room. They can do this by coming in through a separate entrance that connects directly into the guest room wing. The bedrooms lie off one long hallway and are just what we would expect of a ski lodge. They are perfectly functional, exceptionally clean, but a little on the Spartan side. We were told that they are going to be refurbished soon. For now, guests can expect to see pretty floral curtains at the windows that match the spread on the bed. Some opt for a room with either a queen bed and a sofa bed or perhaps a pair of adjoining rooms with a kitchenette. The kitchenettes are a good option, because they come with a small refrigerator, a sink, and a two-burner stove top that allows guests to create a few simple lunches and dinners. At the end of the hall, there is a private hot tub that guests are welcome to use.

In the winter, the emphasis is obviously on skiing, both downhill and cross-country. This place isn't huge, yet somehow there are 81 runs and 2,500 vertical feet packed onto the mountain. The inn also offers a High Altitude Training Center; this attracts members of the Canadian Ski Team, who like to train here. There is also plenty of après ski activity, with an old-fashioned saloon, along with a theatrical group known as the Silver Star Players. Just across from the inn, visitors will find Doc Willies, which is outfitted with a swimming pool and a Jacuzzi and spa for loosening up tired muscles at the end of the day. Within walking distance of the inn is Brewers Pond, for ice skating.

The summer months are not quite as busy, but they are an equally enticing time for mountain bikers and Rollerbladers, who come to test their mettle on these hills. The chair lift will transport people up the mountain; they can mountain bike back down again. Dogs can walk just about anywhere their human friends want to go, and there are plenty of hiking trails that lead through forests, near creeks, and into scenic valleys. It is fine to have a dog here and to ski as well. The mountain is so small that it is easy to ski for a couple of hours, come back to the inn for lunch, walk the dog, and then head back out again while the canine naps.

# The Empress

721 Government Street
*Victoria, B.C., Canada V8W 1W5*
*(800) 441-1414, (604) 384-8111, (604) 381-4334*

*General Manager: John Williams*
*Rooms: 451 doubles, 30 suites*
*Canadian Rates: Doubles $170-260 (EP) Suites $335-1,220 (EP)*
*Payment: AE, CB, DC, DSC, JCB, MC, and VISA*
*Children: Welcome, special children's programs are available*
*Dogs: Welcome, special dog programs are available that include a*
   *canine menu*
*Open: Welcome*

It is quite an undertaking to write about The Empress, it is, after all, the grand dame of Victoria and has been since 1908. The hotel was designed by Francis Mawson Rattenbury, who also designed the equally impressive Parliament Buildings situated along Victoria's waterfront. It took four years, and plenty of manual labor to erect this gracious building, whose walls, in places, are 30 inches thick. When it was all done, this chateau needed a name befitting its stature, and so they called it The Empress, after Queen Victoria, the Empress of India.

As with anything historic, there are a fair number of stories to tell about The Empress. One of the more famous is Operation Teacup, launched in 1966, after there was talk of tearing the hotel down because it lacked certain modern amenities — namely, heat.

There arose such a ruckus, from across the country, that restoration was soon favored over demolition. Its most recent renovation occurred in 1989, when a special design team was hired to restore the hotel to its turn-of-the-century grandeur. They spent months studying original drawings and pictures of the rooms, and searched high and low for historically accurate fabrics and colors from the Victorian period. The hotel's overall look is still a classic one, but one that emphasizes the lavish designs of this era. Plasterers spent five months recreating original moldings, and then stripping and refinishing existing moldings. The most spectacular discovery of all, though, was in the Tea Lobby and adjacent ballroom, where intricately detailed plaster ceilings had been covered up for years. In the Tea Lobby, the beautiful stained glass dome was also restored. The Empress contains more intrinsic historic treasures than we could possibly ever begin to mention here, in fact entire books have been written about the hotel's history.

The lovely, atrium lobby is quite modern in design; however, the rest of the hotel has held onto its traditional spirit. The Tea Lobby and Palm Court are two of the hotel's most gracious rooms. As those who have visited Victoria know, these impressive chambers are the best places to sip afternoon tea. The Tea Lobby, which is fashioned with bright pink walls, is able to nicely combine the vibrant wall treatment with the traditional cornices, pillars, and Victorian antiques. Sample a pot of the Empress' own tea blend, served from silver teapots, and dine on fresh berries served in crystal goblets. The three-tiered china caddie holds delicate tea sandwiches of smoked salmon, deviled egg, cucumber, and watercress. Honey-toasted crumpets and scones are served with thick, Jersey cream. Soft music, playing in the background, completes this elegant scene. High tea at The Empress is as fine as anyone is likely to experience outside of London.

The Empress Dining Room is equally stunning, if not baronial. It's 20-foot high carved mahogany ceiling, tapestry walls, and crackling fire set the tone for this elegant space. It was once one long room, but has been split into the intimate dining room and an equally lavish lounge across the way. (A Death by Chocolate buffet is served here each evening.) We dined by candlelight to a memorable meal, created with ingredients native to British Columbia. Dining patrons may start with the smoked quail wrapped in pancetta; the Dungeness crab struedel with a spicy mango and roma tomato salsa; or the marinated grilled prawns on endive with a spinach-herb cream. Entrées included the roasted pork tenderloin with an apple-gooseberry chutney, halibut set on a crisp herb potato cake and topped with diced lobster and a tomato chervil sauce; or the Oriental spiced rack of lamb with a sweet potato-carrot purée and sherry sesame lamb jus. The dessert cart was brimming with over 125 offerings, and the award winning wine cellar featured 350 different vintages.

Just so your canine companion does not feel slighted, the executive chef has also created a new canine menu as well. Appetizers include domestic and imported cheeses; a country style paté with fruit chutney; or the veal liver tartar with raw egg and capers — all accompanied by doggy biscuits. Entrées featured ahi tuna, lamb loin, or tenderloin of beef combined with steamed rice and vegetables. Older dogs who might be watching their weight, can opt for the low fat version of this menu. Sherbet, dog cookies, and ice cream — all made with dogs delicate digestive systems in mind, are found on the dessert menu. While dogs cannot take their meals in the dining room, they can have an equally fine time by ordering these lavish affairs from room service.

Exceptionally wide hallways, triple the width of most, lead to the guest rooms. Many of the existing chambers were converted from apartment suites and consequently each is quite unique. We loved the high ceilings, delicate moldings, and deep window wells. Much of the furniture was recreated using designs taken from some of the original pieces found in the hotel, so that all of the rooms have a traditional look to match the historic ambiance of the hotel. The color schemes vary with the room, but expect rich colors and plenty of florals. Everything is perfectly coordinated, whether on the quilted spreads, tailored dust ruffles, or full length draperies. Suites are fashioned with decorative fireplaces and enormous living rooms. All the modern amenities are also in place, including heat (air conditioning has not yet been installed, but they do have fans). Guests can expect terry robes laid at the end of their turned down beds, chocolates awaiting on a tray, and a full complement of toiletries in the modern bathrooms.

Children, as well as dogs, should be treated to a stay at The Empress. In addition to a full children's program, most kids will thoroughly enjoy the wading pool, which is set next to the 40-foot lap pool in the atrium. Afterwards, the whole family can head out to explore the grounds and the beautiful town with their canine cohorts. The Empress lies on 20 beautifully manicured acres, and is within easy walking distance of just about anything one might want to do in Victoria. Put Bowser on a leash and stroll along the waterfront. You can walk for miles along the sea wall, or venture down some steps to one of Victoria's beaches. A short walk in another direction leads to one of Victoria's many parks — Beacon Hill Park. Follow the cliff to grassy Clover Point or take a trip out to the Fisgard Lighthouse at Fort Hill Road. All are great oceanside areas that are ideal for picnics, reading, or throwing a ball for your canine companion. Runners and their dogs will thoroughly enjoy the forested trails around Beaver and Elk Lakes. In short, a stay at the Empress is an experience not to be missed by guests of any stripe — two-legged or four-legged. This place has character and pizzazz, qualities almost impossible to find in hotels in this day and age of national chains.

---

# Dashwood Manor

*One Cook Street*
*Victoria, B.C., Canada V8W 3W6*
*(604) 385-5517*

*Hosts: Derek Dashwood and Family*
*Rooms: 14 suites*
*Canadian Rates: $75-285 (B&B), Weekly and monthly rates available*
*Payment: AE, MC, and VISA*
*Children: Welcome*
*Dogs: Welcome*
*Open: All year*

Dashwood Manor. The name alone conjures up images of aristocracy and great wealth. The story behind this Edwardian Tudor Revival home is not of the idle rich, but of a dedicated young man working to fulfill a dream. The house was built in 1912 in a neighborhood of other lavish homes that line a bluff overlooking the Strait of Juan de Fuca. Little expense was spared when building this manor, with slashed grain fir paneling in the main hallways and white oak paneling in the dining room. As with most houses of this era, the ornate plaster work was reserved for the public spaces; today's guests can still find some of it in the Windsor Oak or Oxford Grand suites.

Although the house changed hands a few times over the years, it was not until the building was converted from a private home to apartments that it really began to deteriorate. Derek Dashwood watched the property's decline and decided to purchase it in 1978. The price tag alone was daunting, but the work that needed to be done was even more so. It nearly bankrupted him, as the rent from the apartment dwellers could not even begin to cover the maintenance costs. Derek carefully planned the building's final restoration and converted the 8 apartments into 14 suites. In the winter months, they are occupied as long term rentals, with returning guests booking into the next century. During the other three months of the year, these suites are rented by the night or the week, opening their doors to guests and their vacationing dogs.

We followed the shoreline drive from Victoria's harbor to the manor. There are faster ways to get from there to here, but this was by far the most scenic. Along the way, we passed all sorts of people and their dogs walking along the sea wall that edges the ocean. At the far end of Beacon Hill Park, we found the Dashwood Manor. From the exterior, this is still an imposing structure, with its dark timber beams and multiple eaves rising up three stories. We suspected that all the rooms facing the ocean have remarkable views — and we were right.

Stepping through the front door is similar to entering a medieval manor. Dark, paneled walls line the foyer and the massive central staircase. Sunlight streams in through the six-foot-high stained glass window at the top of the landing, and down the stairwell into the foyer. The air was faintly scented by wood smoke drifting out from the stone fireplace. We spent some time admiring the engravings of the English countryside, along with the antique brass plates that lined the walls, before beginning our tour of the Dashwood Manor.

Guests with dogs might want to think about reserving one of the first-floor bedrooms, as these have the easiest access to the outdoors. The Oxford Grand suite offers fabulous views of the ocean, through a plate glass window inset with stained glass. This was the house's original parlor, a place where the men used to gather after dinner. In similar fashion, suite guests may come back here in the evenings and relax before the fire. An adjacent alcove, separated from the parlor by a wide arch, holds a queen bed and an antique bureau. The colors in this suite are a dusty pink, and the furnishings, while antique, are a bit on the worn side. Across the hall is the Windsor Oak Room, which has just as much character. The simple furnishings are surrounded by beamed ceilings, oak paneling, and a fireplace. The room overlooks Beacon Hill Park, and also has glimpses of the ocean.

The remaining suites are found upstairs, with the most newly renovated chamber situated on the second floor, and the most original located on the third floor. What the third floor rooms may lack in modern amenities, they more than make up for in unparalleled ocean views. The most recently refurbished suites have light oak reproduction furnishings, while the older rooms contain a combination of antiques and comfortably worn pieces. Cambridge is one of these newly restored spaces — in fact, it still smelled like freshly cut timber. It is a corner suite, with a tiled Jacuzzi tucked into one corner. Dark green colors combine with the natural wood paneling to create a garden room setting. When Derek described these second-floor suites, he also shared with us the names of some who once slept here. For instance, the light and festive Chelsea Room was Arthur Lineham's bedroom. (He commissioned the house). The Tudor Room is a bachelor suite today, but was once Miss Madigan's bedroom, the nanny to the Lineham's children. We liked the cozy feeling of the Tudor Room, with its plush, green carpet and brass bed tucked up against a half wall. Guests look through the large windows for indirect ocean views. Those staying in the third-floor suites see only the sea and sky. Camelot is one of these expansive suites, set up in the third floor's eaves. This space could use new carpeting; however, it is the most versatile suite, with a queen bed and two sofa beds. The best combination of views and luxury are found in the Somerset, as the remodeled bathroom is huge and contains a Jacuzzi. Guests also have a private balcony to sit on, where they can easily enjoy the sunset over the sea and mountains. Access to the third-floor chambers can be attained through an outside staircase, making them acceptable choices for those who are concerned about making too much noise walking their dogs late at night.

We were impressed with the thoughtful amenities in all the suites. The bathrooms, both new and old, have a full complement of Lord and Mayfair soaps and shampoos. Guests can be totally self-sufficient, as all suites have full kitchens that are stocked with everything they might need to create their own breakfasts. Eggs, bacon, bread, juice, and coffee are some of the basics, which can be supplemented with a few goodies from the local bakeries and food shops.

We really like the Dashwood Manor's location, and not just because of its views. It is easy to walk dogs here — we just stepped out the front door and across the street to the promenade that winds along the sea. The Manor is also right next door to Beacon Hill Park, a lovely place with all sorts of intriguing areas for a dog to investigate. There are 185 acres to visit, including formal gardens, ponds, and fountains, all intertwined with paths. A twenty-minute walk through the park puts visitors and their dogs in downtown Victoria. Since parking can be difficult, this is an ideal and energetic option. Another possible outing is to climb up Moss Rock on Fairfield Hill — or walk along Dallas Road back toward Victoria. Along the way, visitors are certain to meet all sorts of local dogs out enjoying the day as well.

# Chateau Whistler Resort

*4599 Chateau Blvd.*
*Whistler, B.C., Canada V0N 1B4*
*(800) 441-1414, (604) 938-8000, Fax (604) 938-2020*

**General Manager:** David Roberts
**Rooms:** 306 doubles, 36 suites
**Canadian Rates:** Doubles $125-250 (EP), Suites $250-1,100 (EP)
**Payment:** AE, CB, DC, DSC, JCB, MC, and VISA
**Children:** Welcome (cribs, cots, high chairs, and baby-sitters available)
**Dogs:** Welcome with a $10 nightly fee
**Open:** All year

The Chateau Whistler was the first mountain resort chateau built in almost 100 years by Canadian Pacific Hotels and Resorts. This place is so extraordinary, that we wouldn't be surprised if it took another 100 years to create anything else comparable. The drive from Vancouver along the Sea to Sky Highway was, as usual, spectacular. Cliffs dropping thousands of feet to the ocean gave way to mountain valleys and snow-capped peaks. We so enjoyed the vistas, that it felt as though we arrived in Whistler before out journey had even gotten under way. The 12-story Chateau Whistler should stand out in this valley, but instead, it is nestled above the main village in the foothills of Blackcomb Mountain. The hotel was all we had imagined a great chateau to be — turrets, spires, and steeply sloping roofs set against this lush, mountainous landscape.

This feeling is carried through to the interior spaces as well, especially in the Great Hall, where even royalty would feel at home. The exposed beams of the vaulted ceilings rise 60 feet above the hall, while below a combination of stone pillars, slate floors, and pecan paneling surrounds the sumptuous sitting areas. Sophisticated French Provincial furnishings, both antiques and fine reproductions, form small sitting areas. Accents are provided by whimsical folk art, dried and fresh flowers, and woven baskets. At the end of the Great Hall, there is a glass wall that begins at floor level and rises to the peak of the ceiling. This chamber is an excellent spot for guests to settle in. Here, we were not only privy to terrific views but also to the cracking and popping fire in large stone hearth. Aprés ski activity is generally at its best, however, next door in the Mallard Bar. Walls of glass also make this an especially sunny space during the day, but at night it is transformed into an intimate chamber with flickering candlelight reflecting off the wall of glass.

A huge stone fireplace, overstuffed chairs, and a warm drink seem like the perfect way to end a day on the slopes.

The resort sits up so high that all guest rooms, whether facing Blackcomb or overlooking the valley, have fantastic views. From the smallest to the most elaborate two-story suites, all these chambers are well appointed. Handmade quilts top down comforters and fine linens. The furnishings are substantial pieces, and reproduced to emulate fine antiques. Unusual carved headboards crown the beds, while long benches lie at their feet. Some rooms are furnished with armoires edged with carved wood that resembles rope. Baskets and an array of folk art are interspersed into these spaces as well, adding delightful decorative touches. In many rooms, quilts line the walls, while in others, an original watercolor or gilt framed botanical print is a highlight. Each of these spacious chambers also has a residential quality to them, with potted plants and a full array of amenities. Some contain French doors that open to terraces, while the majority have walls of windows that provide panoramic views. Well-designed bathrooms offer a full complement of toiletries, along with terry robes, thick towels, and hair dryers. This luxurious setting is also an environmentally correct one, utilizing an extensive recycling program that includes blue bins in the bathrooms, donating unused toiletries to charity, and giving guests the option to go a day without fresh towels.

Wildflowers is the premier restaurant at the hotel, and executive chef Bernard Casavant is renowned for his fine cuisine. The adjoining dining rooms have walls of glass and are decorated in a French Provincial motif, with accents provided by Audubon prints, antiques, and lavish arrangements of fresh flowers. We enjoyed perusing the menu, as much for the innovative offerings as for the lovely watercolor wildflowers printed upon it. The seasonally changing dishes always feature local ingredients and the wine list includes an impressive array of British Columbia vintages. Some might choose to start with an appetizer such as the wild mushroom and ricotta turnover served with a grilled sweet pepper salad; a warm tomato and sundried olive tart with a balsamic essence and basil pesto; or a traditional Caesar salad topped with either baby shrimp, smoked salmon, or roasted garlic. Entrées on the fall menu included a barbecued duck breast with sundried cranberry crepes; a rack of lamb with a sweet mustard and a wild mint crust, or the Harvest buffet. The latter includes fresh seasonal salads, baked wild salmon, roast prime rib, harvest vegetables, and the best of all, the dessert buffet. The breakfast buffet is equally lavish.

Dogs and Whistler seem like natural extensions of one another. Canines can walk the Valley Trail that winds by the resort and throughout the valley. In the summer, people Rollerblade along this trail and in the winter it becomes a cross-country ski trail. We suggest taking Bowser on a hike to either Joffre Lakes, Rainbow Lake, or Singing Pass. More leisurely outings are available in any of the area's provincial parks. If this is a family trip, we can recommend a number of good hikes for children and dogs. Follow the Lost Lake Trail, which can be picked up in the village, for an easy day hike with young ones. The Cheakamus Lake Trails can be found off the Cheakamus Lake Road, just off Highway 99. Follow this trail to the Singing Creek Trail. Everyone will enjoy a visit to the Ancient Cedars of Cougar Mountain. Drive up Cougar Mountain to Showh Lake. The short trail leads to a forest of ancient cedar trees that are so big a family would have to link hands just to surround one.

Less dog-oriented options include skiing in the winter, and golf in the summer months on the resort's Robert Trent Jones course. Windsurfing, mountain biking, river rafting, and Rollerblading are also very popular diversions at Whistler. At the end of the day, when the muscles have had just about enough, we recommend investigating the fabulous spa at Chateau Whistler. This is, without a doubt, the place for some lavish pampering. The indoor/outdoor swimming pool is complemented by a soaking tub, hot tubs, saunas, steam rooms, and a weight room. The spa offers a full range of services, including massage therapy, herbs for detoxification, and facials. Now all they need to do is implement a comparable doggie program and we would almost feel a little less guilty for enjoying all these facilities as much as we do.

---

# Listel Whistler Hotel

*4121 Village Green*
*Whistler, B.C., Canada V0N 1B0*
*(800) 663-5472, (604) 932-1133, Fax (604) 932-8383*

*Manager: Brian Ennis*
*Rooms: 100 doubles, 4 suites*
*Canadian Rates: $149-229 (B&B), Suites $155-395 (B&B)*
*Payment: AE, ENR, DC, DSC, JCB, MC, and VISA*
*Children: Welcome; under 16 years of age are free of charge when*
*          sharing a room with their parents*
*Dogs: Welcome*
*Open: All year*

The Listel Whistler Hotel came as a complete surprise to us. We arrived in Whistler prepared to write about the Delta Hotel Whistler, but were drawn instead to this far more intimate hotel, which is also situated in the village. The Delta is an enormous and somewhat impersonal hotel that does in fact take dogs; however, we preferred the more reasonable rates and intimate character of the Listel Whistler Hotel.

The Listel Whistler is set in the village at the base of Whistler and Blackcomb mountains. Brightly colored international flags line the rooftop of this attractive, three-story building. The small lobby is as welcoming as its staff. After acquainting us with the hotel, they showed us a range of accommodations. We walked down wide hallways painted an appealing shade of salmon, lined with hunter green carpets. Prospective guests may choose between rooms facing the ski mountains or rooms looking over the valley. Regardless of choice, most should be pleased with these chambers, even though they are a little on the cozy side. We suggest requesting a king bedded room, as the standard rooms with two queen beds have just enough additional space for the bureau and a small table flanked by a pair of chairs. We liked the interesting eaves in the top-floor bedrooms, and the fact that the windows were designed to resemble the shape of the dormers.

Beds are covered with festive and contemporary Northwest native-patterned spreads. Chairs are constructed out of light woods with caned backs. Remote controlled televisions offer movie systems, and clock radios and direct dial telephones add to the list of standard amenities. Families will need two rooms, or they may request one of the larger suites. The most spacious of these is the Executive Suite, which has a king-bedded room separated from a fireplaced living room by a pair of French doors. The two couches in the living room fold out and a large table can easily accommodate the family's breakfast needs. The junior suite, on the other hand, is equipped with a bedroom with a good-sized sitting room. In the morning, a Continental breakfast is waiting downstairs, but guests who happen to wake up a little early can also take advantage of the coffee maker in the room to brew a cup of coffee. (Starbucks is in the village — for those who want to buy a package of gourmet coffee, or who would just prefer for someone else to make their morning coffee.) Guests can also store drinks and snacks, or cans of dog food, in the small refrigerators. Some will be pleased to know there is a valet and guest laundry.

These features are all typical of a larger property, but in a hotel of this size they are an unexpected pleasantry. We also enjoyed the outdoor, heated swimming pool, Jacuzzi, and saunas. Alpine and Nordic skiers will be happy to know that they may store their skis in a special area, so they don't have to worry about lugging them up to the rooms. Convenient underground parking is available to hotel guests, for a small fee. After skiing or a day spent hiking, guests tend to gravitate to the intimate Rodeo Bar. This is a welcoming space, where people hang out in front of the fire, along the intimate bar, or over by the dart boards. Parents would even feel comfortable relaxing in here with their children before heading around the corner for dinner. There are, of course, plenty of other great restaurants within walking distance of the Listel, but after a long day of exercise it is sometimes nice just to eat in.

O'Doul's is the café-style restaurant, which resembles something out of the Caribbean, with its festive green and peach wall treatment, tropical plants, and ceiling fans. Two walls of windows look out towards the golf course or up to the mountains. Some guests might start their meal with the West Coast seafood chowder, escargots Provençale, or the prawns St. Tropez. The latter are fried with cayenne and red peppers, then seasoned with white wine and lemon. The salads and pastas looked excellent; but then again, so did the fresh trout stuffed with Dungeness crab and the fisherman's stew of prawns, scallops, mussels, salmon, clams, and shrimp. Those with a hearty appetite can request the filet mignon with mushrooms and Bernaise sauce, the rack of lamb with a sweet vermouth sauce, or the delicious prime rib.

Dogs love it at Whistler. They have mountains to climb and rivers to explore in the immediate vicinity, and more provincial parks situated in the outlying area than they could visit in a year. The Valley Trail is a paved trail that starts at one end of the valley and encircles it. Fun day hikes can be taken to Singing Pass-Russet Lake and to Rainbow Lake. Another popular option that is a bit shorter and easier than most, leads dogs and their human counterparts to Lost Lake Park. With the onset of snow, many of these trails become fine cross-country ski trails. Guests can either cross-country or downhill ski in the morning, make a short trip back over to the hotel at lunch time, and pick up Bowser for a little impromptu walk about the village.

# Chain Hotels/Motels-800 Numbers

Best Western: (800) 528-1234
Budgetel Inns: (800) 4-BUDGET
Comfort Inns: (800) 228-5150
Canadian Pacific: (800) 441-1414
Days Inn: (800) DAYS INN
Delta: (800) 268-1133
Econo Lodge: (800) 446-6900
Embassy Suites: (800) 362-2779
Fairfield Inn: (800) 228-2800
Four Seasons Hotels: (800) 332-3442
Guest Quarters: (800) 424-2900
Hampton Inns: (800) HAMPTON
Hawthorne Suites: (800) 527-1133
Hilton Hotels: (800) HILTON
Holiday Inn: (800) HOLIDAY
Homewood Suites: (800) 225-5466
Howard Johnson: (800) 654-2000
Hyatt Corp: (800) 228-9000
La Quinta: (800) 531-5900
Loews: (800) 445-6937
Marriott Hotels: (800) 228-9290
Motel 6: (800) 466-8356
Quality Inns: (800) 228-5151
Radisson Hotels: (800) 333-3333
Ramada Inns: (800) 2-RAMADA
Red Roof Inns: (800) 843-7663
Residence Inn: (800) 331-3131
Ritz-Carlton: (800) 241-3333

Sheraton Hotels: (800) 325-3535
Shoney's Inns: (800) 222-2222
Super Eight: (800) 800-8000
Travelodge: (800) 255-3050
Westin: (800) 228-3000
Wyndham Hotels: (800) 822-4200

## Helpful Telephone Numbers

American Animal Hospital Association...........................(303) 986-2800
American Humane Association........................................(800) 227-4645
A.S.P.C.A..........................................................................(212) 876-7700
Assistance Dogs International ........................................(303) 234-9512
Guide Dog Foundation for the Blind ...............................(800) 548-4337
Humane Society for the U.S. ...........................................(202) 452-1100
National Animal Poison Control Center ..........................(800) 548-2423
Pet Loss Support Hot line ...............................................(916) 752-4200
Pet Finders .......................................................................(800) 666-5678
Tattoo-A-Pet International ...............................................(800) TAT-TOOS

# The Best of the Rest

## B&Bs, Inns, Hotels, and Motels

# Oregon

**ALBANY**
> **Best Western Pony Soldier**
>> 315 Airport Rd. SE
>> (503) 928-6322
>
> **Motel Orleans**
>> 1212 SE Price Rd.
>> (503) 926-0170

**ASHLAND**
> **Ashland Valley Inn**
>> 1193 Siskiyou Blvd.
>> (541) 482-2641
>
> **Best Western Bard's Inn**
>> 132 North Main St
>> (541) 482-0049
>
> **Best Western Heritage Inn**
>> 434 Valley View Rd
>> (541) 482-6932
>
> **Quality Inn Flagship**
>> 2520 Ashland St
>> (541) 488-2330
>
> **Windmill's Ashland Hills Inn**
>> 2525 Ashland St
>> (541) 482-8310

**ASTORIA**
> **Bayshore Motor Inn**
>> 555 Hamburg St
>> (503) 325-2205
>
> **Crest Motel**
>> 5366 Leif Erickson Dr
>> (503) 325-3141
>
> **Red Lion Inn**
>> 400 Industry St
>> (503) 325-7373

**BAKER CITY**
> **Quality Inn**
>> 810 Campbell
>> (503) 523-2242

**BANDON**
> **Inn at Face Rock Resort**
>> 3225 Bandon-By-The-Sea
>> (800) 638-3092

**BEAVERTON**
> **Greenwood Inn**
>> 10700 SW Allen Blvd.
>> (503) 643-7444

> **Shilo Inn**
>> 9900 SW Canyon Rd
>> (503) 297-2551

**BEND**
> **Best Western**
>> 19221 Century Dr
>> (541) 382-4080
>
> **Best Western Woodstone**
>> 721 NE 3rd
>> (541) 383-1515
>
> **Comfort Inn**
>> 61200 S Route 97
>> (541) 388-2227
>
> **Hampton Inn**
>> 15 NE Butler Rd
>> (541) 388-4114
>
> **Red Lion Inn**
>> 1415 NE 3rd St
>> (541) 382-7011
>
> **Shilo Inn**
>> 3105 O B Riley Rd
>> (541) 389-9600

**BOARDMAN**
> **Nuggett Inn**
>> Hwy 84 & Boardman Rd
>> (541) 481-2375

**BROOKINGS**
> **Best Western Beachfront Inn**
>> Lower Harbor Rd
>> (541) 469-7779
>
> **Harbor Inn Motel**
>> 15991 Rte 101
>> (541) 469-3194

**BURNS**
> **Best Western Ponderosa**
>> 577 W. Monroe
>> (503) 573-2047
>
> **Royal Inn**
>> 999 Oregon Ave.
>> (503) 573-5295

**CAMP SHERMAN**
> **Cold Springs Resort**
>> Cold Springs Resort Lane
>> (541) 595-6271

**CANNON BEACH**
Best Western
Ocean Front
(503) 436-2274
Tolvana Inn
Beach Loop
(503) 436-2211
**CLACKAMAS**
Clackamas Inn
161010 SE 82nd
(541) 650-5340
Cypress Inn
9040 SE Adams
(541) 655-0062
**COOS BAY**
Edgewater Inn
275 E. Johnson
(541) 267-0423
Red Lion Inn
1313 N. Bayshore
(541) 267-4141
**CORVALLIS**
Harrison House B&B
2310 NW Harrison
(541) 752-6248
Shanico Inn
1113 NW 9th Ave
(541) 754-7474
**COTTAGE GROVE**
Comfort Inn
845 Gateway Blvd
(541) 942-9747
Econo Lodge
1601 Gateway Blvd
(541) 942-1000
**ENTERPRISE**
Ponderosa Motel
102 SE Greenwood
(541) 426-3186
**EUGENE**
Best Western Greentree
1759 Franklin Blvd.
(541) 485-2727
Best Western New Oregon
1655 Franklin Blvd.
(541) 683-3669
Eugene Hilton
66 E 6th St
(541) 342-2000

Holiday Inn
225 Coburg Rd
(541) 342-5181
The Valley River Inn
100 Valley River Way
(541) 687-0123
**GOLD BEACH**
Best Western
1250 So. Hwy 101
(541) 247-6691
**GOVERNMENT CAMP**
Mt. Hood Inn
87450 E.Government Camp
(541) 272-3205
**GRANTS PASS**
Best Western
111 NE Agness
(541) 476-1117
Holiday Inn
105 NE Agness
(541)471-6144
Riverside Inn
971 SE 6th St
(541) 476-6873
River's Reach B&B
4025 Williams Hwy
(541) 474-4411
**GRESHAM**
Holiday Inn Express
2323 NE 181 St
(541) 492-4000
Quality Inn
1545 NE Burnside
(541) 666-9545
**HOOD RIVER**
Best Western
1108 E. Marina Way
(541) 386-2200
Vagabond Lodge
4070 Westcliff Dr
(541) 386-2992
**JOHN DAY**
Best Western
315 W. Main St
(503) 575-1700
**KLAMATH FALLS**
Best Western
4061 South 6th St
(503) 882-1200

**LAKE OSWEGO**
　Best Western
　　15700 SW Upper Boones
　　(503) 620-2980
　Holiday Inn
　　14811 Kruse Oaks Blvd
　　(503) 624-8400
**LAKEVIEW**
　Best Western
　　414 N. G St
　　(503) 947-2194
**LINCOLN CITY**
　Best Western
　　535 NW Inlet
　　(503) 994-4227
　Coho Inn
　　1635 NW Harbor
　　(503) 994-3684
　Dock of the Bay Motel
　　116 SW 51st St
　　(503) 996-3549
**MADRAS**
　Sonny's Motel
　　1539 Rte 97
　　(503) 475-7217
**MCMINNVILLE**
　Best Western Vineyard Inn
　　2035 SW 99W
　　(503) 472-4900
**MEDFORD**
　Best Western Medford Inn
　　1015 S. Riverside
　　(541) 773-8266
　Best Western Pony Soldier Inn
　　2340 Crater Lake Hwy
　　(541) 779-2011
　Holiday Inn
　　2300 Crater Lake Hwy
　　(541) 779-2623
　Red Lion Inn
　　200 N. Riverside
　　(541) 779-5811
　Windmill Inn
　　1950 Biddle Rd
　　(541) 770-1234
**MOUNT HOOD**
　Mount Hood Inn
　　87450 E. Gov. Camp Loop
　　(541) 272-3205

**Red Lion Inn**
　　3612 So. 6th St
　　(541) 882-8864
**LA GRANDE**
　Best Western
　　2612 Island Ave
　　(503) 963-7195
**NEWPORT**
　Best Western Hallmark Resort
　　744 SW Elizabeth St
　　(541) 265-8853
　Val-U- Inn
　　531 SW Fall St
　　(541) 265-6203
　Whaler Motel
　　155 SW Elizabeth St
　　(541) 265-9261
**OAKRIDGE**
　Best Western Oakridge Inn
　　47433 Rte 58
　　(541) 782-2212
**ONTARIO**
　Best Western
　　251 Goodfellow St
　　(541) 889-2600
　Howard Johnson Lodge
　　1249 Tapadera Ave
　　(541) 889-8621
　Super 8 Motel
　　266 Goodfellow St
　　(541) 889-8282
**OREGON CITY**
　Val-U Inn
　　1900 Clackamette Dr
　　(541) 655-7141
**PENDLETON**
　Red Lion Inn
　　304 SE Nye Ave
　　(541) 276-6111
**PORTLAND**
　Best Western Fortniter
　　4911 NE 82nd Ave
　　(503) 255-9771
　Best Western Heritage Inn
　　4319 NW Yeon
　　(503) 497-9044
　Best Western Inn
　　420 NE Holiday
　　(503) 233-6331

**Best Western Inn**
1215 N. Hayden Meadows
(503) 286-9600
**Delta Inn**
9930 N. Whitaker
(503) 289-1800
**Imperial Hotel**
400 SW Broadway
(503) 228-7221
**Marriott Hotel**
1401 SW Front Ave
(503) 226-7600
**Oxford Suites**
12226 N. Jantzen Dr
(503) 283-3030
**Quality Inn (Airport)**
8247 NE Sandy Blvd
(503) 256-4111
**Ramada Inn (Airport)**
6221 NE 82nd Ave
(503) 255-6511
**Red Lion Hotel**
310 SW Lincoln
(503) 221-0450
**Red Lion Hotel**
1401 N. Hayden Island Dr.
(503) 283-2111
**The Riverside Inn**
50 SW Morrison
(503) 221-0711
**REEDSPORT**
**Best Western Salbasgeon Inn**
1400 Rte 101
(541) 271-4831
**Salbasgeon Inn of Umpqua**
45209 Rte 38
(541) 271-2025
**ROCKAWAY BEACH**
**Silver Sands Motel**
South 2nd Ave
(541) 355-2206
**Tradewinds Motel**
523 N. Pacific Ave
(541) 355-2112
**ROGUE RIVER**
**Best Western Inn**
8959 Rogue River Hwy
(541) 582-2200

**SALEM**
**Phoenix Inn**
4370 Comercial SE
(541) 588-9220
**SISTERS**
**Best Western Ponderosa Lodge**
505 W Rte 20
(541) 549-1234
**THE DALLES**
**Best Western Tapadera Inn**
112 W. 2nd
(541) 296-9107
**Lone Pine Motel**
351 Lone Pine Rd
(541) 298-2800
**Quality Inn**
2114 W. 6th
(541) 298-5161
**Shilo Inn**
3223 Bret Clodfelter Way
(541) 298-5502
**TIGARD**
**Best Western Inn Chateau**
17993 Lower Boones Ferry
(541) 620-2030
**Embassy Suites**
9000 SW Washington Sq.
(541) 644-4000
**Shilo Inn**
10830 SW Greenburg Rd
(503) 620-4320
**TILLAMOOK**
**Western Royal Inn**
1125 N. Main St
(503) 842-8844
**Whiskey Creek B&B**
7500 Whiskey Creek Rd.
(503) 842-2408
**TROUTDALE**
**Phoenix Inn**
477 NW Phoenix Dr
(541) 669-6500
**TUALATIN**
**Sweetbriar Inn**
7125 SW Nyberg Rd
(503) 692-5800
**WARM SPRINGS**
**Kah-Nee-Ta Lodge**
100 Main St
(541) 553-1112

WARRENTON
Shilo Inn
1609 E. Harbor Dr
(541) 861-2181
WILSONVILLE
Holiday Inn
25425 SW Boones Ferry Rd
(541) 682-2211
WINCHESTER BAY
Winchester Bay Friendship Inn
390 Broadway
(541) 271-4871

YACHATS
The Adobe Motel
1555 Hwy 101
(541) 547-3141
Fireside Motel
1881 Hwy 101
(541) 547-3636

---

# Washington

ABERDEEN
Nordic Inn
1700 S. Boone St
(360) 533-0100
Olympic Inn
616 W. Heron St
(360) 533-4200
Red Lion Inn
521 W. Wishkah
(360) 532-5210
ANACORTES INN
Anacortes Inn
3006 Commercial Ave
(360) 293-3153
Islands Inn
3401 Commercial Ave
(360) 293-4644
ARLINGTON INN
Arlington Motor Inn
2214 Route 530
(360) 652-9595
AUBURN
Best Western Pony Soldier Inn
1521 D St NE
(206) 939-5950
Nedels Inn
102 - 15th St NE
(206) 833-8007
Val-U Inn
9 - 14th Ave NW
(206) 735-9600
BELLEVUE
Best Western Bellevue Inn
11211 Main St
(206) 455-5240

Red Lion Inn
300 - 112th Ave SE
(206) 455-1300
West Coast Bellevue Hotel
625 - 116th Ave NE
(206) 455-9444
BELLINGHAM
Lions Inn Motel
2419 Elm St
(360) 733-2330
Quality Inn
100 E. Kellogg Rd
(360) 647-8000
Rodeway Inn
3710 Meridian St
(360) 738-6000
Val-U Inn
805 Lakeway Dr
(360) 671-9600
BOTHELL
Residence Inn
11920 NE 195th St
(206) 485-3030
BREMERTON
Dunes Motel
3400 - 11th St
(360) 377-0093
Flagship Inn
4320 Kitsap Way
(360) 479-6566
Quality Inn at Oyster Bay
4303 Kitsap Way
(360) 405-1111

BUCKLEY
Mountain View Inn
Route 410
(360) 829-1100
CASHMERE
Village Inn Motel
229 Cottage Ave
(509) 782-3522
CASTLE ROCK
Timberland Motor Inn
1271 Mt. St. Helens Way
(360) 274-6002
CENTRALIA
Ferryman's Inn
1003 Eckerson Rd
(360) 330-2094
Huntley Inn
702 W. Harrison Ave
(360) 736-2875
Peppertree West Motor Inn
1208 Alder St
(360) 736-1124
CHEHALIS
Pony Soldier Motor Inn
122 Interstate Av.
(360) 748-0101
CHEWELAH
Nordlig Motel
101 W. Grant St
(509) 935-6704
CLE ELUM
Stewart Lodge
805 W. First St
(509) 674-4548
Timber Lodge Motel
301 W. First St
(509) 674-5966
COULEE DAM
Coulee House Motel
110 Roosevelt Way
(509) 633-1101
COUPEVILLE
Coupeville Inn
200 Coveland St.
(206) 678-6668
EAST WENATCHEE
Fours Seasons Inn
11 W. Grant Rd
(509) 884-6611

EDMONDS
K & E Motor Inn
23921 Route 99
(206) 778-2181
ELLENSBURG
Best Western Inn
1700 Canyon Rd
(509) 925-9801
Nites Inn
1200 S. Ruby
(509) 962-9600
EVERETT
Cypress Inn
12619 - 4th Ave West
(206) 347-9099
Travelodge
3030 Broadway
(206) 259-6141
Holiday Inn
101 - 128th St SE
(206) 745-2555
Ramada Inn
9602 - 19th Ave SE
(206) 337-9090
Westcoast Everett Pacific Hotel
3105 Pine St
(206) 339-3333
FEDERAL WAY
Best Western Inn
31611-20th Ave S
(206) 941-6000
FIFE
Best Western Inn
5700 Pacific Hwy E
(206) 922-0080
Days Inn
3021 Pacific Hwy E
(206) 922-3500
Econo Lodge
3518 Pacific Hwy E
(206) 922-0550
Royal Coachman Inn
5805 Pacific Hwy E
(206) 922-2500
FORKS
Pacific Inn Motel
352 Route 101
(360) 374-9400

FREELAND
Harbour Inn Motel
1606 Main St
(360) 331-6900
GOLDENDALE
Ponderosa Motel
775 E. Broadway St
(509) 773-5842
HOQUIAM
Westwood Inn
910 Simpson Ave
(360) 532-8161
KELSO
Best Western Inn
310 Long Ave.
(360) 425-9660
KENNEWICK
Cavanaugh's at Columbia Cntr
1101 N. Columbia Center
(509) 783-0611
Comfort Inn
7801 W. Quinault
(509) 783-8396
Shaniko Inn
321 N. Johnson St.
(509) 735-6385
KENT
Best Western
1233 N. Central
(206) 852-7224
Cypress Inn
22218 84th Ave., South
(206) 395-0219
Val U Inn
22420 84th Ave., South
(206) 872-5525
KIRKLAND
Best Western
12223 Northeast 116th
(206) 822-2300
La Quinta
10530 Northeast Northup
(206) 828-6585
LACEY
Capital Inn Motel
120 College St., SE
(360) 493-1991

LEAVENWORTH
Bayern On the River
1505 Alpen
(509) 548-5875
Der Ritterhof Motor Inn
190 Route 2
(509) 548-5845
Obertal Motor Inn
922 Commercial St.
(509) 548-5204
LONG BEACH
Anchorage Motor Court
22 Northwest Blvd. N
(360) 642-2351
Nendels Edgewater Inn
409 10th St. SW
(360) 642-2311
Our Place at the Beach
1309 South Blvd.
(360) 642-3793
LONGVIEW
Lewis and Clark Motor Inn
838 15th Ave.
(360) 423-6469
The Townhouse
744 Washington Way
(360) 423-1100
LYNDEN
Windmill Inn Motel
8022 Guide Meridien
(360) 354-3424
LYNNWOOD
Best Western
4300 200th St. S.W.
(206) 775-7447
Residence Inn
18200 Alderwood Mall
(206) 771-1100
MARYSVILLE
The Village Motor Inn
235 Beech St.
(360) 659-0005
MOCLIPS
High Tide Ocean Beach Resort
4890 Railroad Ave.
(360) 276-4142
MONROE
Best Western
19233 Route 2
(360) 794-3111

**MORTON**
  Seasons Motel
    200 Westlake
    (360) 496-6835
**MOSES LAKE**
  Best Western
    3000 Marina Dr.
    (509) 765-9211
  Holiday Inn
    1735 East Kittleson
    (509) 766-2000
  Shilo Inn
    1819 East Kittleson
    (509) 765-9317
**MOUNT VERNON**
  Best Western
    300 West College Way
    (360) 424-4287
  Best Western
    2300 Market
    (360) 428-5678
  Mount Vernon Travel Lodge
    1910 Freeway Dr.
    (360) 428-7020
**OAK HARBOR**
  The Auld Holland Inn
    5861 North Rte. 20
    (360) 675-2288
**OCEAN SHORES**
  Discovery Inn
    1031 Discovery Ave., S.E.
    (360) 289-3371
  Gitche Gumee Motel
    648 Ocean Shores NW
    (360) 289-3323
  Grey Gull
    651 Ocean Shores
    (360) 289-3381
**OLYMPIA**
  Best Western
    900 Capitol Way
    (360) 352-7200
  Deep Lake Resort
    12405 Tilley Road South
    (360) 352-7388
  Quality Inn
    2300 Evergreen Park Dr.
    (360) 943-4000

Ramada Inn
    621 South Capitol Way
    (360) 352-7700
**OROVILLE**
  Red Apple Inn
    1815 Main St.
    (509) 476-3694
**PACKWOOD**
  Woodland Motel
    11890 Rte 12
    (360) 494-6766
**PASCO**
  Hallmark Motel
    720 West Lewis St.
    (509) 547-7766
  King City Truck Stop
    2100 E. Hillsboro Rd.
    (509) 547-3475
  Red Lion Inn
    2525 N. 20th Ave.
    (509) 547-0701
**PORT ANGELES**
  Red Lion Bayshore Inn
    221 North Lincoln St.
    (360) 452-9215
**PORT TOWNSEND**
  Annapurna Inn
    538 Adams St.
    (360) 385-2909
  Harborside Inn
    330 Benedict St.
    (360) 385-7509
  Port Townsend Inn and Spa
    2020 Washington St.
    (360) 385-2211
  The Tides Inn
    1807 Water St.
    (360) 385-0595
**POULSBO**
  Cypress Inn
    19801 N.E. 7th St.
    (360) 697-2119
  Poulsbo's Inn
    18680 Rte. 305
    (360) 779-3921
**PROSSER**
  Best Western
    225 Meriot Dr.
    (509) 786-7977

**PULLMAN**
  Quality Inn
    1050 Bishop Blvd.
    (509) 332-0500
**PUYALLUP**
  Northwest Motor Inn
    1409 South Meridian
    (206) 841-2600
**RAYMOND**
  Maunu's Mountcastle Motel
    524 Third St.
    (360) 942-5571
**RENTON**
  Nendel's Inn
    3700 E. Valley Rd.
    (206) 251-9591
**RICHLAND**
  Columbia Center Dunes
    1751 Fowler Ave.
    (509) 783-8181
  Red Lion Inn
    802 George Wash. Way
    (509) 946-7611
  Shilo Inn
    50 Comstock St.
    (509) 946-4661
**RITZVILLE**
  Best Western
    1405 Smitty's Blvd.
    (509) 659-1007
  Colwell Motor Inn
    501 West First St.
    (509) 659-1620
  The Portico
    502 South Adams
    (509) 659-0800
**SAN JUAN ISLAND**
  Inn at Friday Harbor Suites
    680 Spring St.
    (360) 378-3031
**SEATAC**
  Airport Plaza Hotel
    18601 International Blvd.
    (206) 433-0400
  Best Western
    20717 International Blvd.
    (206) 878-3300
  Comfort Inn
    19333 Pacific Highway S.
    (206) 878-1100

  Seattle Marriott
    3201 South 176th St.
    (206) 241-2000
**SEATTLE**
  Best Western
    200 Taylor Ave North
    (206) 448-9444
  Days Inn
    2205 7th Ave
    (206) 448-3434
  Executive Residence
    2400 Elliott
    (206) 329-8000
  Hotel Vintage Park
    (206) 624-8000
    1100 Fifth Ave.
  Quality Inn
    2224 8th Ave
    (206) 624-6820
  Residence Inn
    800 Fairview Ave North
    (206) 624-6000
  Stouffer Madison Hotel
    515 Madison St
    (206) 583-0300
**SEDRO-WOOLLEY**
  Three Rivers Inn
    210 Ball St
    (360) 855-2626
**SEQUIM**
  Best Western
    268522 Rte 101
    (360) 683-0691
  Econo Lodge
    810 E. Washington St
    (360) 683-7113
  Red Ranch Inn
    830 W. Washington
    (360) 683-4195
**SNOHOMISH**
  The Countryman
    119 Cedar Ave.
    (360) 568-9622
**SOAP LAKE**
  Notaras Lodge
    236 E. Main St
    (509) 246-0462
**SPOKANE**
  Cavanaugh's River Inn
    N. 700 Division St
    (509) 326-5577

Comfort Inn
6309 E Broadway
(509) 535-7185
Days Inn
1919 N. Hutchinson
(509) 926-5399
Quality Inn
8923 E. Mission St
(509) 928-5218
Ramada Inn
Spokane Intrnl. Airport
(509) 838-5211
Sheraton Hotel
322 North Spokane Falls Ct
(509) 455-9600
SULTAN
Dutch Cup Motel
918 Main St
(206) 793-2215
SUNNYSIDE
Nendel's Motor Inn
408 Yakima Valley Hwy
(509) 837-7878
TACOMA
Best Western
6125 Motor Ave NW
(206) 584-2212
Best Western
8726 S. Hosmer St
(206) 535-2880
La Quinta Inn
1425 E 27th St
(206) 383-0146
Ramada Hotel
2611 East E Street
(206) 572-7272
Sheraton Hotel
1320 Broadway Plaza
(206) 572-3200
Tacoma Travelodge
8820 S. Hosmer
(206) 539-1153
TONASKET
Red Apple Inn
1st Street
(509) 486-2119
TOPPENISH
Toppenish Inn Motel
515 S. Elm St
(509) 865-7444

TUKWILA
Doubletree Suites
16500 Southcenter Pkwy
(206) 575-8220
Homewood Suites
6955 Southcenter Pkwy
(206) 762-0300
Marriott Residence Inn
16201 W. Valley Hwy
(206) 226-5500
TUMWATER
Best Western
5188 Capitol Blvd.
(360) 956-1235
Tyee Hotel
500 Tyee Dr.
(360) 352-0511
TWISP
Idle-A-While Motel
505 N. Rte 20
(509) 997-3222
UNION
Alderbrook Resort
E. 7101 Rte 106
(360) 898-2200
UNION GAP
Huntley Inn
12 E. Valley Mall Blvd.
(509) 248-6924
VANCOUVER
Best Western
7901 NE 6th Ave.
(360) 574-2151
Quality Inn
7001 NE Rte 99
(360) 696-0516
Red Lion Inn
100 Columbia St
(360) 694-8341
Residence Inn
8005 NE Parkway Dr
(360) 253-4800
Shilo Inn
401 E. 13th St
(360) 696-0411
Shilo Inn
13206 Rte 99
(360) 573-0511

WALLA WALLA
Comfort Inn
520 N 2nd Ave
(509) 525-2522
Pony Soldier Motor Inn
325 E. Main St
(509) 529-4360
WASHOUGAL
Econo Lodge
544 - 6th St
(360) 835-8591
WENATCHEE
Best Western Inn
1905 N. Wenatchee
(509) 664-6565
Holiday Lodge
610 N. Wenatchee
(509) 663-8167
Orchards Inn
1401 N. Miller St
(509) 662-3443
Red Lion Inn
1225 N. Wenatchee
(509) 663-0711
WESTPORT
Coho Motel
2501 N. NYHUS
(360) 268-0111

WINTHROP
The Marigot Hotel
960 Rte 20
(509) 996-3100
The Virginian Resort
808 N. Cascade Hwy
(509) 996-2535
WOODLAND
Lewis River Inn
110 Lewis River Rd
(360) 225-6257
Scandia Motel
1123 Hoffman St
(360) 225-8006
Woodlander Inn
1500 Atlantic St
(360) 225-6548
YAKIMA
Cavanaugh's at Yakima Center
607 E. Yakima
(509) 248-5900
Econo Lodge
510 N. 1st St
(509) 457-6155
Red Lion Inn
818 N. 1st St
(509) 453-0391

# British Columbia

ABBOTSFORD
Best Western Bakerview
1821 Sumas Way
(604) 859-1341
Holiday Inn Express
2073 Clearbrook Rd.
(604) 859-6211
Quality Inn
1881 Sumas Way
(604) 853-1141
BLUE RIVER
Mike Wiegele Heli Ski Village
Hartwood St.
(604) 673-6381
BOSWELL
Mountain Shores Resort
Route 3A
(604) 223-8258

401 Motor Inn
2950 Boundry Rd.
(604) 438-3451
Lake City Motor Inn
5415 Loughheed Hwy
(604) 294-7545
BURNS LAKE
Burns Lake Motor Inn
Route 16 E
(604) 692-7545
CACHE CREEK
Tumbleweed Motel
Hwy 97
(604) 457-6522
CAMPBELL RIVER
Anchor Inn
261 Island Hwy.
(604) 286-1131

Austrian Chalet Resort
462 S. Island Hwy.
(604) 923-4231

Campbell River Lodge
1760 Island Hwy
(604) 287-7446

**CHETWYND**
Stagecoach Inn
5413 South Access Rd.
(604) 788-9666

**CHILLIWACK**
Comfort Inn
45405 Luckakuck Way
(604) 858-0636

Cottonwood Inn
45466 Yale Rd.
(604) 792-4240

Holiday Inn
45920 First Ave.
(604) 795-4788

**CLEARWATER**
Jasper Way Inn
57 E. Old Thompson Rd.
(604) 674-3345

Wells Gray Inn
5 Village Rd.
(604) 674-2214

**CLOWHOM**
Clowhom Lake
Box 2720
(503) 226-4044

**COURTENAY**
Arbutus Hotel
275 8th St.
(604) 334-3121

Collingwood Inn
1675 Cliffe Ave.
(604) 338-1464

Kingfisher Beach Resort
4330 S. Island Hwy.
(604) 338-1323

**CRANBROOK**
Inn of the South
803 Cranbrook St.
(604) 489-4301

**DAWSON CREEK**
The George Dawson Inn
11705 8th St.
(604) 782-9151

Trail Inn
1748 Alaska Ave.
(604) 782-8595

**DELTA**
Best Western Tsawwassen
1665 56th St.
(604) 943-8221

Delta Town and Country
6005 Hwy 17
(604) 946-4404

**DUNCAN**
Falcon Nest Motel
5867 Trans-Canada Hwy.
(604) 748-8818

Silver Bridge Inn
140 Trans-Canada Hwy.
(604) 748-4311

**FERNIE**
Cedar Lodge Motel
101 7th Ave.
(604) 423-4622

Park Place Lodge
742 Hwy 3
(604) 423-6871

**FIELD**
Kicking Horse Lodge
100 Centre St.
(604) 343-6303

**FORT NELSON**
Coachouse Inn
4711 50th Ave. S.
(604) 774-3911

**GOLDEN**
Golden Rim Motor Inn
1416 Golden View Rd.
(604) 344-2216

Prestige Inn
1049 Trans-Canada Hwy
(604) 344-7990

**HARRISON HOT SPRINGS**
Harrison Hot Springs Hotel
On the Lake
(604) 796-2244

**KAMLOOPS**
Courtesy Inn Motel
1773 Trans-Canada Hwy.
(604) 372-8533

Kamloops Travelodge
430 Columbia St.
(604) 372-8202

Panorama Inn
610 W. Columbia St.
(604) 374-1515
Roche Lake Resort
Route 5A
(604) 828-2007
KELOWNA
Alpine Lodge
1652 Gordon Dr.
(604) 762-5444
Big White Motor Lodge
1891 Parkinson Way
(604) 860-3982
Lodge Hotel
2170 Harvey Ave.
(604) 860-9711
Prestige Inn Park Lake
1675 Abbott St.
(604) 860-7900
LADYSMITH
The Loyalist B&B
10890 Chemainus Rd.
(604) 245-2590
MALAHAT
Malahat Bungalows Motel
Malahat Dr.
(604) 478-3011
MANNING PARK
Manning Park Resort
Hwy 3
(604) 840-8822
MAPLE RIDGE
Best Western Maple Ridge
21735 Lougheed Hwy
(604) 463-5111
Travelodge Maple Ridge
21650 Lougheed Hwy
(604) 467-1511
MERRITT
Merritt Motor Inn
3561 Voght St.
(604) 378-9422
NAKSUP
The Selkirk Inn
210 West 6th.
(604) 265-3666
NANAIMO
Best Western
6450 Metral Dr.
(604) 390-2222

Harbourview Days Inn
809 Island Hwy. S.
(604) 754-8171
100 MILE HOUSE
Red Coach Inn
170 Cariboo Hwy.
(604) 395-2266
OSOYOOS
Bella Villa Resort Motel
6904 64A Ave. E
(604) 495-6751
PENTICTON
Bel-Air Motel
2670 Shaka Lake Rd.
(604) 492-6111
Coast Lakeside Resort
21 Lakeshore Dr.
(604) 493-8221
Golden Sands Resort
1028 Lakeshore Dr.
(604) 492-3600
Waterfront Inn
3688 Parkview St.
(604) 492-8228
PORT ALBERNI
Alberni Inn
3805 Redford St.
(604) 723-9405
Timberlodge
Port Alberni Rd. South
(604) 723-9415
Village Motel
4151 Redford St.
(604) 723-8133
PRINCE GEORGE
Connaught Motor Inn
1550 Victoria St.
(604) 562-4441
Holiday Inn
444 George St.
(604) 563-0055
PRINCE RUPERT
Best Western Highliner
815 First Ave.
(604) 624-9060
Crest Motor Hotel
222 First Ave. W.
(604) 224-6771

**QUALICUM BEACH**
**Old Dutch Inn**
  2690 Island Hwy W.
  (604) 752-6914
**RADIUM HOT SPRINGS**
**Cedar Motel**
  7593 Main St. W.
  (604) 347-9463
**Sunset Motel**
  4883 McKay St.
  (604) 347-9464
**REVELSTOKE**
**Best Western Wayside Inn**
  1901 LaForme Blvd.
  (604) 837-6161
**Regent Inn**
  112 Victoria Rd.
  (604) 837-2107
**RICHMOND**
**Delta Pacific Resort**
  10251 St. Edward's Dr.
  (604) 278-9611
**Radisson President Hotel**
  Cambie Rd.
  (604) 276-8181
**Travelodge-Vancouver Airport**
  3071 St. Edwards
  (604) 278-5155
**SALMON ARM**
**Shuswap Inn**
  Trans-Canada Hwy.
  (604) 832-7081
**Travelodge**
  2401 Trans-Canada Hwy.
  (604) 832-9721
**SIDNEY**
**Best Western Emerald Isle**
  2306 Beacon Ave.
  (604) 656-4441
**Hotel Sidney Waterfront**
  2537 Beacon Ave.
  (604) 656-1131
**VANCOUVER**
**Georgian Court Hotel**
  773 Beatty St.
  (604) 682-555
**Holiday Inn Hotel/Suites**
  1110 Howe St.
  (604) 684-2151

**Vancouver Renaissance**
  1133 Hastings St.
  (604) 689-9211
**Westin Bayshore**
  1601 Georgia St.
  (604) 682-3377
**VERNON**
**Best Western**
  5121 26th St.
  (604) 549-2224
**Coast Vernon Lodge**
  3914 32nd St.
  (604) 545-3385
**Prestige Inn**
  4411 32nd St.
  (604) 558-5991
**Vernon Travelodge**
  3000 28th St.
  (604) 545-2161
**VICTORIA**
**Admiral Motel**
  257 Belleville St.
  (604) 388-6267
**Executive House Hotel**
  777 Douglas St.
  (604) 388-5111
**Ocean Pointe Resort**
  45 Songhees Rd.
  (604) 360-2999
**Oxford Castle Inn**
  133 Gorge Rd. E.
  (604) 388-6431
**Red Goat Lodge**
  Hwy 37
  (604) 234-3261
**WHISTLER**
**Delta Whistler Resort**
  4050 Whistler Dr.
  (604) 932-1962
**Tantalus Resort Condominium**
  4200 Whistler Way
  (604) 932-4146
**Whistler Fairways**
  4005 Whistler Way
  (604) 932-2522
**YELLOWPOINT**
**Inn of the Sea Resort**
  3600 Yellowpoint Rd.
  (604) 245-2211

# Regulations for National and State Parks, Forests and Recreation Areas

## Oregon

Dogs are allowed in the Crater Lake National Park, as well as in the Hells Canyon and Oregon Dunes Recreation Areas. They are allowed in all of Oregon's national forests and areas run by the Army Corps of Engineers. They are also allowed in most of Oregon's state parks. The following state parks and lakes **do not allow** dogs:

| | |
|---|---|
| Ainsworth | Cape Blanco |
| Bastendorff Beach | Cape Kiwanda |
| Beachside | Casey |
| Benson | Emigrant Springs |
| Beverly Beach | Pioneer Park |
| Cape Arago | William M. Tugman |

For further information about Oregon's national forests please call the national forest service at 503-326-2877. For further information about Oregon's state parks and recreation areas please call 503-378-6305.

## Washington

Dogs are **not allowed** in any of Washington's national parks, recreation areas, or lands run by the Army Corps of Engineers. (The only exceptions are the Coulee Dam and the Olympic National Forest where leashed dogs are allowed.) They are allowed in most of Washington's state parks. The following state parks and lakes **do not allow** dogs:

| | |
|---|---|
| Cascade | Moses Lake R.V. Park |
| Chief Looking Glasss | Phil Simon Park |
| Columbia | Point Defiance Park |
| Connelly | Samish Park |
| Entiat | Semiahmoo County Park |
| Lake Gillette | Silver Lake County Park |
| Lake Sacajawea | Skamokawa Vista Park |
| Lighthouse Marine | Sunny Beach Point |
| Mayfield Lake County Park | Thornton A. Sullivan Park |
| McNary Loch and Dam | Washington Park |
| Montlake Park | |

For further information on Washington's national parks and forests please call 206-220-7450. For more information on Washington's state parks and recreation areas please call 360-753-2027.

**Washington State Ferries:** Animals are not allowed in terminals, above the car decks, or on the passenger ferries unless they are in a container.

# Regulations for British Columbia's National and Provincial Parks

## U.S. and Canadian Regulations for Transporting Dogs Across the Border

Dogs and cats from the United States, more than three months of age, must be accompanied by a certificate signed by a licensed veterinarian of Canada or the U.S. certifying that the animal has been vaccinated against rabies during the preceding 36 months. The certificate must have a description of the animal and date of vaccination. For further information contact: Agriculture Canada, 620 Royal Avenue, New Westminster, BC V3L 5A8 (604) 666-8750

## National and Provincial Parks

Dogs are allowed in virtually all of British Columbia's national and provincial parks. The following is a list of the provincial parks where dogs **are not allowed.** (While this list might seem extensive, keep in mind that British Columbia has over 20 million acres of land set aside for parks. Of the 380 provincial parks, only 26 of these prohibit dogs.) They are as follows:

Andrews Bay
Bowron Lake
Bull Canyon
Canyon Hot Springs
Creston Valley
Dioisio Point
Emory Creek
Eskers
Fairmont Hot Springs
Garibaldi
Grohman Narrows
Harrison Hot Springs
Kalamalka Lake
Kawkawa Lake
Kickininee
Kootenay Lake
Monkman
Nakusp Hot Springs
Nairn Falls
Niskonlith Lake
Okanagan Falls
Okanagan Mountain
One Island Lake
Stake-McConnell Lakes
Sunnybrae
Whytecliff Park
Wistaria

**British Columbia Ferries:** BC Ferries will transport your pet free of charge. Pets must remain in your vehicle or be kept on leashes on the vehicle decks as they are not allowed above the car decks.

# Index

# On the Road Again
## With
# Man's Best Friend

## Reader Input

We research extensively to bring you the best places to stay with a dog. We also appreciate any assistance our readers can give us. Therefore, if you find an interesting B&B, inn, hotel, or resort that welcomes guests traveling with a dog, please let us know. We enjoy hearing from our readers, and are always impressed with their perceptive comments on where to go and what to do with a dog.

If, after researching your suggestion, we include that entry in our next edition of *On The Road Again With Man's Best Friend*, we will send you a complimentary copy of that book.

Please send your information to:

Allison Elliott
Dawbert Press, Inc.
P.O. Box 2758,
Duxbury, Massachusetts 02331

Our e-mail address is Dawbert @ aol.com
Fax: (617) 934-2945

You may also call us directly at
(800) 93-DAWBERT

We look forward to your input!